IN THE NAME OF GOD,

THE COMPASSIONATE, THE MERCIFUL

American Crescent

American Crescent

A MUSLIM CLERIC ON THE POWER
OF HIS FAITH, THE STRUGGLE AGAINST
PREJUDICE, AND THE FUTURE OF
ISLAM AND AMERICA

Imam Hassan Qazwini

   Random House   New York

Published in the United States by Random House, an imprint of The Random House Publishing Group, a division of Random House, Inc., New York.

RANDOM HOUSE and colophon are registered trademarks of Random House, Inc.

Library of Congress Cataloging-in-Publication Data

Al-Qazwini, Sayid Hassan.
  American crescent : A Muslim cleric on the power of his faith, the struggle against prejudice, and the future of Islam and America / Imam Hassan Qazwini
    p. cm.
  Includes bibliographical references.
  ISBN 978-1-4000-6454-0
1. Al-Qazwini, Sayid Hassan. 2. Muslims—United States—Biography.
3. Islam—United States. I. Crawford, Brad. II. Title.
  BP80.A5296A68 2007
  297.8'2092—dc22
    [B]   2007010345

Printed in the United States of America on acid-free paper

www.atrandom.com

9 8 7 6 5 4 3 2 1

First Edition

Book design by Carol Malcolm Russo

To my teacher, role model, and father,
Ayatollah Sayed Mortadha Qazwini

Preface

ISLAM'S POWER LIES in action. I could not write a book about Islam without telling the story of Muslims who passionately practice the faith, and I could not imagine writing about my own life without telling how Islam has shaped it. Through news reports, graphic television footage, blogs, and the abstraction that comes from being on the other side of the world from the events of the day, "Islam" unfortunately has become a loaded word in America, synonymous with aggression and anti-western rhetoric. My own experience as a Muslim raised in the cradle of Shia Islam, guided through twelve years of seminary study, and schooled in American sociology has provided a very different understanding, which I have gained through my lineage, upbringing, and migration to America.

Lineage. My relationship with Islam began with the very origins of the faith. The Prophet Muhammad, the messenger of Islam, is my great-great-ancestor through thirty-nine generations. In the Middle East, where memory is deep, a person is not an individual. He is one square in a social fabric that stretches to the horizon, and he connects to that fabric through the common thread of family.

Family is family, no matter how far removed in time or space. So when I read the verses of the Qur'an, I feel honored to count God's messenger as one of my own, and when I assemble for prayer behind my father, an ayatollah in Karbala, Iraq, I know that his words and counsels have been passed down from father to son for fourteen hundred years. The life of the Prophet Muhammad has inspired so many people—the world has 1.5 billion Muslims today—that I chose to write my first book, in 1989, about his personal ethics, his response to the quandaries of everyday life, not only his epic decisions as a prophet.

Upbringing. As I was growing up, my parents did not take my religious education for granted. My father was careful to lead by example and to impart Islamic principles without being heavy-handed. I never felt pressured to attend seminary or to pursue the life of an imam. I feel so proud when I meet people who know me only through my father. As soon as I mention his name, I see their neutral expressions change to ones of admiration and respect, even before I have earned their regard. My father has conferred his reputation upon me by association, and my only method of repayment is to live up to his ideals and transmit them to my children to develop their own character.

Migration. Islamic and pre-Islamic history is filled with stories of migration. Abraham migrated from Iraq to Judea at God's command. Moses migrated from Egypt to the Sinai, and Jesus traveled around Galilee and to Perea to preach his message of love and charity. The Prophet Muhammad's harrowing migration from Mecca to Medina in A.D. 622, forced by the violent response to his preaching of Islam, was such a defining point in the history of Islam that the Islamic calendar begins with that year. Out of his migration came the establishment of a new society: the Islamic judiciary, philosophy, politics, and military that still influence much of the world today. Islam has by no means remained static; successive cultures that embraced Islam incorporated it into their cultural framework, each one's brilliant scholars adding texture and depth to our religious understanding.

There's something inherently spiritual about migration: the uncertainty and hardship of the journey, the reshaping of an old identity, the integration into a new society, and the personal reckoning that reveals universal truths. I have migrated three times, twice because of political persecution of my father, and once for the sake of religious opportunity. I moved with my family from Iraq to Kuwait at age six, from Kuwait to Iran at age fifteen, and from Iran to the United States at age twenty-eight. The third move affected me most profoundly, despite being voluntary. Leaving the Middle East put Islam's relation to the entire world in a context I could not have appreciated otherwise. Suddenly the beliefs and customs I had taken for granted collided with a society that placed few limits on how I ought to behave. I could see a clear distinction between my own character and the expectations that surrounded me. With Islam as the guide, I had to find my own way.

Some people think that being transplanted to a foreign environment restricts a person. I don't believe that is true. I view myself as being like a tree that needs only the proper conditions to survive, wherever these might be. In the early 1900s, growers brought Algerian date palms to the Indio and Coachella areas of southern California, not terribly far from my first home in America, and they have thrived there in the desert ever since. All they really require is lots of sun, and roots deep enough to reach groundwater. Sometimes what appears to be a grove of palms is actually separate trunks sharing a single root system.

This is the story of the human being himself. Few would choose to uproot their lives and rebuild amid a confusing and unfamiliar culture, but whether they do so willingly or under threat, these immigrants adjust and, with help from family, thrive—for adaptability is one of our defining characteristics as people. Imam Ali, the cousin and son-in-law of the Prophet Muhammad and the second most important figure in Shia Islam, knew something about hard journeys and felt a person could go anywhere he felt at home in his head. "Your country does not belong to you more than any other country," he said. "The best country is the one that treats you well."

My third migration has made me who I am today, an amalgam of East and West. In America I have found the best country, and I have found an unexpectedly dynamic interpretation of Islam. Here, amid a flurry of distortions and assumptions about the faith, industrious, freedom-loving Muslims are proving Islam's compatibility with democracy and civil rights. More than my own biography, it is that ongoing interplay between America and its most misunderstood religion, Islam, that I wish to describe and celebrate.

CONTENTS

American Crescent

CHAPTER 1

Husayn vs. Hussein

The most excellent jihad is the uttering of truth
in the presence of an unjust ruler.[1]
—*The Prophet Muhammad*

ONE NIGHT IN early 1971, my father came home at nine o'clock
to find an urgent message from the governor of Iraq's Karbala
province, Shabib al-Maliki. He returned the call, and their conversation was brief, which made it either more ominous or less, I'm
not sure. Governor Maliki wanted to see him right away. Nine
o'clock was late for Karbala; in the Middle East lunch, not dinner,
is the main meal of the day, and the first call to prayer comes at
dawn. My father's experiences over the previous ten years, and especially in the two and a half years since the Baath party had
come to power, had taught us that a request for a late-night meeting could signal nothing positive.

Two days earlier, a close friend of my father's, Ayatollah Mohammad Shirazi, had fled the country after learning of a plot to
assassinate him. Ayatollah Shirazi was one of Iraq's most learned
and trusted scholars of Islamic jurisprudence, a *mujtahid,* and he
unflinchingly criticized the Baathists, a dangerous practice under
an anti-Shia regime whose ideology and rule were based on consensus through fear. Baathist assaults frequently targeted the

outspoken and the charismatic. The more influential the critic, the more savage the government's response. It might start with legal harassment and escalate to overt threats. Then anonymous agents of the Mukhabarat, the secret police known as the "visitors of the dawn," would knock on your door in the pre-waking hours when witnesses were few and the element of surprise high. If you were lucky, they administered a beating. If you were not, they took you to headquarters for interrogation, torture, or execution, depending on whether you told them what they wanted to hear. Detainees at Abu Ghraib, the British-built sixties-era facility where the Baathists held many of their political prisoners, experienced cruelty of the most imaginatively ghoulish varieties: scalding with boiling water in their most sensitive areas, branding, crucifixion, blinding with insecticides, feet-first insertion into an industrial grinder. They were dissolved in acid baths while their wives were forced to watch. Some simply vanished.

.   Upon learning of his impending fate, Ayatollah Shirazi made the sensible decision to avoid torture or death and instead struck out for Kuwait under cover of darkness. He told no one of his plan.

At the governor's office soon after receiving the message, my father joined a secretary and Governor Maliki himself, who didn't waste any time in revealing his agenda: Where is your friend Shirazi? Why did he leave? My father could take some comfort in the fact that Governor Maliki had seemingly called this meeting to discuss Ayatollah Shirazi and not his own criticisms of the regime, which were frequent.

I don't know where he went, my father said—and it was true; he did not—but I can tell you that Ayatollah Shirazi left because he feared for his life.

Two years earlier, Ayatollah Hassan Shirazi, Mohammad's brother, had written poems mocking the regime and openly denounced those in power as thugs and gangsters. He was arrested, tortured, and nearly executed. Only widespread public outrage at his treatment saved him. (He fled to Lebanon, where one of Saddam Hussein's agents assassinated him in 1980.)

Governor Maliki pretended for my father's benefit that Aya-tollah Mohammad Shirazi had overreacted. Shirazi was very safe in Karbala, he said. He had no reason to worry.

You're right, my father said, and the best proof of what you say is the two sheikhs, Ayatollah Shirazi's associates, who were arrested at the doorstep of Imam Husayn's shrine yesterday. (The shrine dated to Karbala's very origins and powerfully symbolized the struggles for justice of all Shia Muslims.)

Governor Maliki retorted that the Iranian sheikhs, who were Shia clerics, had been deported for lack of proper documentation.

My father had known the governor, a Shia lawyer, for years before the Baathists came to power, and he knew he could not win this argument. Though not a Baathist himself, Maliki was accountable to them, and the future awaiting a governor who de-fied the regime would be dark, and short. The secretary left the room, and Governor Maliki fell silent. When he spoke again, his officious tone had disappeared.

Sayed Mortadha, he said, I love you, and I don't want you to get hurt. He shook his head. I should not give you this advice. My position requires that I not give you this advice . . . *You will be next.* If Shirazi had stayed, he would not be alive right now. You should go.

The next morning my mother woke us up at four o'clock in-stead of the usual seven and told us there would be no school that day. We were going on a trip to Basra. I was six years old and so happy about not going to school that I didn't think to question why we had to rise so early. We took only what we would need for a few days: a change of clothes and some snacks for the car. Everything else, including my father's extensive library, stayed behind. Before we left, my grandfather Ayatollah Mohammad Sadiq Qazwini stopped by the house, and my father knelt to kiss his hand. As they embraced, I sensed that it would be a long time before they saw each other again.

A Mercedes-Benz cab pulled up after morning prayers and all seven of us squeezed inside: my father, my mother, my three older brothers, my one older sister, and me. A ten-hour drive away, Basra was the largest city in southern Iraq, a somewhat ragged old port town once known as the Venice of the Middle East for its extensive canal system. Founded as a garrison a few years after the death of the Prophet Muhammad, it seemed to be continually caught in the middle of conflict, probably because of its strategic position on the Shatt al-Arab, the union of the Tigris and Euphrates rivers, near the Persian Gulf. All of Iraq's oil exports passed this way, and the borders of both Iran and Kuwait were less than thirty miles away. Later the city would be hit hard in the eight-year Iran-Iraq War, the Gulf War, and the Iraq War.

The tone in the car was not at all somber. For my siblings and me, this was a field trip. My father, however, remained quiet throughout the drive, looking serious and preoccupied. Occasionally he paged through a Qur'an he held on his lap and whispered a few prayers. We stopped only for bathroom breaks, and those weren't frequent enough.

North of Basra, the road forks; one road leads downtown, and the other, the route we took, leads southwest to Safwan, a village near the Kuwaiti border. We all noted the change in plans, but none of us was brave enough to ask why we weren't, in fact, going to Basra. The closer we came to the border, the quieter my father got. Iraq and Kuwait have a historically uneasy relationship. In the days when the Ottoman empire controlled southeastern Europe, most of the Middle East, and the Mediterranean coast of Africa, the two lands were one, though for centuries Kuwait had a semiautonomous sheikhdom. Iraq surrendered its claim to Kuwait when the former escaped British rule in 1932 but was unaware at that time of its neighbor's vast petroleum reserves. When Kuwait shed its status as a British protectorate in 1961, Iraq's prime minister, Abdul Karim Qasim, disputed the claim of independence and mobilized troops on the border. War appeared imminent. The British dispatched their military, backed by Arab countries, to defuse the situation, and Prime Minister Qasim backed off.

As a well-known preacher and authority on Islamic principles, my father had traveled to at least half a dozen countries to
speak; those engagements accounted for most of our household
income. He refused to accept a salary for teaching at the seminary, believing that work to be one of his fundamental religious
obligations. In a fortunate quirk of timing, he was already scheduled to speak in Kuwait in two weeks, so the idea that we were
crossing as a family in advance of his lecture might have seemed
plausible to officers manning the checkpoints. At the border, my
father warned us to keep quiet and stay in the car. He strode to
the office and got his passport stamped. We passed through a second checkpoint, then a third. Border guards would ask a few routine questions, compare faces with passports, and wave us
through. Perhaps having a private driver lent the journey an air of
legitimacy. Whatever the reason, we entered Kuwait without incident, without the rest of us even appreciating the risk involved.

Later, at my uncle's house in Kuwait City, I overheard my
uncle telling my father, "You were right. You did the right thing,
and you got out safely." But if one of Saddam's spies had observed
our flight and called ahead to the border checkpoint . . .

Governor Maliki, certainly an intelligent man, must have calculated that the government would attribute our disappearance
to fear in the wake of Ayatollah Shirazi's preemptive exile. Not
only did the governor never face punishment for his tip to my father, he also became the minister of justice a decade later, when
the name of that ministry held even fewer promises for those at
odds with the regime. The border guards discovered too late that
we were not supposed to leave the country, but what punishment they suffered for their oversight, I cannot say.

BIRTH OF THE SHIA

Whenever he deemed it useful, Saddam would kill Muslims,
Christians, Communists, and anyone else without regard for
their beliefs. In the 1950s he was so notorious as a hot-tempered

gangster on the streets of Sunni-dominated Tikrit, a rough-and-tumble city to begin with, that the Baath party recruited him as an enforcer while he was still in his teens. A few years later, they chose him to lead the assassination of Prime Minister Qasim, who had gained power through a coup himself the year before. Saddam failed (and took a bullet in the process), but not for lack of effort. Religion did not matter much to him, except as a tool to manipulate the pious or as a threat to his secular rule. It was this second consideration—principles, not theology—that bred his special hatred for the Shia.

He rarely trusted Shia with any significant responsibility in his regime because Shia believe that it's better to divide for truth than to unite in error, an article of faith that dates to the seventh century. The full tale is long, and some of it has been disputed or lost to history, but it began at an oasis outside Mecca after the Prophet Muhammad's last trip there, known as the Farewell Pilgrimage, two months before his death. (Though a visionary and shining ethical model, the Prophet Muhammad *was* mortal.)

The Prophet Muhammad already had become remarkably influential and won many admirers in the region. By the end of his life, he held sway over the entire Arabian Peninsula, and he was able to unify Arabs under his leadership. For those who had religious or ethical questions, he was there to provide guidance and further define the faith. But as the Prophet grew visibly weaker toward the end of his days, the question of who would succeed him loomed large, and he knew that for the sake of his community and Islam's future, he would have to answer it. He did this following the Farewell Pilgrimage at Ghadir Khum, a small stream marking the crossroads between Mecca and Medina where pilgrims parted company with their fellow Muslims. The Prophet Muhammad sent word to those far ahead to return and waited for the stragglers to catch up, so that by the time he began speaking, more than 100,000 of his followers had gathered around him. At the climax of his speech, he said:

It seems the time approaches when I shall be called away [by God] and I shall answer that call. I am leaving for you two precious things and if you adhere to both of them, you will never go astray after me. They are the Book of God and my progeny, that is, my *Ahlul-Bayt*. The two shall never separate from each other until they come to me by the Pool [of Paradise].[2]

The Prophet then reminded his people that he would be watching over them, and he raised the hand of his cousin and son-in-law and said, "Whoever I am his master, Ali is his master. O God, love those who love him. Be hostile to those who are hostile to him. Help those who help him. Forsake those who forsake him. And keep the truth with him where he turns."[3]

This was a momentous proclamation, but not surprising. The Prophet Muhammad's cousin was his closest male heir and almost universally respected as a pious, fair, capable, and deeply intellectual leader. We call him Imam Ali, "imam" being a reverential term for the early line of Shia leaders. Imam Ali's father, Abu Talib, had been the head of a small but influential clan in Mecca and had taken care of the orphaned Prophet Muhammad for much of his childhood; the Prophet returned the favor almost three decades later by taking in Imam Ali when Abu Talib could no longer afford to care for him.

When the Prophet Muhammad turned forty and began receiving messages from God about Islam, Imam Ali was the first person to convert after the Prophet's own wife. He was the only one permitted to enter and leave the Prophet Muhammad's house at will and the only male who prayed behind the Prophet Muhammad in the Kaaba, the rectangular stone edifice that now stands draped in black curtains at the center of the Grand Mosque in Mecca. Both of the Prophet Muhammad's sons had died at a young age.

If there was any doubt about the significance of the Prophet

Muhammad's speech at Ghadir Khum, he eliminated it with a final statement, a Qur'anic verse revealed to him at the time: "This day have I perfected for you your religion and completed my favor on you and chosen for you Islam as a religion."[4] The Prophet Muhammad asked all of the tens of thousands present, including a prominent Muslim named Abu Bakr, to swear an oath of allegiance to Imam Ali. Narratives from Islamic tradition tell us that Abu Bakr congratulated Imam Ali on his new role. "Well done, Ibn Abi Talib!" he said, referring to him by his last name (literally, "son of Abu Talib"). "Today you became the leader of all believing men and women."

Not everyone accepted this announcement without complaint. Different clans vied against one another for power, and it was apparent to all that whoever succeeded the Prophet Muhammad as leader of the Muslim people would be powerful indeed. If anyone in the Hashim, the tiny clan of the Prophet Muhammad and Abu Talib, succeeded the Prophet, the balance of power would skew heavily toward the Hashim and set the scene for a string of Hashemite leaders. Even worse, some contenders aspiring to succeed the Prophet Muhammad feared, if Imam Ali became the successor, the position could become hereditary, forever locking them out of the Muslim leadership.

Upon the Prophet Muhammad's death, the Muslim community fractured over who should lead and what his role would be. One faction hewed to the Prophet Muhammad's speech at the Farewell Pilgrimage and other statements the Prophet had made that Imam Ali was to be the successor. Logically, then, the leader of the Muslims would always be a member of the Prophet Muhammad's family, his *ahlul-bayt,* and would serve as the community's political and religious authority, though without the Prophet's status as God's messenger.

The Muslims who disputed Imam Ali's assumption of leadership said there was no evidence that the Prophet Muhammad had ever intended to name a successor. They felt entitled to name their own successor from among the Prophet Muhammad's companions. In Medina, the social epicenter of the young Muslim community, several influential companions formed an alliance to make Abu Bakr the new leader; they secured the approval of a key minority in the community and then extracted the majority's endorsement. Abu Bakr was a respected elder, an old friend of the Prophet Muhammad and an early convert to Islam. He promptly gave himself the title "Successor to the Prophet of God," or, in an abbreviated transliteration from Arabic, Caliph.

The result was chaos. Some who had converted for appearance' sake saw the Prophet Muhammad's death as an opportunity to return to the old ways, where trade and profit trumped morality. Many of the Prophet's companions had imagined themselves capable of filling his shoes, and they were reluctant to give up their chance. Abu Bakr's supporters feverishly made the rounds to build acceptance of his leadership. Those who couldn't be persuaded intellectually were physically intimidated. A minority of Muslims, those in the Hashim clan and others close to the family of the Prophet, continued to protest Abu Bakr's selection heatedly. Not only had the Prophet Muhammad clearly designated Imam Ali as his successor, but also the companions who backed Abu Bakr had met in secret and intentionally excluded Imam Ali, who was washing the Prophet's body in preparation for burial at the time.

After months of peaceful dissent, Imam Ali reluctantly and only formally accepted Abu Bakr as caliph to avoid rending the community in two. For the time being, he would advise Muslims as a respected but unofficial leader, and he would uphold the traditions of the Prophet Muhammad through worship, charity, and service to others. The Prophet Muhammad himself had named the group that supported Imam Ali: he had once pointed to several loyalists walking with Imam Ali and said, "This man and his followers will be the winners on the Day of Judgment." In Arabic, "followers of Ali" is *Shi'atu Ali*—the Shia.

Imam Ali's followers might have been outwardly subdued, but they did not give up their belief that he was the rightful heir of the Prophet Muhammad. Regardless of who headed the Islamic caliphate, the Shia looked to Imam Ali as their true spiritual leader and commander. "Study the Qur'an," the Prophet Muhammad had exhorted Muslims at Ghadir Khum after the Farewell Pilgrimage. "Reflect on its clear verses and do not presume the meaning of the ambiguous verses. For, by Allah, nobody can properly explain them to you its warnings and its meanings except me and this man whose hand I am lifting up in front of me [Imam Ali]."[5]

Muslims who accepted Abu Bakr's caliphate had a different interpretation of Prophet Muhammad's speech at Ghadir Khum. They felt he was expressing loyalty and affection for Imam Ali; in Arabic, the word that means "master" can also in rare cases mean "friend"—"Whoever I am his friend, Ali is his friend," the Prophet Muhammad is meant to have said. Even though all Shia and some Sunni books, such as Tirmidhi, profess otherwise, these Muslims argue that the two items the Prophet Muhammad left his people were not the Qur'an and Prophet Muhammad's family, but the Qur'an and Islamic traditions—the sayings and acts of the Prophet Muhammad. These traditions are known as the sunna, and from it the Muslims who accepted a transfer of authority to companions derived their name: the Sunni.

THE BATTLE OF KARBALA

Sunni and Shia both acknowledged Imam Ali's wisdom and righteousness. At times, this translated to accommodation of the Shia view and a share of power for Imam Ali. After twenty-four years and transfers of power to two subsequent caliphs, a council of leaders, a *shura,* named Imam Ali the fourth caliph of Islam by overwhelming consensus. But the virtue and prestige of the family of the Prophet Muhammad also presented a threat. The Muslim world was expanding rapidly, presenting any caliph with the potential for great wealth and prestige. Military might held sway over moral vision. Ironically, within fifty years of the Prophet Muhammad's death, the caliphate had become a dynasty. What had begun as an effort to decentralize religious authority and choose leaders by consultation had opened the door to tyranny.

The further the caliphate strayed from the ideals of Islam, the more righteous the Prophet's family's claim to leadership appeared. The watershed moment for Shia came in my hometown of Karbala in 680. The Prophet Muhammad had been dead for forty-eight years. Islam had spread beyond the Arabian Peninsula to Egypt, Iraq, Syria, Iran, and the Holy Land, but a rival clan of the Hashim, the Umayya, ran the caliphate from Damascus. The Shia were, as before, a small, mostly dispossessed minority (even today, the Shia compose only about 15 to 20 percent of Muslims) whose greatest numbers were now in Iraq and Persia, on the fringes of the Muslim world. They expressed skepticism about the tyrannical caliphate's authority. In Damascus the new caliph, a lewd, immoral man named Yazid, had inherited his position from his father without any consultation from the community, and in defiance of a treaty guaranteeing that an open council would select the next caliph.

Yazid made a conflict inevitable by demanding that the charismatic Imam Husayn, Imam Ali's son and the Prophet Muhammad's grandson, appear before the governor of Medina, where he lived and preached, to take an oath of allegiance to the Umayyad caliph. The ascension to power of the lubricious Yazid had particularly enraged many Muslims in Kufa, a city south of Baghdad and not far from Karbala. Imam Ali had based his caliphate in Kufa years before and still had many supporters there. The Kufans plotted a rebellion, promised support for Imam Husayn in asserting his rightful claim to the caliphate, and summoned him from Medina for help. In response, Imam Husayn traveled to Mecca and bided his time there in religious sanctuary, contemplating his limited options. Though he knew the Kufans might waver, especially if Yazid's massive army attacked them, he saw little choice but to stand up to the false caliph and correct a wrong plaguing the Muslim community: tyranny and corruption, as well as marginalization of the Prophet Muhammad's family, and thus of the

Shia. Imam Husayn decided to go to Kufa, whatever the cost, with his wife, his sisters, his sons and daughters, his nephews and nieces, his companions, and any soldiers he could muster, and there he would make a statement that Muslims from that day forward could not ignore.

Roughly 150 set out from Mecca on the eighth day of Thul al-Hijja, the last month of the Muslim calendar year; they crossed the dusty Arabian plains south of Iraq as caravans streamed toward Mecca for the start of the annual pilgrimage. Imam Husayn's departure had attracted the attention of Meccans; it was no secret where he had gone, and Umayyad messengers promptly relayed word of his movements to the caliph in Damascus. Periodically, Imam Husayn would ask the pilgrims en route to Mecca what news they had to share, and so he developed a picture of what lay ahead. In this way, well before he reached his destination, Imam Husayn learned that Yazid had sent soldiers to Kufa to besiege the city and seal it off. Under an Umayyad campaign of terror and fear, the Kufans had abandoned any plans to rebel against the empire, and more than a dozen commanders leading a combined thirty thousand soldiers rode out from Kufa to engage Imam Husayn's band.

Imam Husayn, with full knowledge of the failed revolt and the enemy legions he would encounter, pushed on toward certain death and encamped at Karbala, about fifty miles northwest of Kufa. For eight days, his alliance held its ground by making camp with hills to the rear to discourage attack and by maintaining a fire-filled trench on the remaining three sides. Their weak point was water. The Syrians had cut off access to the Euphrates, and with their supplies depleted, Imam Husayn's family and companions could not survive. The children began wailing; many died of thirst. On the ninth night of the new year, Imam Husayn addressed what followers remained.

> I do not think that there will be [any further] days [left]
> to us by these men. I permit you to leave me. All [of you]

go away with the absolution of your oath [to follow me], for there will be no [further] obligation on you from me. This is a night [whose darkness] will give cover to you. Use it as a camel.[6]

None of those under Imam Husayn's command accepted his offer. Each swore allegiance freely and vowed to die in battle before the imam did. The following morning, with his people's demise almost complete, Imam Husayn gathered his strength and prepared to meet his opponents in battle. Yazid's armies, the Syrians and complicitous Kufans, fought gingerly, for they recognized their overwhelmingly favorable odds, and none wished to be the man responsible for killing the Prophet Muhammad's grandson.[7] As the number of companions in Imam Husayn's band dwindled, one by one, the warriors standing with him greeted him and advanced into the fray, where each was cut down until only Imam Husayn's family was left among the men. His elder sons and nephews died in similar fashion, or were killed by bow shot.

Imam Husayn was gravely injured; blood poured through his cap from a sword wound, and arrows pierced him from all sides. In a final act of defiance, he charged toward the nearest traitors and swiped at them with his sword, scattering them. The army general Omar bin Saad called for more archers, who rained arrows on Imam Husayn until he could no longer stand. At Omar's command, soldiers then descended on him from every side, assailing him with swords and spears and hacking indiscriminately at his body. A soldier named Shimr ibn Thul-Jawshan approached and beheaded him, and Omar ordered the bodies of all of Imam Husayn's fallen companions and family beheaded along with him. Of Imam Husayn's seventy-two male companions, only one, his son Ali bin al-Husayn, survived, because he was too sick to fight and because God intervened in his enemies' many attempts to kill him. Scores of women and children, some of them Imam Husayn's sisters, cousins, and nieces, also survived to see

Imam Husayn's head paraded through the streets of Kufa and then Damascus as a warning to any who dared oppose the empire, and then delivered to Yazid as a trophy.

SADDAM'S PURSUIT OF POWER

When the Baath party came to power through a coup d'état on July 17, 1968, no one knew it would reign for more than three decades or that 3 million Iraqis would lose their lives. Among the first people targeted by the new government's policies were Shia religious scholars, a tactic that foretold the party's operating principle for the duration of its control over Iraq: the elimination of all dissent. Shia scholars had set the religious and political agendas for more than 60 percent of the country's population.[8] Silencing them, the logic went, would go far toward suppressing the opposition. President Ahmed Hassan al-Bakr, a cousin of Saddam's, began by severely limiting how many non-Iraqis could attend Najaf's thousand-year-old seminary, the world's center for Shia religious study and also home to the shrine of Imam Ali. To an outsider, the restriction might have appeared understandable, an extension of the Baathists' advocacy for freedom from foreign control. For Shia, however, it was tantamount to a declaration of war.

About 70 percent of the seminary's students were non-Iraqis, mostly from Iran, which has 60 million Shia, compared with Iraq's 17 million. Pro-Baathist Iraqis doubted the Shia's national loyalty, accusing them of identifying more strongly with Iran's ethnically Persian Shia than with their fellow Arabs. The ban on foreign students wouldn't close the seminary, but it would have the desired effect of diminishing Najaf's prestige and influence, and insulting Iraqi Shia by isolating them from supposedly corrupting influences, all under the guise of national security. The Shia ayatollahs and imams were not shy about arguing against the measure or against the increased violence and arrests taking place in the streets. The new regime had begun cracking down on dissidents all over the country, Sunni and Shia alike.

Saddam Hussein was thirty-one at the time of the coup. He was only one of five figures who had engineered the overthrow of Abdul Rahman Arif's regime, but less than two weeks afterward he staged his own coup, marching into the office of the new prime minister, Abdul Razzaq al-Nayif, with a gun and a group of officers and advising him to leave the country if he wanted to live.[9] Nayif chose Spain, then London; ten years later, Saddam ordered the military detail that always accompanied Nayif to kill him, and it complied. The minister of defense, Ibrahim al-Dawood, who was also the head of the Republican Guard, was pushed out; the subsequent minister of defense, Hardan al-Tikriti, was exiled and later killed.[10] That left al-Bakr as president and prime minister. For a while, Saddam was content to serve as al-Bakr's vice president and deputy while he built alliances and learned the basics of governance, but long before he took over as president, Saddam was running the country.

Saddam rewarded loyalty with advancement, and those who had proved trustworthy, often thugs from his hometown of Tikrit, lurked in all areas of the government and military, ears to the ground for plots against the regime, criticisms, and petty insults. Iraqis spoke with care on the phone and often used coded language to avoid harassment. One well-known anecdote tells of a woman with a son named Saddam complaining to a friend on the phone of all the trouble he had been causing. Assuming her criticism was aimed at the president, the Mukhabarat came to question her, found her story was true, and consequently backed off.

We have heard so much about Saddam's brutality and heinous crimes, from bizarre tortures to the annihilation of entire towns and villages, that the stories have begun to sound exaggerated and incredible. Yet I know they are true, because my family, friends, and neighbors have lived them. After Saddam formally assumed the presidency in 1979, the Mukhabarat broke into my aunt's house in Karbala in the middle of the night looking for my cousin Hassan al-Tiaef. They beat each member of her family, including her seventy-year-old husband, and demanded to know which one was Hassan. The agents seized him, then left with no explanation. His little brother, Quswar, who was eleven, was traumatized and died of a high fever shortly afterward. My aunt lay sick in a hospital for a month as a result of the incident.

Eight months after Hassan was taken, a car drove by and dumped him, barely alive, in the street in front of their house. His brothers rushed him inside to tend to his wounds, and as they did so, he explained how he had been tortured and interrogated throughout his incarceration. The Mukhabarat released him only when they realized they had the wrong Hassan—a very common Arabic name—but told him not to tell anyone. Where I come from, almost everyone has a story like this.

IN THE PRESENCE OF IMAM HUSAYN

Our house in Old Town Karbala stood just across the street from the shrine of Imam Husayn, a magnificent structure in the center of the city that marks the graves of the Imam and his companions who fell there. A shrine in some form has existed on the site since 684, a year after the Umayyad caliph Yazid died. A blue-tiled wall surrounds the massive courtyard, which can hold ten thousand people for Friday prayers and various ceremonies. Along the inside edges of the wall, merchants sell trinkets, pictures of Imam Husayn, and related religious artifacts, the most popular of which are small clay tablets and beads, made from the soil of Karbala, that Shia around the world use in prayer. This is hallowed ground. Two lofty minarets flank a grand, gold-plated dome that matches them in height. When the afternoon sun hits that dome, the light is visible for miles. I can remember looking out my bedroom window at dawn and being able to see flocks of flamingos stirring in their nests in the shrine's minarets. This is where I first learned to love my religion.

Karbala is an ancient holy city sixty miles southwest of Baghdad known for its religious scholarship and its date industry. The more than 4 million palm trees along the Euphrates River once made Karbala province one of the largest date producers in the world. Essentially all of Karbala is Shia, but the shrine draws millions from around the globe every year, from Iran, Pakistan, Afghanistan, India, and the West, giving the city a cosmopolitan feel not unlike Mecca's. Sunnis also recognize Karbala as an important holy site. Though it was a bustling and highly successful town of 100,000 people in 1971, because it is a holy city, its entertainment was limited. There were no bars, nightclubs, or movie theaters. Many of our neighbors had TVs, but we didn't. For adults, free time meant exchanging stories and jokes over a cup of tea in one of the city's many cafés. At five or six years old, I was not allowed to go in, but I would pass by on the way to or from school or prayers and catch the sweet scent of hookah smoke wafting out open windows.

With four brothers, one sister, seventy or eighty cousins, and few distractions, I was never far away from my family. When he wasn't traveling, my father would speak at the shrine of Imam Husayn or at Al-Hindiya, a religious school, before large crowds, and he would take a few of my brothers with him. There were five of us children living in the house at any one time, so we could not all go at once. When I did get to go, I was struck by how attentive his audiences were. Afterward, I would hear people speak of his influence on their lives and his eloquence, and it filled me with pride. Even when I started first grade at Imam al-Sadiq School, I was surrounded by family. My father had founded the school, the first modern, full-time Islamic school in the city, and also served as the principal and taught classes. My older brothers also attended, and many of my cousins were teachers. Wherever I went, I was watched, nurtured, and loved.

You could argue, however, that dwelling in such a tightly circumscribed world didn't inhibit my creative troublemaking. I often played with my brother Mohammed, who was two years older. The Old Town area, where we lived, is a warren of centuries-old row houses and tenements along narrow streets, the tightest of which were unpaved and could accommodate only two abreast. In the winter they would turn muddy. Above the second floor of the house, rather than an attic and gabled roof, we had a veranda filled with plants that was perfect for sleeping on hot summer nights; our veranda was connected to that of every other house on the block, so that anyone on that row could race across the rooftops from one end of the street to the other with only the lip of each house's exterior walls to impede him. One summer afternoon, our mother charged Mohammed and me with watering the myriad plants on the veranda, not an unenjoyable task since we got to horse around outside and splash each other with the water we poured from large ceramic vases into each pot. I don't recall whose idea it was, but one of us leaned over the roof, spotted an older, balding gentleman strolling directly below us, and decided it would be fun to give him a drink as well. Together we hoisted a giant vessel up over the low wall and emptied the entire contents on his head. Well, in Karbala we would say he cursed like a horse-cart driver. We disappeared before he could look up to see who had soaked him, and thanks to all the interconnected roofs, he couldn't be sure that someone from our house was responsible. We took advantage of his uncertainty by scrambling down three flights of stairs to the basement to hide before he pounded on the front door. My father answered and apologized, my mother suggested checking the roof, and one of them went upstairs to see whether anyone was there. Not long after, the door closed, the man left unsatisfied, and we lived to scheme another day.

Hiding in the basement was the best alternative because, aside from the obvious benefits of not being caught, we would not have to look my father in the eye and lie if he asked us whether we had done it. If he had confronted us, we would have had to tell the truth. My father did not discipline with threats or yelling. Rather, we knew he had high standards for us, and we didn't wish to disappoint or embarrass him. In our culture, the actions and stature of one person reflect on the entire family, just as the family's reputation reflects on the individual. Job offers and marriage proposals can come based on family name. So my father always carried himself with a great deal of dignity and seriousness, and in turn he commanded a tremendous amount of respect. Rarely did we joke or banter.

My mother was softer, our advocate and also the family liaison. When we wanted something, our strategy was to plead the case with my mother and have her approach my father. And when he had made any sort of family decision, she would carry the message to the rest of us. My mother gave birth to six of us at home, including me, and at those times the family dynamic shifted. Men are not allowed to assist in childbirth; a midwife would tend to my laboring mother while some of our female relatives would come to offer prayers and supplications. As children, my brothers and I could stay in the house during delivery, but not in the same room. We would wait in the kitchen or a nearby room to fetch items as needed. Middle Eastern mothers tend to be emotional and to nurture an almost excessive attachment to their children. They are the linchpins of all domestic matters, and my mother was no different. If one of us was late in coming home, she would don her black abaya, a full-length, hooded overgarment worn in public, and stand on the porch keeping watch until we arrived, as if waiting there would bring us back earlier. She must have spent that time preparing a lecture for our return, because she always had one ready.

The boundaries between nuclear family and extended family are blurry in my culture. My aunts displayed as much love and concern for us as my mother did; I even referred to my mother's youngest sister as Mama. Young couples often live in the husband's parents' house until they are more established. As a young boy, I saw much of what here we would call my extended family every day and played with my cousins just as I would with my brothers, sometimes staying the night.

Soccer and marbles were popular pastimes in Karbala, but with my cousins our favorite activity was flying kites. Kids of all ages flew them. On windy days, once school was out, you could look across the horizon and see thousands in all colors dotting the sky. Parents liked it because they could keep watch on the children, restricting them to the rooftops or yards; we liked it because we could test the kites to see whose was best. These were not store-bought kits but creations of our own making, diamond-shaped kites with thick coated paper stretched over wooden crosspieces. Though simple, they flew well. The rooftops of the connected houses allowed plenty of room to launch and maneuver a kite through the constellation of those already aloft. The better fliers could send a kite up a hundred feet or more, higher even than the shrine of Imam Husayn.

For some of the older, tougher boys, flying and competing weren't enough. They would use glue to coat their strings with tiny shards of glass and attack other kites' strings to cut them loose—kite wars. Unless potential challengers were willing to risk chasing their kite off to some distant neighborhood or losing it altogether, they would lower theirs in a hurry and watch the wars, some eagerly and some with resignation.

THE QAZWINIS OF KARBALA

My full name is Imam Sayed Hassan al-Qazwini. I come from a long line of religious scholars. *Imam,* the Arabic word for "religious leader," comes from an Arabic phrase meaning "leader of the congregational prayer." The second part of my name, Sayed, means "master" in Arabic and is an honorary title given to those who can trace their lineage back to the Prophet Muhammad. Like thousands of Muslims around the world, I am his direct descendant, thirty-nine generations removed. My given name, Hassan, is that of the Prophet's eldest grandson. "Al" is the definite article in Arabic, the equivalent of "the" in English. And the surname Qazwini literally means "one who comes from Qazwin," a Persian city Anglicized as Caspian and situated on the sea of the same name in Iran.

Three hundred years ago, my grand-ancestor Abdul Karim fled to Qazwin from western Arabia to avoid religious persecution. The people of Qazwin loved him greatly, married him to one of their daughters, and after his death built a shrine in his honor. When his two sons, religious scholars both, came of age, they abided by the wishes expressed in his last will and testament and moved to Karbala to study. There the Qazwini name took root, and my ancestors' history unfolded.

For seven generations, my forefathers have studied Islamic philosophy, jurisprudence, and logic in Karbala and have worshipped there. The stories that I know, the stories of my family, are the stories of Iraq. My ancestor Ayatollah Ibrahim Qazwini was a prominent writer on the principles of jurisprudence in the mid-1800s. My great-great-grandfather Ayatollah Hashim Qazwini held the most esteemed position among Karbala's scholars in the early 1900s. In the early 1920s, my great-uncle Ayatollah Hussein Qazwini and my grandfather Ayatollah Mohammad Sadiq Qazwini, then only twenty years old, joined with other religious scholars to rise up against the post–World War I British occupation of Iraq and help bring King Faisal I to power. My grandfather went on to become a prominent ayatollah and one of Iraq's most popular and esteemed mujtahids, responsible for interpreting Islamic law. I did not get to spend much time with him because of our exile to Kuwait, but I clearly remember his imposing presence and the holy glow about his face. He led prayers at one of the oldest mosques in Karbala, and when I joined him on his walks there, people would stop him on the street to kiss his hand, a sign of deep reverence.

My respect for my father echoes the respect he paid to his own. In the Arab world, fathers are not simply fathers: they are the leaders of the extended family and retain authority long after their children have become socially and financially independent. From a young age, my father lived on the bare minimum and turned over almost all of his earnings to my grandfather. My grandfather and grandmother taught my father, Ayatollah Mortadha Qazwini, to recite and understand the Qur'an from infancy. At age twelve, he enrolled in seminary in Karbala, a privilege usually reserved for sixteen-year-olds. By age eighteen, he was teaching there. In his early twenties, he began speaking outside Iraq, in Lebanon, Bahrain, the United Arab Emirates, and Kuwait.

He was quiet and respectful toward benevolent authority but did not hesitate to speak out against injustice where he saw it. When I was born, in the fall of 1964, he was exiled in the town of Zakho, in northern Iraq, for excoriating the enfeebled government of Abdul Salam Arif, a well-known anti-Shia figure who advocated pan-Arabist unification with Egypt and Syria. Through my father's political connections, my mother managed to take all five of us children—I was only three months old at the time—to Zakho to visit him. He was there ten months.

Six years earlier, he had found himself opposing Abdul Karim Qasim's revolutionary republic, which had overthrown the old western-aligned monarchy in a 1958 military coup. He disliked the new government's Communist bent; though it wasn't a Communist regime, the Iraqi Communist party gained influence after the coup and also received funds and assistance from the Soviet Union. The secular Communists had developed a reputation for disrespect of Islamic law and launched terror and intimidation campaigns that resulted in casualties in Mosul and Baghdad. In street demonstrations, Communist activists invaded Iraq's holy cities and chanted slogans against Islam.

For Shia, the final straw was an editorial cartoon in the Iraqi Communist party's newspaper likening the Grand Ayatollah Sayed Muhsin al-Hakim, the highest Shia scholar in the world at the time, to a donkey. Just before the cartoon appeared, Ayatollah Hakim had issued a fatwa, a binding Islamic ruling, forbidding Muslims from joining the Iraqi Communist party and dismissing Communism as "nothing but atheism and blasphemy." The ruling was a slap in the face to the party, whose membership had to that point been increasing at a record pace. Shia responded to the donkey cartoon with the fiercest protests yet, some of which broke down into riots; Communist party offices were set ablaze.

Street support for Communism began dwindling, and Ayatollah Hakim's fatwa helped sap its strength.

Amidst more conflict, in 1962, Prime Minister Qasim attempted to placate Shia interests by inviting a quorum of Shia scholars, including my father, to an Iftar dinner (an evening meal that breaks the fast during Ramadan) in Baghdad. Before the dinner, the scholars selected my father to be their spokesman in a meeting with the prime minister. He didn't let the pomp and circumstance of the occasion dissuade him from criticizing Qasim's policies. He recited a list of demands, the gist of which was (1) stop attacking Shia holy cities; (2) stop overriding Islamic law, particularly in courts of marriage and divorce; and (3) return property taken from landowners as part of a land redistribution plan. When Prime Minister Qasim resisted, instead offering a "grant" to the Shia seminary in Najaf as consolation, my father, incensed, refused to attend the dinner.

Prime Minister Qasim was not anti-Shia per se—his family background was both Sunni and Shia—and both groups opposed some of his policies, so in standing up to him, my father was speaking not just for Shia but on behalf of the entire Iraqi society. Word spread rapidly in Karbala and the Shia holy cities that my father had stood up to Qasim in Baghdad and rejected his bribe. Within days, Ayatollah Hakim summoned my father to Najaf to hear the story firsthand. A week after the dinner, police arrested my father and took him to a detention center in Baghdad, so he became the first religious leader to be arrested for political reasons under the Qasim regime.

. Thanks to pressure from Ayatollah Hakim, the government released him, yet it wasn't prepared to send him home the victor. Instead it transported him to Tikrit, Saddam's hometown and a Sunni stronghold. No doubt the idea was to expose my father to a sharply different point of view and perhaps subject him to street justice in the Tikrit tradition. The plan backfired. Sunnis there befriended my father and openly invited him to stay in their homes. He became something of a local sensation. When

Prime Minister Qasim pardoned him three months later and permitted him to return to Karbala, thousands turned out in the streets to welcome him home.

"EVERY DAY IS ASHURA"

In Karbala, the apex of the year comes in the first month of the Arabic calendar, Muharram. In the first ten days of the new year, we observe Ashura ("tenth" in Arabic), a commemoration of the period of Imam Husayn's struggle against Yazid's overwhelming forces at the Battle of Karbala. Just after sunrise on the final day, the anniversary of the day Imam Husayn was martyred, thousands turn out to watch a hundred to a hundred and fifty young men sweep through the streets with swords in hand and clad in white robes and headbands that represent funeral shrouds. "We will never forget Imam Husayn!" they cry out. Some strike their own heads with swords or flagellate their backs with chains. Less aggressive marchers beat their chests. Men call out the names of Imam Hassan and Imam Husayn and carry green and black banners: green for Islam and black for mourning. Women dress in black and weep for Imam Husayn, and some also march. Critics decry the ceremony as barbaric, but the number of men who actually cut themselves is small.

More important than the act is what it represents to the Shia, a victory of blood over the sword. Through solidarity with Imam Husayn, we atone for the brutal injustice that took place the day he was killed and simultaneously pledge vigilance to prevent it from happening again. "Every day is Ashura. Every place is Karbala," we say. There are public Ashura gatherings throughout Shia lands, but thousands who come to Karbala for Ashura walk from their homes, sometimes hundreds of miles, to prove their commitment. Townspeople who live near major routes to Karbala set up aid stations with chairs and water to assist pilgrims in their journey to the shrine of Imam Husayn.

When I commemorate Imam Husayn's life and death, my

reverence for him and attachment to him is so passionate that I cannot hold back my tears. I grew up in this great man's shadow and know him not just as a figure from history, but as a forefather, a direct ancestor through thirty-seven generations. Contemplating his sacrifice for Islam, as I did in my years in Karbala and as I have since, is a continual source of inspiration for me. Then and now, Imam Husayn is my absolute hero.

The symbolic power of his sacrifice resides so deep in the Islamic psyche that a catch-22 confronted all of Iraq's venal elite: slander Imam Husayn, and they appeared unjust; venerate him, and they emboldened the vigilant citizens who resisted their crimes. In the mid-1970s, Saddam was busy consolidating his power and insulating himself from coup attempts. He secured from al-Bakr the rank of four-star general without undergoing any military training, expanded the Baathist army under his control to counterbalance the regular Iraqi army, and ushered more party loyalists into decision-making positions. During Ashura celebrations in early 1977, Shia clergy in Najaf and Karbala reacted to this stifling of opposition and persecution of their scholars by leading tens of thousands of pilgrims in chants against the regime. Iraqi troops flooded into the two cities and arrested about two thousand marchers; an unknown number died.[11] Saddam set up a special court to try scholars accused of organizing the demonstration. Fifteen received life sentences, and eight received death.[12] Public observations of Ashura were never again permitted under Saddam's rule.

After the trials, Saddam manufactured a defense against accusations that he was the contemporary Yazid. He publicly professed that he, as a descendant of Imam Husayn, traced his lineage to the Prophet Muhammad, made sure footage of his praying and visits to holy cities appeared on television, and placed a few Shia in government roles.[13] No one I know confused the gestures with a true shift in policy. Too many incidents contradicted these massive efforts at deception, as when Saddam exiled Ayatollah Ruhollah Khomeini in 1978 or executed the high

Najaf scholar Ayatollah Muhammad Baqir al-Sadr and his sister Bint al-Huda in 1980. In 1983, he executed sixty-six scholars, family members of the late Grand Ayatollah Muhsin al-Hakim. The shrine of Imam Husayn, above whose entrance hung a picture of Saddam during his rule, in particular epitomized Saddam's contradictory gamesmanship. A friend of mine visited the shrine after the Gulf War, when Iraqis attempted to overthrow the regime and suffered heavy reprisals once Saddam's troops crushed the resistance. He had gone once in the morning and returned in the afternoon for a second visit, and someone from the Mukhabarat placed a hand on his shoulder. "Were you not in the shrine today?" he asked. My friend said that he was. "Get out," the officer ordered. "Once is enough."

In the wake of that 1991 uprising, five hundred had taken refuge in the shrine as soldiers overran the city, and Saddam ordered the shrine bombed, leaving a gaping hole in the golden dome that was attributed to American aircraft, and quickly repaired the damage. His son-in-law Hussein Kamel led his army into the shrine and slaughtered those who remained there. Witnesses recalled seeing blood pooled on the floor and stray dogs foraging among the dead, and Kamel, outfitted in combat boots, is said to have kicked the cage surrounding Imam Husayn's silver catafalque and issued a challenge: "You're Husayn and I'm Hussein. Get up and see who's winning."

If Saddam Hussein has rivals in his crimes against humanity, he has none in his single-handed destruction of a country. Through lavish private spending, quixotic military ambitions, and international payoffs, Saddam made Iraq one of the poorest countries in the world at a time when it could have been one of the wealthiest. The black joke among sympathetic Iraqis is "The only thing that grew under Saddam's rule was cemeteries."

CHAPTER 2

Struggle in Iran

O man! Surely you must strive [to attain] to your Lord,
a hard striving until you meet him.[1]
—*Holy Qur'an*

AT SIX YEARS of age, I found living in a new country a shock. I was not old enough to remember most of the anxiety and uncertainty that went along with Karbala's opposition to the regime. My memories growing up were positive. In Iraq we had the bulk of our family, including all four grandparents, our familiar old house near the shrine of Imam Husayn, and my classmates at Al-Sadiq school. Kuwait City, where two of my uncles, my father's brothers, lived, and where we fled upon leaving Karbala, was more westernized than Iraq. The students at our new school wore pants, shirts, and jackets, not robes, and they laughed at my Iraqi accent. Al-Sadiq had been within walking distance. Here the trip to school entailed a thirty-minute bus ride.

Kuwait in 1971 was a relatively peaceful oasis. Many Arabs, especially Iraqis, who suffered under oppressive governments found safe haven there. As the second-largest oil exporter after Saudi Arabia, it also drew foreign workers to its petroleum industry, the main reason that 52 percent of its residents were foreign born.[2] As I grew more comfortable with life in Kuwait and grew up a little,

I came to appreciate the country's differences. Kuwait had applied some of its petro-wealth to infrastructure and society's essentials. It had better health care, better police, better roads, and much more freedom than Iraq. The ruling Al-Sabah family held regular elections for parliament and took care to share the country's riches with its citizens. Shia could live comfortably there, undisturbed under a majority Sunni government, provided they did not engage in politics or unsettle the status quo.

From fourth grade on, I would take part of my 100-fils allowance (about 30 cents) to buy a Kuwaiti newspaper called *Al-Watan* ("The Nation"), mostly to follow soccer but also to learn about the wider world. I memorized the name of Britain's prime minister at the time (Harold Wilson), the U.S. presidents from Nixon on, and Henry Kissinger's biography down to the year he emigrated from Germany. I reveled in American culture. I knew the exotic landscapes of the desert Southwest from watching TV westerns with Arabic captions at friends' houses. I remember being mesmerized by the sweeping brass soundtracks that accompanied them. I was familiar with Texas and Hollywood and the Marlboro Man. I saw John Wayne grimacing from Kuwait City marquees.

Islam was expanding. Already the grounding of daily life and culture in much of Asia, Africa, and the Middle East, it was gaining more exposure in traditionally Christian countries such as Germany, France, Britain, and the United States. Through their colonies and importation of Muslims to rebuild after World War II, European countries' Muslim populations grew drastically in the second half of the twentieth century. By 2002, western Europe had more than 15 million Muslims.[3] Talk of "Islam and the West" was becoming less accurate: sometimes the two were one and the same. In the fall of 1976, a friend of my father's from seminary, Imam Mehdi Khorasani, came to dine with us while on a visit from San Francisco, where he had founded the Islamic Society of California. Seventeen years earlier, he had started the Islamic Society of London.

He spoke lovingly of the beauty of the countryside around San Francisco, the opportunities for spiritual growth, and the progress the Islamic Society of California had made. When we had dinner guests, custom obligated my brothers and me to retire to our bedrooms to complete homework while the adults sat in the living room and talked. We were astonished, then, when our father summoned me and two of my older brothers, Moustafa and Mohammed, and said that Imam Khorasani wanted a word. What could such an important man want with teenagers and children? We were excited and nervous as we filed downstairs to face him. "As-salaamu alaikum," he said, using the traditional Arabic greeting: *Peace be with you.* Imam Khorasani asked us whether we had given thought to our careers. My oldest brother, Ali, was already in the United Kingdom studying to be an engineer. Moustafa and Mohammed suggested that this path, engineering, or perhaps law or medicine, might be right for them. Being older, they faced the bulk of the questions.

Consider going to seminary, the imam suggested. Our people need you. Become an imam, he said. If you want to travel the world, become an imam. If you want to foster Muslim culture, become an imam. If you want to enjoy this life and the next life, and advance the religion, become an imam. I was awed by this slight yet imposing man, so full of conviction and carrying God's message to the other side of the world. My eyes must have gone wide. Being an imam means being a doctor of the spirit, he told us. Then he turned to me and said, "Someday, many years from now, you will come knock at my door, introduce yourself, and announce that you're an imam."

In 1978, a former student of my father's came to Kuwait to deliver a lecture on Islam in America that I attended, and he told the audience that Islam there was in its crawling stage, an infant faith. The rest of the world already knows about Islam's mighty contributions to science, math, and medicine, he said, but Americans don't. Afterward, he presented me with a gift, an Arabic version of a book about Imam Ali called *The Brother of the Prophet,* written by Imam Mohamad Jawad Chirri. (When the first Muslims left the hostile trading hub of Mecca to start a new society in Medina, the Prophet Muhammad referred to Meccans as the Immigrants and to Medinans as the Supporters and matched up pairs from the two communities to care for each other as brothers. He assigned Imam Ali no brother, however, and when Imam Ali questioned him, the Prophet Muhammad said, "I have left you for myself, for you are my brother and successor.")[4] The ex-student, then in his early thirties, had spoken in Dearborn, Michigan, where Imam Chirri (pronounced "Shur'-ee") had founded the Islamic Center of Detroit and was leading an enthusiastic and growing Muslim community.

Imam Chirri had impeccable credentials and was held in high esteem in the United States. He had graduated from the Najaf seminary. But I could tell that Imam Chirri was different from the imams my father met with in Iraq and Kuwait. In his author photo, he wore a shirt and tie underneath his dress robe, something I had never seen before. His biography stated that he spoke, wrote, and taught in English as well as Arabic. And he had met with Presidents Nixon and Carter as well as with major Arab leaders, such as President Gamal Abdel Nasser of Egypt. Here was someone who had made great personal sacrifices to follow his beliefs and managed to reconcile the traditions of West and East, with tolerance and wisdom. I still did not know what course my life might take, but I was genuinely inspired by this man.

THE TWELVE SHIA IMAMS

The term "imam" has multiple meanings in Islam. In its simplest sense, and to both Shia and Sunnis, the imam is the leader of a congregational prayer, usually a respected elder member. Islam lacks the hierarchy of Catholicism; clerical positions are often determined by consensus, and most any capable Muslim can lead the prayer. He or she is an imam *only in the act*. The title has no permanence.

In the clerical sense, an imam is an Islamic priest, the spiritual leader of an entire congregation, who gives the Friday-afternoon sermon, runs the mosque, counsels Muslims, and serves as a community liaison. These imams generally have extensive knowledge of the Qur'an and the traditions of the Prophet Muhammad and have undertaken years of study.

The final meaning is that of a divinely inspired leader. Prophet Muhammad was the last messenger of God, but in the Shia view, the spark of divine blessing and spiritual perfection passed from him, to Imam Ali, to his eldest son, Imam Hassan, and then to Imam Husayn, each unerringly stewarding the words and intentions of the Prophet Muhammad from one generation to the next. This went on for nearly 250 years. The Prophet Muhammad alluded to the imams' coming: "The Imams [successors] after me are twelve," he said. "The first of them is Ali son of Abu Talib and the last of them is the Qaem [Al-Mahdi, the Guided One]. They are my successors, trustees, guardians, and the proofs of God on my nation after me."[5] Collectively, these men are the Twelve Revered Shia Imams (see pp. 259–62 for more on each), sinless and divinely appointed. The Shia include the traditions (the sunna) of the Twelve Imams alongside those of the Prophet Muhammad in the Islamic canon. The Imams' sunna only reinforce the teachings of the Prophet Muhammad. They do not contradict them.

Islamic law derives from the Qur'an but depends more heavily on the sunna and specifically the hadith, which are specific sayings from the Prophet Muhammad and the Twelve Imams. Hadith are part of the sunna, which also encompasses behavior and stories from the Prophet and the Imams. Muslims generally do not accept all of the sayings now attributed to the Prophet Muhammad, however, because some of them are apocryphal. A few centuries after the Prophet's death, one could verify a hadith by documenting the parties through which the saying had passed. (Several companions were known to have fabricated hadith for political advantage or material gain.) By the mid-ninth century, Muslims had compiled about 700,000 hadith on everything under the sun, many of which contradicted other hadith or ran counter to principles established in the Qur'an.[6]

Authentic hadith can be regarded as equal in authority, though not in sanctity, to passages from the Qur'an. Unfortunately, the separation of authentic hadith from false hadith is an inexact science. Sunni and Shia Muslims agree that hadith from unreliable sources should be rejected, but they do not agree on which sources are unreliable. The most effective fabricators ascribed their sayings to upstanding, respected Muslims to mask the unreliable content.[7] Mu'wayiah, the first caliph of the Umayyad dynasty (A.D. 661–750), developed a committee to manufacture false hadith for political purposes. One says, "My companions are like stars. With whomever you follow, you shall be guided," which effectively put every companion on the level of the Prophet Muhammad and also tidily legitimized Mu'wayiah's questionable rule, as he himself was a companion.

In the centuries after the Prophet Muhammad's death, these false sayings supported the worst kinds of governments. Another concocted hadith from the Umayyad dynasty: "Put up with whatever conduct you do not like of your rulers because if you abandon the Jama'a [group] even the distance of one foot and then die, you will die as unbelievers."[8] Corrupt rulers publicized such sayings so effectively that even major Sunni scholars accepted them. Today, mainstream Sunnis still say that Muslims have no right to revolt against Muslim tyrants, one reason why so many Muslim countries have abominable rulers.

THE SHIA WAY

The differences between Shia and Sunni are both more significant and less significant than the average non-Muslim might expect. Culturally, and in terms of our religious rites, there is little that separates us. Distinguishing Shia from Sunni on the street is not like distinguishing horses from zebras. Clothing and hairstyles aren't radically different. Someone's accent or last name can suggest his or her affiliation, but neither is a giveaway. Iraqis tend to have tribal names that originate from certain areas, and because some regions are more Shia or Sunni than others (western Iraq is Sunni territory, for example, and Shia dominate in the south), an observer can make an educated guess. But, just as among many races, ethnicities, and religious groups around the world, Shia and Sunni have intermarried, blurring the lines for those who insist on making the distinction.

When praying toward Mecca, Shia pray with their arms extended; Sunnis keep them close to their sides with elbows bent. Sunnis perform their prayers five times each day, at dawn, noon, afternoon, sunset, and evening, while Shia combine the noon/afternoon prayers and sunset/evening prayers and pray three times a day (but still perform all five prayers). Both schools have historical justifications for their practices, but the truth is that some Muslim traditions, like so many other religions' practices, have multiple interpretations that developed over centuries. We are more alike than different.

Certain hard-line Muslims exaggerate and distort Shia Muslim views to estrange them from their brethren. They characterize Shia reverence for the family of the Prophet Muhammad and visitation to Prophet Muhammad's grave and the shrines of the Imams as idol worship and polytheism. They view Shi'ism as a later development somehow separate from Islam itself. They decry the "innovation" of the Imams and contemporary ayatollahs because Shia doctrine allows for reinterpretation of legal precedents (*ijtihad*), whereas Sunni jurisprudence has not changed since the ninth century. In some Sunni eyes, Shia are apostates.

Once, while on a shuttle bus during the hajj, the pilgrimage to Mecca, I encountered a Sunni brother who identified me as Shia by my turban and asked me why we worship rocks. A primary stylistic difference between Shia and Sunni is that Shia prefer to worship on clean earth or that which grows on it—"Earth has been made a place for prostration and a substance for purification," the Prophet Muhammad said—whereas Sunni will pray on carpet or wool rugs.[9] Shia handle the obvious logistical challenge by carrying prayer mats woven from plant fiber or clay tablets, like those Karbala vendors sell near the shrine of Imam Husayn—the rocks my fellow pilgrim on the bus was derisively referring to. I explained that we do not *worship* rocks but pray *over* them symbolically, that his literal interpretation was akin to characterizing someone who kisses the Qur'an as worshipping sheepskin. He would not hear of it.

I see two philosophical reasons for the animosity toward Shia, and the first is built on the second. Polytheism and idol worship are the gravest of sins in Islam. To practice them deliberately and sincerely is to denounce Islam entirely. The Shia's regard for the Prophet Muhammad's family is not idol worship, but among a subset of Muslims who despise Islam's diversity, any worship that does not conform to their narrow interpretation is *haram*—forbidden. The second reason lies in Islam's sense of community. The common values and dearly held beliefs among Muslims naturally foster close ties. But Shia have always been candid that the majority of Muslims, those who accepted rule by companions, took the wrong path, obviously an unpopular belief to publicize.

Regrettably, their paths diverged almost at the very origin of Islam, so Sunnis and Shia have lived very different histories—unlike Catholics and Protestants, who have hundreds of years of common history. Sunnis can point to the caliphate and the grand halls of emperors bearing their version of the faith to cities halfway around the world; they created the flourishing arts, culture, and philosophy of the Abbasid dynasty (A.D. 750–1258) during Islam's golden age. Shia, mostly shut out of government since Islam's revelation, have their school of thought, their sacrifices for ideals as exemplified by Imam Husayn, and the belief that justice will be reinstated in the future.

The fundamental division between Shia and Sunnis is surmountable, but the systematic persecution that grew out of this division has exacerbated their differences over the centuries. Between A.D. 846 and 861 the Abbasid dynasty attempted to destroy the shrine of Imam Husayn four times in hopes of suppressing Shia views and ending pilgrimages there, but Shia rebuilt it each time. Mohammad ibn Abd al-Wahhab, the eighteenth-century founder of the Wahhabi movement, renewed the fanatical opposition to Shia through extensive raids on Najaf and Karbala in the early 1800s, looting the shrine, desecrating the tombs of Imam Ali and Imam Husayn, and killing two thousand Shia in Karbala on Ashura.

All of the Shia Imams were persecuted to varying degrees. Some went into hiding to escape threats or were cautious about whom they would see. Several were poisoned, and Imam Ali was slain by an extremist who felt he had not taken a harsh enough position with an enemy army that surrendered in battle. The last Imam, Muhammad ibn al-Hassan, went into occultation in 874, at age five, when the eleventh Imam died. Shia know him as the Hidden Imam, Al-Mahdi, the savior who awaits the proper time to reveal himself and launch a campaign of justice and reform. Most Sunnis also believe in the return of Al-Mahdi before the Day of Judgment, though not as the twelfth Imam. Islamic texts say he will return in a time of war, false prophets, and the nullification of Islamic law and will appear in the Grand Mosque in Mecca in concert with Jesus to rid the world of tyranny.

SHIFTING ALLIANCES: WEST AND EAST, PERSIAN AND ARAB

In 1979 two landmark events took place in the Middle East:

The first, in February, was that Ayatollah Ruhollah Khomeini fueled the overthrow of the Shah of Iran, Muhammad Reza Pahlavi, and started the Islamic Revolution. My father was so relieved to see the end of the Shah's blundering and corrupt reign that he joined the first delegation to Iran to congratulate the ayatollah. The Shah's deposal seemed inevitable. Opposition had been building since the United States and Britain engineered removal of the popular prime minister of Iran, Mohammad Mossadegh, in

1953 amid concerns that, in American eyes, he was too vulnerable to Communist influences.[10] Ayatollah Khomeini had condemned the Shah's monarchy going back to 1963. Iranians chafed at both the Shah's western-oriented reforms and positions, including co-operation and trade with Israel (the Shah was one of only two leaders of Muslim countries to recognize Israel), and the clandestine trials and murder of political opponents. At Qum's Feiziyeh School of Theology in 1963, on the anniversary of the death of Imam Jafar al-Sadiq, the sixth Shia Imam, the Shah's Imperial Guard had disrupted a remembrance ceremony; the episode then escalated into violence and led to the deaths of three seminary students and the beating of an ayatollah's son-in-law, who was mistaken for the ayatollah himself. Two months later Ayatollah Khomeini, in an Ashura sermon before thousands, foretold ignominy for the Shah if he didn't change course:

> O Mr. Shah, dear Mr. Shah, abandon these improper acts. I don't want people to offer thanks should your masters decide that you must leave. I don't want you to become like your father [whom the Soviet Union and England had forced off the throne, fearing that he would side with Germany in World War II]. When America, the Soviet Union and England attacked us, people were happy that [your father] went. Listen to my advice, listen to the clergy's advice, not to that of Israel. That would not help you. You wretched miserable man, forty-five years of your life have passed. Isn't it time to think and reflect a little, to ponder about where all this is leading you, to learn a lesson from the experience of your father?[11]

Two days later, SAVAK (the National Organization for Information and Security), the Shah's secret police, arrested the ayatollah at his home. After an imprisonment lasting eight months, he was expelled from the country and spent most of the next fourteen years in Najaf, Iraq. He traveled to Karbala weekly to visit and lecture. The Iraqi president, Ahmed Hassan al-Bakr, and Saddam closely watched Ayatollah Khomeini and the political climate in Iran during those years for signs of unrest. They feared that Iran's dissenting spirit could spread to Iraq and threaten their control, and that if it did, the Shia scholars of Najaf and Karbala would be its catalysts. In Iran, clerics, merchants, western-leaning intellectuals, and Communists were calling for new rule. As Iranians rebelled more openly against the Shah, they met with violent reprisals, sometimes through SAVAK, and such crackdowns precipitated more vigorous rebellion in a spiral of suppression and backlash.

The second major event of 1979 was Saddam's assumption of the presidency from a frail al-Bakr in July. As al-Bakr's deputy from 1968 to 1979, Saddam had wielded more power than most top world leaders. He oversaw the country's vast security operations, he co-signed executive orders, and he functioned as co-president. Yet in that role he still had to maintain a pretense of deference to al-Bakr, a position he wouldn't have wanted to hold indefinitely. After Saddam's takeover, nothing could interfere with his plans to dominate the Middle East.

As the Islamic Revolution got under way that year, Saddam's agents were omnipresent in Iraq and busily gathering intelligence in Kuwait and Iran. A month after my father returned to Kuwait City from marking Ayatollah Khomeini's victory in Iran, he was fired on while driving past the Iraqi embassy. A bullet struck his car, and though he was unhurt, my older sister and her baby had been riding with him. Probably it was my father's continued vocal opposition to Saddam's regime—he was emboldened by the victory of the Islamic Revolution in Iran—that led to greater scrutiny than he had received in the past. But he couldn't go to the authorities because Kuwait was itself overwhelmed by the struggle to neutralize the Baathists' influence. The Kuwaiti government didn't have the resources to seal its borders with Iraq, and Saddam had been building up his military in anticipation of conflict with Iran. A week before the shooting, another scholar in

Kuwait, Abdul Munem Shawki, had been abducted by Iraqi forces and spirited off to Iraq; he was executed weeks later. My father could no longer be confident of our safety in Kuwait.

Suddenly it was 1971 all over again. No matter where we went, it seemed, Saddam's shadow followed us. (Upon assuming power in 2004, the former prime minister of Iraq Ibrahim al-Jaafari sent my father an eight-hundred-page file he had retrieved from the old Mukhabarat headquarters. From it, we learned that agents had been following my father while we lived in Kuwait. Even some visitors and dinner guests, probably under duress, were gathering information about our family for the Mukhabarat. The file documented all kinds of information: visitors to our house, my father's travel schedule, photos of family members.) That spring, my mother came to all of us and said, "Your father is considering moving to Iran. What do you think?" We were shocked. By now, we had grown to love Kuwait. It was home to us. I raised my hand and said, "What? Iran?" We didn't have any idea what day-to-day life might be like, though we knew that Kuwait's standard of living was higher. Where would we settle, we wanted to know. Tehran? Qum?

Once school let out for the summer in 1979, we took a trip to Iran. For me and my brothers and sisters, the trip was exploratory, but my father felt he could wait no longer. He bought a house in Qum (pronounced "Kohm") and settled in while we completed a final year of schooling in Kuwait. Qum was an old town, with 350,000 people at the time, and a holy site because of the presence of the elegant shrine of Hadrat Fatimah Masoumah, the sister of the eighth Shia Imam, Imam Ali al-Redha, who lived during the eighth and ninth centuries.

Much of what goes on in Qum revolves around its seminary, often called by its common name, the Hawza, the same title used for Najaf's. The largest seminary in Iran, the Hawza comprises more than one hundred schools and institutions, not counting two entirely separate seminaries, one for women and one for international students, who come from almost eighty countries.

Ayatollah Abdul Karim al-Haeri, a Najaf graduate, founded the seminary in the early 1920s. Residents there were bombarding him with pleas to establish a seminary. Ayatollah Haeri conducted an *istikhara,* a prayer for guidance followed by a random consultation of the Qur'an. The passage he found was so encouraging that he immediately decided to heed the Persians' wishes and remain in Qum. Traveling overland to Najaf in those days represented a considerable hardship, and the local seminary grew quickly. It began to rise to prominence in the mid-twentieth century. Roughly the same number of students attended Qum and Najaf at the time, but Najaf had the more prestigious scholars. Al-Bakr and Saddam can take responsibility for tipping the scales in favor of Qum. Qum's ranks swelled in the late 1960s, after al-Bakr limited the number of non-Iraqi students who could attend Najaf, and in 1980 Saddam changed those caps to an outright ban, a reflection of how suspicious he had grown of Shia influence from Iran. In 1970 about five thousand students attended Najaf; by 1981, the number was little more than two hundred. Qum, by comparison, had thirty-five thousand.[12]

The shift was no secret. Shia leaders, feeling unsafe in Iraq, were leaving the country in droves. A massive purging operation staged in the spring of 1980, as I was completing my sophomore year in Kuwait, elevated the fears. In April, nine months after Saddam became president, he deported about forty thousand Shia who, he claimed, were ethnically Persian, including some of my relatives.[13] Over the course of the war with Iran, which stretched from 1980 to 1988, that number rose as high as five hundred thousand.

On April 8, 1980, one of my father's sisters called to tell us that fourteen members of our family, mostly my first and second cousins, had been arrested in Karbala. My grandfather Ayatollah Mohammad Sadiq Qazwini was among those taken. The roundup had taken place with the briefest of warnings. The day before, agents of the Mukhabarat invited my grandfather to join a delegation of religious leaders requested to pay their respects—really, their allegiance—to Saddam. "If you don't agree to come," one agent warned my grandfather, "you will pay a heavy price."

At midnight that same night, there was a knock at the door. My grandfather refused to answer, so the agents went to a neighbor's house and broke in through the rooftops. First they beat him, with my grandmother looking on, and then they took him wearing only his sleeping robe, left my grandmother in the street, and burned his entire personal library—thousands of volumes. The Mukhabarat sealed the house, and we never saw my grandfather again. In 1984 Amnesty International named him the world's oldest political prisoner. He was eighty-four.

My uncle Abdul-Hussein was leading the dusk and nightly prayers at Al-Gallaf, a suburban mosque in Kuwait City where he had taken over as imam for my father, when I received the call from my aunt with the news. Among the members of our family, my uncle was the only one who could fully appreciate what these arrests meant. He, too, had been ensnared by the Mukhabarat, and the memories still haunted him. My uncle had told me that in 1972 he and eighteen other seminary students in Karbala were arrested by Iraqi troops as part of a crackdown on the Shia establishment and a larger war on Islam. Al-Bakr wanted to shut down all the seminaries. Major Sunni leaders, such as Abdul Aziz al-Badri, were also killed during this campaign. Agents took the students to the headquarters of the Mukhabarat, who wanted my uncle to confess to planning a coup d'état. The secret police sought out conspiracies with zest, and they found them wherever they went. When confessions didn't come readily, they found ways to persuade.

There were no cells, just a single room with a ceiling only thirty inches high, too low to sit with one's head raised. No one dared, or bothered, to talk. The only sounds were screaming, crying, and laughing, which occurred in unison when other prisoners were taken to an adjacent room for torture sessions. Guards knew very well that the cries of the tortured could be heard by other prisoners and expected them to confess more readily after listening to what they were about to endure. But the interrogators must also have taken enough sadistic pleasure in their crimes that such tactics could well have been used for their own sake. In response to agonized cries of "Muhammad," desperate pleas to God's messenger, guards would respond, "Oh, you are calling for Muhammad?" and a guard named Muhammad would join in the abuse.

One torture involved tying the suspect upside down from a ceiling fan. The interrogators would start at the lowest speed, level one, and demand a confession. When it didn't come, the speed was increased—two, three, four—sometimes with beatings to go along. Either for the sake of expediency or because it was more humiliating to be tortured in the presence of another prisoner, the guards at times interrogated two simultaneously. Uncle Abdul-Hussein once looked on, horrified, as the head officer stood laughing in front of a man who was hung upside down from a fan, and then urinated in his face.

After twenty-eight days, they reassigned my uncle to Al-Fudhaylia, a prison in the Baghdad suburbs that until the 1958 Qasim coup had been the Iraqi royal family's personal stable; prisoners slept on the floor in horse stalls. Compared with headquarters, it was a five-star hotel, but the inhumanity continued. Once a month my grandfather would visit, which the guards permitted but discouraged by requiring him to remove his turban and robes and inspecting him in his underwear. For him, the visit, must have been worth any price. My uncle, however, could not stomach the humiliation of his father. "You don't come here anymore," he told him. "I don't want to see this done to you."

Every few days at Al-Fudhaylia, an intelligence officer would come in like a butcher eyeing sheep. He would motion a prisoner out of the room; sometimes the selected individual came back, and sometimes he did not. Over time, my uncle and the other prisoners grasped the routine. If the officer said, "Come with me," that meant you were being called in for a session of torture. If he said, "Pack up," you were going to be killed. Those seconds of not knowing, between the time the officer entered the room and spoke his orders, must have been the most tense, frightening moments of my uncle's detention. Down through the months, the pool of prisoners dwindled, with every officer's appearance carrying a greater weight. "For years, we never knew when our time would come," Uncle Abdul-Hussein told me.

After two and a half years, Saddam pardoned him in a spurious and improbable show of high-mindedness that saw a number of scholars released. My uncle realized, however, that he could never be safe in Iraq under Saddam, that he had merely traded a small prison for a larger one. At the first opportunity, he applied for a hajj visa, the only way to leave the country legally, and he did not return. Like so many, he fled to Kuwait, where my father helped him get a visa and housing in 1976.

Four years later, here I was at Al-Gallaf reintroducing the nightmare to him. He was leading the combined evening and night prayer, which included a five- or ten-minute break with informal prayers and supplications. I waited for the break, then reluctantly revealed to him what my aunt had told me, that fourteen in our family, including my uncle's own father and many of his nephews, had been taken by the Mukhabarat. I saw tears well in his eyes, and nothing I said or did could soften the blow. If they had been arrested and detained, he said, in light of the furor over Iran, they were not just being held. They had been killed. He was sure of it, and although he continued on with the second prayer, he did so with great difficulty.

DOWN THE PATH OF THE IMAM

In July 1980, the rest of us joined my father in Qum. I was entering my junior year of high school and so had two years to go, but at sixteen, students also are eligible to enter the seminary. I did both. During the day, I studied at the seminary. At night, I attended classes from five to ten o'clock in order to complete my

Struggle in Iran   45

formal high school education. A few other seminary students did the same. From a young age, I had aspired to be like my father, and in my teens my desire to pursue that life only grew stronger.

Arriving in Qum with the dream of becoming an imam was like being a star-struck high school soccer player who has been given a ticket to the World Cup. Acquaintances of mine had begun joining the seminary months before and spoke of it as the best thing they had ever done. The summer before, in 1979, I had attended an orientation while the city was abuzz with the possibility of the Islamic Revolution and images of Ayatollah Khomeini adorned public buildings. Journalists, supporters, and independent observers from all over the world clustered in Qum to take in the scene. It felt like the center of the world. I was more overwhelmed by the scale of the Hawza. The University of Michigan's enrollment today would equal that of Qum's Hawza—but only if you counted the fourteen thousand people on its Flint and Dearborn campuses as well as those in Ann Arbor. In Kuwait, my father taught seminary classes to fifteen or twenty students at a time. Here I saw thousands of students strolling through squares and quadrangles in between classes, their robes swishing purposefully with each step.

Exquisite buildings, modeled after the great seminaries of Morocco, Tunisia, and Iraq, dotted the campus. One of the oldest schools at Qum was Feiziyeh, the site of Ayatollah Khomeini's famous 1963 address spurning the Shah. Built in the early 1800s, Feiziyeh served as a student center for all the seminaries. If you really wanted to know what was going on around campus, you went to Feiziyeh and checked the bulletin boards for announcements. At Feiziyeh, a student could listen to classmates' impassioned speeches in the courtyard, collect his monthly stipend, or study in a grand, wood-paneled library on the order of the Vatican Library.

Early on, the opportunity to go to seminary was, for me, the only positive aspect of our move to Qum. Everything else was heartache. The fourteen of our family the Mukhabarat had taken were all men. Their wives and children met us in Iran and did their best to move on without really moving on, never certain whether they were families in waiting or widows and orphans. Their faces reminded me daily of what should not be.

Even though Iran welcomed us—and many other Iraqis in the years to come—the country presented its own challenges. Iran is Persian, not Arab, and the national language is Persian, also called Farsi. In order to participate in and pass my classes at Sadooq High School, I would have to learn it. The languages are not dissimilar—most of the letters are the same, and 50 percent of Persian uses Arab vocabulary—but an Arabic speaker does not understand a Persian speaker, and vice versa. My father was fluent in Persian but did not speak it with us at home, so my exposure was limited. I compensated by reading Iranian and Persian newspapers, such as *Kayhan* ("The World") and *Itila-at* ("Information"), as well as reading Persian novels and taking Persian literature and poetry classes.

Persian-speaking people find it harder to learn Arabic than Arabic speakers do to learn Persian, yet the Persian-to-Arabic transition is more common for the simple reason that Arabic is the language of Islam. The Prophet Muhammad and Islam's early adherents spoke Arabic; the Qur'an was revealed in Arabic (which is also known as the language of angels). The most important and influential Shia leaders are not only masters of jurisprudence, logic, and Islamic history, they also are supremely eloquent. For Muslims, the Qur'an is more than the faith in written form; it is also the preserver of the Arabic language. In the Arab world, Qur'an recitation contests are common, and those who have memorized its entire contents are held in high esteem.

Even most non-Muslim Arab political leaders speak Arabic and know the Qur'an, and non-Arab Muslim imams and leaders usually speak Arabic as well. In seminary, we were required to study Arabic language, grammar, eloquence, and speech for four years.

Language distinguishes Qum's seminary from Najaf's as much as geography does. In the latter, texts and instruction are in Arabic, period. In the former, 70 to 80 percent of the classes are taught in Persian, using Arabic texts. Outside the seminary, students and Qum residents mostly speak Persian.

Seminary life was humble, intense, and rigidly scheduled. Classes started at six A.M. I would attend five sessions, one after another, and stop at noon for prayer. Lunch brought a two- to three-hour break, and classes resumed in mid-afternoon and ran until sunset, when we would perform a congregational prayer. Evenings were times of study and preparation for the next day's classes. I also used this time for my high school coursework. Wednesday night was my favorite time of the week. That was the traditional holy night to visit a mosque called Jamkaran, just outside Qum. After finishing afternoon classes, a few friends and I would take the bus there to complete the day's prayers. Then we would spend the rest of the night joking with each other and discussing spirituality and philosophy. Local stories say that Imam Mahdi came to Jamkaran's architect in a dream and told him to build the mosque, so it is believed to enjoy Imam Mahdi's blessing.

On any given day, travelers unfamiliar with the seminary's setup would gawk in surprise at seeing packs of students, anywhere from fifty to eight hundred of us, clustered in one half of a mosque listening to a lecture, or engaged in boisterous debate. There were no projectors or movie reels, no chalkboards or easels, and no desks or chairs. Each instructor had a pulpit and a microphone. We would follow along as he read passages from texts hundreds of years old and offered his interpretation of the historical scholarship. With such a bare-bones approach, the teachers' passion and rapport with the class were essential. Some teachers were animated and engaging. Some, I regret to say, were boring. As students advanced, they had more freedom to sample various instructors and stick with those they learned from best.

Qum's seminary had (and still has) the largest and most eminent Shia faculty in the world. To varying degrees, these were men of worldwide acclaim with devoted followings and decades of study behind them. They included men like Ayatollah Muhammad Husayn Tabataba'i, the most famous Muslim philosopher of the twentieth century, and Ayatollah Hussein Ali Montazeri, Ayatollah Wahid Khorasani, and Ayatollah Jawad Tabrizi, all well-known jurists and scholars who studied under either Qum's Ayatollah Husayn Burujirdi (the highest Shia scholar from 1947 to 1961) or Najaf's Ayatollah Abu al-Qasim Khu'i (the highest Shia scholar from 1970 to 1992). These four also taught ethics, the domain of the most pious and respected faculty. Held to the absolute highest standards of behavior, ethics instructors drew crowds of four hundred to five hundred students, many of whom would cry as they listened to the lectures. I would hear some of these instructors in the coming years, as I progressed to higher-level classes, all of which stressed the importance of self-examination and true humility. Remember why you're here, our teachers would say. Some of you will become well-known. But if you think of yourselves as celebrities, then you are not serving God. If you become preoccupied with your own stature and advancement, you have already failed. We were urged not to be impressed by the trappings of success, which would disappear soon enough. Instead the focus was on personal reckoning. Ethics classes were not mandatory, but most students attended anyway.

Once a student is accepted to the seminary, he is permitted, though not required, to wear the robe and turban of a religious leader. Most do so within the first two or three years of study. You can see the change a student undergoes when he begins wearing his seminary attire. He becomes more disciplined and dignified. Gone are the ribald jokes, loud laughing, fast walking, casual eating (say, an apple on the way to class), and any reaction to insults or taunts. These proscriptions stem from the belief that formal seminary garb represents the dress of the Prophet, and that while wearing it one must behave accordingly.

There is a title for students who dress this way: the Disciples of Al-Mahdi, the last Revered Imam. Eager to start down the path of an imam, I opted to wear my robe and turban at the first opportunity, toward the end of my first year. For me, in addition to being a student and scholar, I felt honored to live out the legacy of my family, put a new leaf on the tree, and demonstrate my commitment to lifelong religious scholarship. Students traditionally consummated this transformation at a formal ceremony, at which a "spinner" would take cloth a student had purchased and create his turban before placing it on the student's head. I planned a ceremony with two classmates at my father's house. A very distinguished scholar who was my father's friend was invited to spin my turban. My father, my brothers, a few of my teachers, and nearly my entire seminary class attended.

Seminary was not the rigid, hierarchical body dictating Islamic knowledge that my descriptions might make it seem. We managed to come away with a broad base of shared knowledge, but the entire structure of the seminary was organic and geared to the individual. Students might study for a few years, or for a dozen or more. There was a rough breakdown of beginner, intermediate, and advanced classes, but no requirement to spend a fixed amount of time at each level. Proficiency and learning determined the pace of one's advancement. The beginner track emphasized Arabic language, grammar, and eloquence, and also command of the Holy Qur'an. The consensus among Muslims has long been that in order to fully grasp the meaning and intent of the words of the Prophet Muhammad and the Twelve Revered Imams, one must master Arabic. Some terms are so rooted in Arab culture that they cannot be adequately translated into other languages. Formal Arabic, the traditional style spoken at the time of the Prophet, is comparable in tone to the English of the King James Bible and is used in all writing and in official speaking, as in news broadcasts or press conferences. Informal Arabic is more modern, and the vocabulary varies among Arabic-speaking regions. (When I give a lecture today, I'll use formal Arabic about 80 percent of the time and mix in informal for the rest, as when relating a side story or telling a joke.) The language is tremendously complex, more so even than English. Without intensive training, even most native speakers don't use it correctly.

ENDLESS CARNAGE

I lived simply in Qum. There, one comes of age at fifteen, and I was determined to be self-sufficient. Rejection of worldly life and ready acceptance of hardship were the most basic lessons of the seminary. My father had paid for the move to Iran and a new house in Qum and was helping, as much as he could, the relatives whose husbands and fathers had been taken in Iraq. The seminary itself helped somewhat: tuition was free, paid for by the tithing of millions of Shia. In addition, students received a small stipend, the equivalent of $75 per month, which covered basic expenses. I accepted money from my father only when he offered it.

By Iraqi standards, I grew up well-off. We lived in a large house (albeit one shared by nine people), had a maid, and attended good schools. An abundance of food was a given. Until he decided it was a material excess and sold it, my father was the first religious leader in Karbala to drive a car—a Chevrolet—in 1965. We took a family vacation once a year, and a few of my brothers and I would sometimes accompany my father on his speaking trips. Only once I enrolled in seminary did my life turn ascetic. I lived in a dormitory and rarely traveled. I drank no soda, ate no fruit, and combined canned foods with fresh bread at meals. I did my own laundry. The last years of my study were less lean as I was able to supplement our income by speaking, but by then my wife and I also had two children to take care of.

The worst part of student life was the public baths. The weather in Karbala and Kuwait City was mostly hot and dry. Qum lies at about the same latitude as Atlanta but at an elevation of three thousand feet, with the Zagros Mountains to the west, along the Iraqi border, and the Elburz Mountains to the north, near Tehran. Until we moved to Qum, I had never seen snow. The winters were bitter cold, and although the shower areas did have hot water, they did not have heat. The alternative was to shower in my own bathroom, which I favored, as it didn't require waiting outside in line. I had a compact gas-powered water heater in my dormitory, but it was tedious to use, so I suffered through a few years of cold showers, jumping up and down the entire time.

Political affairs in the early 1980s gave me another reason not to use the water heater. Iraq's invasion of Iran in September 1980, which coincided with my entry into the seminary, destabilized Gulf oil shipments. Gas was difficult to obtain and available only on the black market. Iraq cited a supposed assassination attempt on its foreign minister, Tariq Aziz (since captured, tried, and imprisoned following the 2003 invasion of Iraq by coalition forces), in April 1980 as justification for declaring war, but everyone knew that the real reason was Saddam's fear that Ayatollah Khomeini's Islamic Revolution would spread to Iraq.

Saddam played up cultural differences by referring to Iranians as Persians and Zoroastrians, followers of an ancient faith that preceded Islam as Persia's dominant religion. Abu Hanifa, founder of the most widely accepted Sunni school of thought in Islam, was Iranian, as were numerous Muslim pioneers in science and medicine, such as the philosopher and physician Avicenna and the poet and mathematician Omar Khayyám, but Saddam did not talk about them.

The Iran-Iraq War, probably the longest conventional war of the twentieth century, was a shameful waste of human life. Iraq had superior military technology and highly trained armies; Iran countered with larger forces in human-wave attacks that were effective but, without significant air and artillery support, disastrous for the attacking soldiers. By the time the two countries agreed to a cease-fire, in 1988, the combined casualties over eight years were estimated at more than one million, comparable to what the North and South together suffered during the American Civil War.[14] Iran bore most of the carnage, about three quarters of the combined casualties.[15]

Though our family did not fight, and we lost no one as a result of the war, images of young people going to their graves overwhelmed us. The soldiers were about my own age, usually between sixteen and twenty years old. Every day we saw the bodies of these teenagers who had fought and died come back to Qum. The soldiers didn't bring just one body at a time; they brought ten, or fifteen, or twenty. Thousands would fill the streets to mourn. There were cries of agony and shouted prayers; people would slap their own faces, a traditional gesture of grief or atonement in Iraq and Iran. Occasionally, if a lot of people had been killed or a seminary teacher or student had been killed, the seminary would close for the day.

As difficult as the war was for Iranian soldiers, I daresay it was worse for Iraqi soldiers. Joining the Iranian army was voluntary. Iraqis were conscripted, and there was little popular support there for the war. Blithely indulging in irony, Saddam dubbed the war Qadisiyyah-Saddam, an explicit reference to the seventh-century Battle of al-Qadisiyyah, in which early Muslims defeated Persian armies and ultimately brought Islam to present-day Iran. At the time of the Iran-Iraq War, the front of the Iraqi 25-dinar note depicted the original Battle of Qadisiyyah, and next to it a resolute, noble-looking Saddam Hussein.

This didn't appear to change the sentiment on the ground: Iraqi soldiers often surrendered at the first opportunity rather than risk dying in combat for a war they didn't believe in, and as a result Iran retained many more POWs than Iraq did, at one point holding 200,000 to Iraq's 20,000. Iranians, on the other hand, did genuinely see the conflict as a holy war, as evidenced by the large numbers who enlisted voluntarily and the spirit with which they plunged heedlessly into battle. An aggressor had violated their country. Anyone killed was considered a martyr, a *sha-heed.*

The idea that Iran's Islamic Revolution might spread to Iraq, Saudi Arabia, or Kuwait made U.S. officials nervous, too. They assumed that an Iran governed according to Islamic principles would necessarily be anti-American, which was partly true, but not because of Islam. The United States had been carefully nurturing discontent for decades, in a country already sensitive to imperialist tendencies. Iran became something of a pawn to the Soviet Union and the West during World War II, when Britain and the Soviet Union invaded it preemptively lest the country, officially neutral, join the Axis powers. The Allies forced Reza Shah off the throne and installed his more pliable son, Muhammad Reza Pahlavi. During the Eisenhower administration of the early 1950s, the United States helped to overthrow the popular Iranian prime minister, and it continued to lend support to the Shah's increasingly repressive government throughout the 1960s and 1970s.

After Iran forced the Shah into exile in 1979, opening the door to a return of Ayatollah Khomeini, President Carter made a tactical mistake in allowing the Shah to come to the United States for medical treatment (he suffered from an advancing lymphoma). Innocuous or not, his admittance here gave the impression of an alliance and fueled speculation that the CIA was planning a coup to reinstall him as leader of Iran, just as it had done after ousting Prime Minister Mossadegh twenty-six years before. The plot to take over the American embassy in Tehran and hold hostages had begun before the United States accepted the Shah for treatment, but the Shah's entry into this country did reinforce suspicions about America.

With the Iran hostage crisis embarrassing him publicly, President Carter subtly encouraged Iraq to attack Iran, and the Reagan administration would later discreetly maintain a pro-Iraq stance, selling Saddam weapons and equipment for his war—only one instance among many of U.S. foreign policy experts believing that if one group or state is America's enemy, any opponent of that group or state must be America's friend. In December 1983, President Reagan sent Special Envoy Donald Rumsfeld to meet with Saddam and extend an offer to normalize relations, which had been severed in 1967. Rumsfeld was actually visiting Iraq in March 1984 when the news service United Press International reported that Saddam had used lethal mustard and nerve gas against Iran in combat. Rumsfeld did not speak out about those chemical weapons, and if U.S. officials disapproved in principle, that didn't prevent them from restoring full diplomatic ties with Iraq in November 1984. The United States afterward provided billions in loans and aid, and sold Saddam dozens of military helicopters—helicopters that intelligence sources later said they believed were used in the 1988 gassing of civilian Iraqi Kurds at Halabja. A Human Rights Watch report on Iraqi Kurds from March 11, 1991, criticized U.S. officials for their selective morality. "Despite the international outcry over this one infamous event, little was heard in the United States about Saddam Hussein's brutal treatment of his own people until his invasion of Kuwait last August 2 [1990]," it said. "Since the outset of the Kuwait crisis, however, Halabja has become a leitmotif for Saddam Hussein's disregard of human rights, and a major rationale for the war"—which was again deployed in the lead-up to the 2003 invasion.[16]

Of course, the Reagan administration also secretly sold arms to Iran, in the events that led to the Iran-Contra scandal: Oliver North and intermediaries took proceeds from the Iranian weapons sales and funneled them to the Contras, a rebel group fighting Nicaragua's socialist government. The U.S. weapons sales effectively kept both Iraq and Iran well equipped in an attempt to prolong the war indefinitely. The administration seemed to fear the possibility that either nation, but especially Iran, might emerge victorious and disrupt the balance of power in the Middle East, and American intelligence endlessly worked both sides to ensure that Iraqis and Iranians, too traumatized to focus on the West, continued killing each other.

Actually, *Shia* Iraqis and Iranians continued killing each other. Iran is nearly 90 percent Shia, and Saddam permitted Shia, who were conscripted, only in the low military ranks, where they performed the most dangerous assignments on the front lines. Officers were Sunni. Saddam had made a chilling calculation. If Iraq won, he would subjugate Iran and become the central power in the Middle East. If Iraq lost, Shia would die anyway.

CHAPTER 3

Sacred Journey

And proclaim the Pilgrimage among men: they will come
to thee on foot and . . . on every kind of camel, lean on
account of journeys through deep and distant mountain
highways.[1]
—*Holy Qur'an*

BY THE TIME I had completed my traditional high school studies,
in the spring of 1982, I was becoming increasingly independent.
My father had been named as a judge in a Tehran family court the
year before, so he, my mother, and my younger siblings were now
living there. I still struggled to meet basic needs at times, but I had
a firm direction for my life, and, without the additional effort of
night school, more time to devote to my seminary studies. I was
ready to take on my next great adult responsibility. I was ready for
marriage.

Islam has no proscription against marriage for religious leaders—or for anyone else. Marriage is not merely desirable or encouraged. It is a Muslim's fundamental obligation to find a suitable
partner. The Prophet Muhammad said, "He who gets married shall
achieve half of his faith [by getting married], so he shall fear God in
the other half," a way of saying that marrying fulfills half of one's
purpose in life and that worship of God fulfills the other.[2] Marriage
in Islamic society is a sacred contract, a way to reach a higher spiritual plane.

My trouble was twofold: First, I did not have any prospects. Our seminary was a strictly male community, and casual association of any sort with females was frowned upon, particularly so in a holy city like Qum. The best and most common way for a Muslim couple to marry is through family connections, the Islamic belief being that one can judge the fruit by the tree, and also judge the tree by the fruit. This, however, presented a second problem. Tradition in the Middle East requires that brothers marry in order of age. The two older brothers closest to me in age were not yet married. In order to enlist my family's help finding a mate and to secure their approval, I would need to find a way around this custom.

I received guidance on my first problem from a friend I had confided in, a man who was married to a daughter of Ayatollah Shirazi. He suggested that I marry his sister-in-law, the younger sister of his own wife. I considered the possibility but feared that the match might seem one-sided. Ayatollah Shirazi was a towering figure in the Shia world, a man of supreme prestige who wrote more than twelve hundred books, articles, and pamphlets during his lifetime. The lineage of his family was equally lofty. I, on the other hand, was an indigent seminary student who, at the moment, had little to offer a girl of such pedigree. This particular fruit looked to be out of reach.

Yet my father had long been friends with Ayatollah Shirazi, and I had spoken to the ayatollah on many occasions. I decided that I would attempt to follow my friend's advice. Protocol mandates that a suitor's father be the one to formally propose marriage to the girl's father. From casually introducing the topic previously, I knew my father felt I was too young to get married, so instead I approached my mother's father. The bonds between relatives by marriage are strong, and Islamic custom requires that a man perform any task his father-in-law asks of him. If I could persuade my grandfather, then I would have my father's agreement as well.

The tactic worked. My grandfather trusted that I was ready

for marriage, and, with his blessing, my father agreed to propose. All of this took place without the young woman and I ever having met, exchanged pictures, or even spoken on the phone. I had asked my mother and sisters about her (they all praised her), and I knew her brothers well. So I felt confident that our match, should it happen, would be a successful one. Handled properly, arranged marriages rarely result in divorce.

Ayatollah Shirazi's official response arrived two months later: Come in two weeks, he said, and you can get engaged. The Shirazis already lived in Qum. It was my family that would have to travel from Tehran for the ceremony. The engagement ceremony is the equivalent of a marriage ceremony in America—the legal aspect comes first in Muslim marriages. Once a couple has become engaged, they are permitted to socialize at the house of the girl's parents, but they cannot go on dates. Ayatollah Shirazi granted us one month to get acquainted and to prepare for the wedding. I visited once a week during that month, and when our time was up, in February 1983, we celebrated at separate dinner parties, each with about two hundred guests. Afterward, my father took me to the Shirazis' home, where I formally greeted my wife and her family. We then moved into a house we had rented.

Initially we had no honeymoon, though later we did go to Syria together. Once we were married, money was tighter than ever. For married couples, the seminary's stipend came to the equivalent of $150, twice the stipend for singles, but now we were renting a small house, not living in a dormitory. When the cold became unbearable, we would retreat to Tehran and my parents' house if I couldn't pay for, or couldn't find, heating oil in Qum. Studying full-time at the seminary, as I was, I did not have much of an opportunity to bring in extra money, and my wife did not work outside the home. In the Muslim world, responsibilities are divided between husband and wife in a traditional way. Men serve as the public face of the family, working outside the home and safeguarding their wife and children. Women are in charge of domestic life, running the household, raising and disciplining the children, and holding the family itself together. Non-Muslims in the United States frequently ask me about the status of women in Islam, sometimes aggressively—"Why do you Muslims mistreat women?" In fact, Islam holds that men and women are absolutely equal, but that they have different talents and should focus their efforts accordingly. Within the traditional Muslim family, women in most countries have broad license to pursue their ambitions. They may go about their business unaccompanied, they may hold jobs (though some choose not to), and they may participate in politics, both as voters and as leaders. Iran, for example, a country widely viewed as a rogue state by the West, has more female members of Parliament on a percentage basis than the United States does in both houses of Congress. And Indonesia, Turkey, Pakistan, and Bangladesh, all overwhelmingly Muslim countries, have had female prime ministers.

My wife was strong and understanding about our meager finances. Middle Eastern tradition still calls for the husband to grant his new wife a dowry, a symbol of his love for her. A dowry may range from $1 to $1 million, or it can be a payment in kind. A story from the Prophet Muhammad tells of a destitute but learned man who agreed to teach his wife to read and write from the Qur'an as a dowry. I settled on the same dowry that Imam Ali gave his wife, Fatima: two thousand grams of silver, about $1,000. The husband need not pay the dowry at the time of the wedding. It can be paid at any time, either when the husband decides or when the wife requests. Fortunately for me, my wife did not ask for her dowry right away!

Somehow, in the face of so few material advantages, our love grew richly during those early years, and in 1985 our first child, Mohamed, was born. I was visiting my family in Tehran when I heard the news of my wife's labor and immediately returned to Qum. One of the challenges of living in a holy city was the lack of qualified doctors: many families prefer to use female OB/GYNs, but Qum did not have enough to handle the demand. Parents-to-be instead put their faith in midwifery, and most babies were born at home. My wife gave birth to Mohamed at her parents' house, after eight hours of labor. By tradition, the husband's father names the family's first son. My father named him not after the Prophet Muhammad but after Imam Mohammad al-Baqir, the fifth Shia Imam, who guided the legions of Muslims gravitating to the Imams after the tragedy at Karbala. Our son was perfectly healthy, and a joy to hold.

THE FOOTSTEPS OF ABRAHAM

Growing up in Karbala and Kuwait City, I had vacationed with my family in much of the Middle East at a young age: Lebanon, Syria, Turkey. I had been to Palestine in 1966, before the Israeli occupation, and to Mecca while still a toddler. By the early eighties in Qum, I rarely had the time or the means to travel, but there was one trip I intended to make regardless of the cost. I wanted to perform the hajj, the pilgrimage to Mecca.

The hajj is one of the fundamental duties of any Muslim. For Shia, it's one of the Ten Branches of Religion. In the Sunni tradition, it is one of the Five Pillars of Islam. (See pp. 255–58 for lists of each.) The hajj is the greater of two pilgrimages to Mecca, neither of which is the same as a mere visit. The *umrah,* the lesser pilgrimage, is short and can be undertaken at any time of year, by both children and adults. Pilgrims on the hajj must have reached puberty and must travel to Mecca during the pilgrimage season, Thul al-Hijja, the twelfth month of the Islamic calendar. They typically join two and a half million other Muslims from all over the world and collectively retrace the steps of the Prophet Muhammad while engaging in rituals whose origins predate even the earliest days of Islam. Islam is an Abrahamic faith—we know him as Ibrahim—just as Judaism and Christianity are. "It is the [faith] of your father Abraham," the Qur'an says. "It is He Who has named you Muslims."[3] We regard Abraham as a prophet of God alongside Noah, Moses, Jesus, and Muhammad and see Islam as a logical extension of Judaism and Christianity—the Old Testament (the Torah) and the New Testament paving the way for the *newer* testament, the Qur'an.

Jews and Christians are said to be descendants of Abraham through Isaac. Arab Muslims are also descendants of Abraham, but through the line of Ishmael, Isaac's half brother. The Qur'an tells Ishmael's story, as does the Torah, in the Book of Genesis, though the accounts vary at points. In the Islamic tradition, Abraham's wife, Sarah, has trouble conceiving, and she urges Abraham to father a child through her Egyptian servant, Hagar. Abraham agrees, and Hagar bears Ishmael. But when Ishmael is born, Sarah becomes jealous and demands that Hagar be banished. At God's behest, Abraham takes Hagar and Ishmael and leaves them in the deserts of Arabia. Their plight soon grows desperate. Out of water, Hagar rushes between two hills, Safa and Marwa, in search of water to quench her baby's thirst. Not having been in the desert before, she doesn't understand that she is seeing mirages. Each time she leaves Ishmael to look for water, he begins to cry, and she returns to comfort him. The seventh time she leaves, Ishmael ceases to cry, and Hagar returns to find out why. The Archangel Gabriel has created a fountain of water, which is bursting forth from the ground near Ishmael. Hagar gathers rock and sand to form a basin and calls out, *"Zamzam,"* a command to stop the water from dispersing; the two are spared.

Once a month, Abraham comes to visit them. When Ishmael is thirteen, God tests Abraham by commanding him to kill his firstborn son. (In the Judeo-Christian tradition, Isaac, not Ishmael, is the one marked for sacrifice.) Abraham tells Ishmael about the vision he has seen, and they both agree to carry out God's will. At a place called Mina, the devil appears three times to Abraham and attempts to persuade him not to kill Ishmael. Each time, Abraham throws seven stones at the devil, who disappears. When at last Abraham, knife in hand, prepares to take his son's life, God calls out, "Thou hast already fulfilled the vision!"[4] God wanted only Abraham's submission, not bloodshed. In Ishmael's place, the Archangel Gabriel provides a ram to be sacrificed. Today at the end of each pilgrimage, most pilgrims, as well as Muslims worldwide, sacrifice a sheep to symbolize the same act Abraham performed so long ago. No rite during the pilgrimage is without meaning.

Every year I had watched my father leave for the hajj, and I longed to go. In summer 1983 I used some savings from our wedding, accepted some extra help from my father, and resolved to make my dream a reality. I traveled alone. Iran limits the number of people allowed to go each year, and success in the lottery system can take ten years, so I flew to Syria to fast-track my trip. I discovered too late that the Saudi embassy in Syria refused to grant non-Syrians visas for the hajj. I had wasted my time, they said. It seemed inconceivable to me that I could get halfway to Mecca and spend so much of my money only to be turned away. But at the embassy I made an appointment with the ambassador and wrote a quick note that quoted the Prophet Muhammad: "He who fulfills one need of his faithful brother in this life, God will fulfill seventy needs for him in the hereafter."[5] The ambassador smiled, pulled out a green pen, and wrote "Okay for hajj" across it. Elated, I showed it to the man who told me I had wasted my time, and not long after, I had a visa for Saudi Arabia.

That should have been the end of that, but the hajj grows more popular every year. At the Saudi Arabian Airlines office in downtown Damascus, I went to agent after agent and discovered that none would have any seats available for a week or two, too late for me to participate. In a twist of good fortune, I bumped into a friend from Qum who tipped me off to a secret that opens many doors, if you can spare it: money. The airlines had no coach tickets available, but they did have business-class seats. For another $50 and a half-hour wait, I could upgrade and fly out. I did so gladly.

Throughout its history, as a pilgrimage site and trade center, Mecca has offered sanctuary to people and property. But before air travel, reaching the city was difficult and often dangerous. Pilgrims journeyed overland by camel or by ship and might need many months to complete the pilgrimage. Bandits and thieves roamed the roads and preyed on the unsuspecting and the moneyed. In the 1860s the wealthy begum (a begum is a Muslim woman of high rank) of Bhopal, India, wrote an account of her contingent's hajj journey that included heavy taxes levied by local Ottoman rulers, continual caravan raids, and the brief kidnapping of her mother.[6] Disease was rampant. Still the pilgrims came.

But you don't have to ride a camel or be robbed to experience the Islamic adventure of a lifetime on the hajj. Just being in the city among Muslims of all races, nationalities, economic strata, and cultures is an incredible adventure. Everywhere you go, signs are in Arabic, English, Urdu, Malay, Chinese, Swahili, French, and Spanish. Even in the most cosmopolitan cities in the world, you would be unlikely to find such a range of languages spoken in the span of a few city blocks. A hundred or a hundred and fifty years ago, it could not have happened anywhere else on earth. For many Muslims, the hajj is their only chance to interact with people from the other side of the world. They come away transformed, with a new respect for the larger brotherhood of Muslims and the power of faith and unity to improve society.

The Grand Mosque is the first stop for a pilgrim beginning the hajj. The mosque is vast, large enough to hold a million people, not including the central courtyard. On every side, the masses flow into the surrounding streets and plazas, standing and kneeling shoulder to shoulder. Every man wears the same clothes, white two-piece robes known as *ihram*. (Women can wear their usual modest dress.) The loose-fitting robe is an equalizer and also helps mitigate the relentless heat. Mecca is fifty miles east of the Red Sea at the base of the Hejaz Mountains, in the Saudi desert, a geography that can produce Mojave-like weather. My first hajj fell in August, when temperatures can hit 120 degrees Fahrenheit.

At the center of the mosque stands the Kaaba, the ancient

stone structure all Muslims face during prayer. Abraham and his son Ishmael rebuilt this sanctuary, which Adam created, to renew worship of the one God and establish the rituals that Muslims would later follow; an adjacent rock still bears Abraham's footprint, encased in gold. Over time Abraham's rituals devolved into a carnival of polytheism and hedonism. Three hundred sixty idols adorned the roof of the Kaaba, representing the various nomadic tribes that traveled there each year to worship and trade. Instead of saying prayers, the pagans would clap and whistle. Merchants displayed prostitutes and sold slaves.

The Prophet Muhammad reinstated the rites of Abraham. A member of the wealthy and prestigious Quraysh tribe, which maintained and governed access to the Kaaba, the Prophet witnessed the corrupted religious practices in Mecca firsthand—the worship of money and power at the expense of the good of the community. Urged on by revelations from God, he preached compassion for orphans and the underprivileged, ethical conduct, and, most important, God's universal singularity. The most important Muslim declaration of faith is "I bear witness that there is no god but God"—"Allah" being simply the Arabic name for God. (Christian Arabs also call God Allah, and in Aramaic, the original language of the Bible, "God" is *Allaha*.) The Prophet's pronouncements threatened the status quo in Mecca, and for this he was exiled to Medina, a small farming village to the north, the only community that would accept him. It was one of the defining moments of his life and among the most traumatic.

Abu Talib, the Prophet Muhammad's well-respected and influential uncle, shielded him from most of the scorn he earned from Meccans for criticizing their polytheistic beliefs and moral lapses. When Abu Talib died, the Angel Gabriel visited the Prophet and warned him that he must leave Mecca. The Prophet Muhammad already had begun sending some of his companions to Medina. As Meccans began noticing the Muslims' absence, the Prophet Muhammad slipped away to a nearby cave and asked

Imam Ali to sleep in his bed in Mecca to thwart a possible attempt on his life. To circumvent individual culpability, the Meccans had chosen ten young warriors from ten different tribes to kill the Prophet with swords in the night. When they found Imam Ali in the Prophet Muhammad's house, they recognized him and abandoned their plan. Instead, a party set out to track the Prophet, but by the time they had followed his footprints to the entrance of his cave hideout, a nesting dove and an intact spider web made it seem that the cave was vacant. The party called off the search and returned to Mecca. Free of pursuit, the Prophet Muhammad took one last tearful look at Mecca and received this verse from God: "Most surely he who has made the Qur'an binding on you will bring you back to the destination."[7] He would not return for eight years.

The two tribes of Medina, the Aws and the Khazraj, had been fighting for a hundred years before the Prophet Muhammad's arrival. He immediately began rebuilding the relationship between the two tribes in the same way that he forged a relationship between the Medinans and the incoming Meccans. He issued a proclamation of brotherhood, matching each Aws with a Khazraj (and, separately, each of them with a Meccan) and requiring that they look out for each other and share financial resources. In time, as they observed each other's daily trials and lent support, the warring ceased. From the moment the Prophet arrived, the people of the city heralded him and gave him rule of the city. His first act was to change its name from Yathrib, as it was previously known, to Medina (literally, "The City"). As he rode into the city after his twelve-day flight from Mecca, the Medinans sang a greeting to him:

> The moon has risen on us from where we give farewell to the
>   beloved ones.
> It has become mandatory on us to express gratitude to God as
>   long as there is one praying to Him.

O you, who have been dispatched to us, you shall attain our
allegiance.
You came to honor Medina, you are most welcome, O you the
best Inviter.[8]

THE PROPHET MUHAMMAD'S MOST
IMPORTANT PILGRIMAGE

The first rite of the pilgrimage, called Turning (*tawaf*), is a counter-
clockwise circumambulation of the Kaaba that makes the holiest
spot in the world for Muslims the pivot point of one's actions. This
is done seven times and in large groups, often with thousands of
people. Next, pilgrims reenact Hagar's search for water in the
desert—at the same spot where she faced her trial—by walking
quickly or at a trot between Safa and Marwa (a ritual known as
saei), which are now enclosed in the Grand Mosque along with the
miraculous Well of Zamzam. Even apart from the travel required
to get to Mecca, the hajj itself is a series of journeys punctuated by
rites. On the eighth day of the pilgrimage month, pilgrims walk or
catch buses and trucks for a five-mile ride east through a valley to
Mina, where a massive tent city houses the swelling ranks pushing
in from Mecca. This is a stopover, a chance to nap and read the
Qur'an before continuing east the next morning to the Plain of
Arafat, another five miles away and the scene of the pilgrimage's
zenith. Arafat is a physically desolate place, a desert wilderness.
But spiritually it is enriching and a site of deep contemplation.
This is where Adam and Eve were brought back together after
being cast out of Eden. At Arafat, pilgrims prepare for the Day of
Judgment, examining their own thoughts and actions and reaf-
firming their faith. In the foreground rests Mount Mercy, where
the Prophet Muhammad issued his Farewell Sermon, in which he
said, "Certainly you shall meet your Lord and He will ask you
about your deeds."[9]

From the Plain of Arafat, the rites of the hajj move west, back toward Mecca. At sundown on the second day, pilgrims make their way to a place called Muzdalifa and encamp once more for an all-night vigil. Each pilgrim collects forty-nine stones, for the next three days' events.

The stoning of the devil at Jamarat might be the hajj ritual non-Muslims know best. Three long rock walls represent the devil in his efforts to dissuade Abraham from fulfilling God's command to sacrifice his son. On the tenth, eleventh, and twelfth days of Thul al-Hijja, pilgrims gather at the walls to symbolically stone the devil. This might be the most dangerous part of the trip. Non-Muslims know of the ritual from news stories about people crushed to death in the ensuing congestion. Outdated infrastructure is part of the problem: the bridge many pilgrims use to cast their stones bears 300,000 people at peak use, three times as many as it was designed to hold, and sections have collapsed on more than one occasion. More striking to me is the remarkable restraint exhibited by the crowds in such close confines. Mecca more than triples in size during the hajj; at every turn, hundreds of people stand at your shoulder, the moist heat radiating from bodies adding to the dry heat everywhere else. This is the largest mass movement of people undertaken anywhere, and it happens annually, with few unpleasant outcomes. There is no fighting or aggression.

After the devil stoning, the pilgrimage is nearly complete. Pilgrims may change out of their *ihram* at Mina, and they mark their spiritual rebirth either by getting their head shaved completely or by having a lock of hair cut. This is followed by the feast of Eid al-Adha, the most important Islamic holiday, on which many Muslims will sacrifice a sheep or other livestock to commemorate Abraham's sacrifice. (Meat from the two and a half million sacrificed sheep is frozen and shipped to destitute parts of Africa.) A three-day ritual and celebration follows, and Muslims worldwide participate. Some pilgrims will linger in Mecca, and some will venture north to visit the Mosque of the Prophet in Medina and the tombs of the Imams, but before they leave Mecca, they return to the Grand Mosque for a final Turning around the Kaaba, which signals the formal end of the hajj.

This is the same route the Prophet Muhammad took when he marched into Mecca, ten thousand companions in tow, eight years after the assassination plot drove him to Medina. He had attempted to make peace with the Meccans in a treaty the previous year, but Meccans violated the treaty by attacking tribes allied with the Muslims of Medina. The Prophet Muhammad felt his only recourse was to retake the city of his birth. Its residents had heard outlandish tales of crazed, zealous cultists who wanted to destroy their city, but when the people of Mecca witnessed the Medinans' dignified and respectful procession into the city, they were so amazed that they ceased hostilities and celebrated the Prophet Muhammad's arrival. Not everyone was pleased with his return, however, and many who had committed vicious acts against his family and people feared retribution. Meccans had attacked his pregnant daughter Zaynib, causing her to miscarry, and they had killed one of his uncles and disfigured his body.

After his peaceful reclaiming of the city, the Prophet Muhammad called the people of Mecca to gather in the Grand Mosque and said, "O People of the Quraysh, what do you think I shall do to you?" They replied, "We think you will do nothing but good. You are a great brother and a great nephew." He fulfilled those expectations, saying, "Go, for I have pardoned you all." Historians say the Meccans dispersed like a people who had risen from their graves and been given new life. The Prophet Muhammad charged a black former slave, Bilal, with giving the call to prayer at the Grand Mosque in Mecca; in the early days of Islam, Meccans had beaten the man for his refusal to renounce his religion, and the Prophet Muhammad had purchased his freedom and forced the abuse to stop. Now the former slave had one of the most coveted jobs in the city. The Meccans had been defeated in battle, and now they had been overcome by peace.

The victory raised some difficult questions. After the Prophet

Muhammad had fled Mecca eight years before, the Quraysh seized his house. Upon his return, he had nowhere to sleep but refused to reclaim the house that had been taken from him. He elected to pitch a tent in the open air, a decision that foreshadowed the answer to another major question: what would he do now? Conventional wisdom predicted he would remain in Mecca and assert his newfound control. For a week the answer remained in doubt; then Muhammad packed up his tent and returned to Medina with his supporters from that city. "I will live with you, and I will die with you," he told the Medinans.

ROAD HAZARDS

The greater ease of travel for the hajj has remade Mecca. In the 1950s, the hajj averaged fifty thousand people a year. The first year I went, it drew more than a million pilgrims for the first time. Now the total approaches 3 million, and the trend shows no sign of relenting. As the numbers have surged, the demographics have changed as well. The hajj used to be the province of the aged fulfilling their once-in-a-lifetime obligation. Pilgrims in their twenties were less common, certainly in part because of the cost, which can easily run to $5,000. Several years ago in Mecca, I spoke to an older Indonesian woman, a college-educated government employee who made $300 a month. It probably took her twenty years to save for her journey, and she was grateful to have done it.

Rising numbers have brought more full-time residents to Mecca to serve the pilgrims, and with them come calls for improved roads, enlarged places of worship—a 1988 expansion of the Grand Mosque added more than 900,000 square feet to the surrounding plaza and 650,000 square feet to the mosque roof—and more hotels and shops. The latest development proposal calls for 32 million square feet of new hotels, shops, prayer facilities, residences, and green space and a central avenue that would dwarf the Champs-Élysées.[10] Such growth has had the unacceptable side effect of encroaching on some of the holiest and most historically important sites in Islam. In Mecca, the house the Prophet was born in has been replaced with a public library. In Medina, the houses of the fourth and the sixth Imams have been razed.

The destruction is no accident. Saudi officials, with pressure from the country's Wahhabi institutions, have used modernization as an excuse to discourage what they see as idolatry. Shia often visit these sites to reflect and offer prayers, which the Wahhabis confuse with worship of figures other than God. (In the past, some Wahhabi scholars have called for the destruction of the Prophet Muhammad's shrine; knowing this would outrage Muslims around the world, the Saudi government did not comply.) When the Wahhabis took over Saudi Arabia in the 1920s, they demolished the decorative domes on graves at Al-Baqeea cemetery, the resting place of Fatima, the Prophet Muhammad's daughter; Imam Hassan, his grandson; and several other Imams, and almost exposed the graves in the process. The Mutawa, the Saudi religious police, don't allow any sort of rituals around the remaining homes of the Imams or, before it was destroyed, the birthplace of the Prophet.

Each year, before I lead our group from the Islamic Center of America to Mecca, I warn them about the Mutawa in their red robes and long beards. They patrol the crowds to ensure that pilgrims perform the rites properly, but this means performing the rites properly *as they see it,* that is, the majority way. The Mutawa have been known to attack Shia who pray with their arms extended or offer any type of Shia supplication. Sometimes they will harangue Shia pilgrims or physically manipulate their bodies to force them to pray like Sunnis. I counsel our group members to be passive if this happens and avoid giving the police a reason to assault anyone. The risk is real. On almost every trip, at least one person in my contingent has had a run-in with the Mutawa. I myself have been yelled at several times for visiting the graves of four of our Revered Imams in Medina.

Shia make up 15 percent of Saudi Arabia's population but

must be especially cautious not to reveal their identity. Just as there are no churches or synagogues in Saudi Arabia, so there are no Shia mosques. The Shia who make their home there, in the land of Prophet Muhammad and Imam Ali, of Imam Hassan and Imam Husayn, pray in Sunni mosques. For me this illustrates how deep the injustice is against the family of the Prophet. After fourteen centuries, the holy family is still not revered the way it ought to be.

Hajj protocol strictly forbids possession of printed materials other than the Qur'an. In 2006, our Young Muslim Association at the Islamic Center of America printed an English-language guidebook on travel strategies and proper conduct on the hajj, a guidebook our group could use during the trip. Every copy was confiscated when we arrived at King Abdul Aziz Airport in Jeddah. Yet the Mutawa sometimes assign people to stand in the middle of the street to pass out millions of copies of their own books—Wahhabi-approved literature. Inevitably, they're waiting at the end of the jetway to hand you such titles as *The Basic Tenets of Islam* when you deplane. The content seems worthy and innocent enough on the surface, but on closer examination, it's rife with biases and accusations. It might venerate monotheism as a cornerstone Islamic principle, for example—"There is no god but God"—but then append commentary straight from the Wahhabi school of thought: "However, there are some Muslims who don't believe in monotheism, and these are Shia." I can only laugh at such propaganda. If I don't believe in monotheism, I am not a Muslim anymore.

EXPLORING THE NEW WORLD

Being a student at the advanced level of studies in Qum is not unlike working as a lower-level university faculty member. At Qum, a student can teach a class as soon as he has taken it and proved that he has a command of the relevant material. In my last years of seminary, I both taught and attended classes, the latter fre-

quently focusing on jurisprudence and ethics. Both endeavors
helped me advance in my studies (nothing fosters learning like
having to explain things to someone else), and I took advantage
of the collegial air in Qum to forge a strong relationship with my
instructors. On Thursdays and Fridays, the weekend in Iran, I
would borrow cassette tapes of previous classes to get ahead.
Often I collaborated with instructors on research, or they would
assign me projects to work on. In 1987, I completed my first
book, a translation of a critical study of two Sunni books of hadith, *Sahih Muslim* and *Sahih Al-Bukhari,* from Persian to Arabic.
Too many Muslims regard these as unquestionably authentic,
and it's true they are more reliable than many other hadith collections, but I explored the inaccuracies that had slipped past the
two eminent compilers.

The following year I launched a quarterly journal called *Al-
Nibras* ("The Eternal Light") and solicited articles from top instructors. Some wrote for free. I found the work rewarding but
the finances just as vexing as my own. Each two-hundred-page
issue cost about $3,000 to publish, and the cover price and en-
couraging letters alone couldn't offset those costs. I published
four issues before money matters became unworkable. As an alternative, I pursued another book project, my first original work,
a study of the Prophet Muhammad's personal conduct and moral
philosophy, emphasizing his human tendencies more than
prophetic standards. I called it *Prophet Muhammad: The School of
Ethics.*

In 1986 my father had attended a conference in Dallas and
saw the acute need for spiritual guidance of the Muslims living in
the United States. They repeatedly asked him to immigrate to
America and work as their imam. He promised to think about it,
and when he traveled to St. Louis for the same conference the
next year, he stayed in the country for many months to explore
the needs of Muslims there and familiarize himself with American culture. After talking it over with my mother and a few
scholars, he purchased a building in Pomona, California, and

founded an Islamic center. I don't think he viewed the move as permanent, but it was a chance to take on new challenges and to help a growing Muslim community in America with little in the way of clerical support. My younger siblings, two brothers and two sisters, who were still underage at the time, moved to Pomona with my parents. My father's regular dispatches from the Islamic frontier captured my imagination.

In America an upper-level student might take on a summer internship before graduation. Qum's seminary had an equivalent known as *tabligh,* which involved traveling to remote Iranian villages during the summer months to stay and preach among the people. Before engaging in such an enterprise, most students have studied all aspects of the religion and its laws, but few have gained any experience in public speaking, one of an imam's most important skills. The *tabligh* gives them the chance to hone their preaching, earn some additional money, and help bring Islamic knowledge to underserved communities.

I chose not to take that route, but I did feel that I needed more speaking experience. I had taken a public speaking class and done very well, but at twenty-five I had never sat in the pulpit. During my last two years of seminary, I accepted invitations to speak in Lebanon during the seminary's two-week break for Ashura. The Lebanese speak Arabic, and I felt that it would be easier to lecture for the first time in my native language than to try to speak Persian in Iran. I went to a village called Al-Dowair, in southern Lebanon. The Lebanese are renowned for their hospitality. I was heartened to see a thousand or more people turn out each night during Ashura for my lectures, and then see people line up afterward to comment and invite me into their homes for lunch or dinner. I stayed at a different house every day and was overwhelmed by Lebanese generosity—and by their meals, which took some getting used to.

I grew up with the cuisines of Iraq and Iran, where rice is the main staple. In Lebanon they rely more on bread and grains and enthusiastically serve a dish called *kibbe nayye,* which is raw beef mixed with bulgur and spices and served in a roll like sushi. I hadn't expected to learn lessons in diplomacy along with public speaking in Lebanon. "Close your eyes and eat," my hosts told me. I reluctantly took a bite. *Oh, no, what have I done?* I thought. Many Muslims have an aversion to raw meat because of the Qur'anic proscription against eating meat tainted with blood. I managed to swallow, and once I did, I got past the texture to the flavor, which was . . . quite tasty. I have since come to look forward to sharing *kibbe nayye* with Lebanese friends on my visits there.

Speaking in Lebanese during Ashura came with its own curveballs. In 1991, I traveled to Adloon, a Lebanese beach town near Tyre. Despite the fact that I was about to address a crowd of fifteen hundred as the keynote speaker, I was calm. For some reason I had unwavering confidence in what I could do. But I learned that eloquent, relevant preaching alone is not always enough. A first- or second-year seminary student had asked the local imam for time to speak before my lecture. The imam consented but asked that the student limit his talk to fifteen minutes. The young man spoke for thirty instead.

The second night, weathering a warning from the imam, he again spoke for thirty minutes, at which point the imam sent a note to the front saying that his time was up. The student read the note, tore it up, and spoke for fifteen minutes more. Murmurs ran through the crowd, and I sensed a rising tension. Then bedlam ensued! One man in the audience began arguing with the speaker, and another charged out of the crowd and punched him. The pulpit for sermons sits high above the audience and requires a flight of steps to reach. The speaker fell fifteen feet to the floor, and I knew I would have to take control. I rushed into the pulpit and tried to calm the crowd, but now people were throwing chairs at each other. Fifty people were brawling, and the circle of chaos was expanding. Two security guards came over to protect me; one was knocked down by a chair. At that point I decided it was best to leave, and I slipped out a back door amid the sounds of gunshots and ambulance sirens. Sometimes there's nothing left to say.

Back at the imam's house, I discovered that the inconsiderate speaker's family had been feuding with another family in town for some time. I don't know exactly what the disagreement was about, but honor and family pride are sacred in the Middle East, and I don't doubt that the speaker's disregard for his time limit was intended to insult someone at the Ashura gathering. The story quickly spread from town to town. I spoke in other villages during Ashura that year, and congregants would approach me and joke about the fireworks I had started by speaking in Adloon.

With the exception of that one night, my experiences speaking in Lebanon were uniformly positive. The people were friendly, I appreciated the culture and lifestyle, and I improved my oratorical style. Some nights, people would approach me and ask me to stay at their mosque for good, and often it didn't seem like a bad idea. Soon I would graduate from seminary with the equivalent of a Ph.D. in Islamic studies, and I would need to apply that knowledge somewhere. Decisions had to be made. Returning to Iraq was not an option. Most of my immediate family had already moved to California with my father and they were encouraging me to join them, but the idea of starting over again, in a new country, with a new language and a new culture, pained me.

I thought of a story I had heard of the sixth Imam, Imam Jafar al-Sadiq. He spoke to a merchant who often traveled to Europe on business and who worried about God's judgment of his priorities. The merchant admitted that he taught Islam to Europeans when he traveled, but at home he said he did not have time to teach. Would God punish him for this? Imam Jafar al-Sadiq smiled and said, "If you die while teaching Islam in Europe, you will be resurrected as a nation by yourself, your light will illuminate your way, and God will place you in the highest abode in heaven."[11] My spirit lay in the Middle East, but Imam Jafar al-Sadiq's counsel made me realize that the region had plenty of good people to serve the Muslim community. By the time I graduated in 1992, enrollment at the Hawza in Qum had reached 55,000. In the West, every duty would potentially have a greater impact. And my heart lay with my family in America.

My father needed my help. The biggest factor in my choice to come to America was my children, Mohamed and Ahmed. I had spent my entire life fleeing oppression, and I wanted them to have stable, secure childhoods and bright futures. I thought about America's pioneering spirit, my father's accomplishments in Pomona, Imam Chirri's work at the Islamic Center of Detroit, and Imam Khorasani's rhapsodies on the beauty of California and his long-ago call to join him as an imam. And I decided to answer.

CHAPTER 4

The Idea of America

We have inherited a large house, a great world house
in which we have to live together—black and white,
Easterner and Westerner, Gentile and Jew, Catholic
and Protestant, Muslim and Hindu—a family unduly
separated in ideas, culture, and interest, who, because
we can never again live apart, must learn somehow to
live with each other in peace.[1]
—*Martin Luther King, Jr.*

PUNDITS WHO DESCRIBE Muslim-Christian relations as a
conflict-ridden interplay between East and West oversimplify our
history. Christians, among them Copts, Chaldeans, and Mar-
onites, have long lived throughout the Middle East. Even after
Islam spread across the Middle East in the seventh and eighth centuries, minority Christian communities coexisted with Muslims
in these places, usually peacefully, for hundreds of years. Muslims
dwelt in Spain as early as A.D. 711 and also on the far west coast
of Africa; from there slave traders later brought them to the New
World to work the farm fields of the South and the Caribbean. Perhaps 15 percent of the African slaves shipped to the Western
Hemisphere were Muslim, about 2.25 million people.[2]

To be sure, the two groups have clashed repeatedly since the
Middle Ages, sometimes spectacularly. Attacks and counterat-
tacks in North Africa, Spain, the Caucasus, and the Holy Land
have fixed in the collective Christian consciousness images of the
fierce Muslim warrior, scimitar in one hand and Qur'an in the
other. (In reality, most lands that came under Muslim control ar-

rived there peaceably, with some even soliciting Muslim rule to wipe out the scourge of their own hateful polities.) But for most of American history, Muslims have been seen as an "other," a group visible but not welcomed. The most famous contemporary Muslim in the West has to be Muhammad Ali, universal adulation of whom has overshadowed some of the American public's former contempt for his flat refusal to serve in Vietnam and identification with the Nation of Islam. "I know where I'm going and I know the truth and I don't have to be what you want me to be," he said when he announced he was joining the Nation of Islam the day after beating Sonny Liston to win the heavyweight title in 1964. "I'm free to be what I want."[3] (The Nation of Islam and Islam are not the same, but Ali did convert to Islam in the 1970s.) Footage of Malcolm X riling crowds with talk of "blue-eyed devils" and armed struggle still frames his image in white America's consciousness more than the language he used after converting to Islam and making the hajj, when he called for racial reconciliation and revised his earlier views.

By the time I immigrated, in 1992, the identity of American Islam had begun a makeover, and perception was catching up with reality. Changes to U.S. immigration policy in 1965 made job skills and family reunification the measuring stick for entrance to America rather than a national-origins quota, and this allowed immigrants from the Middle East and South Asia, many of them Muslims, to come in large numbers for the first time. An immigrant class with unprecedented wealth and education, these Muslims set about adapting their faith to their new surroundings. Islam in the 1990s had become the fastest-growing religion in the United States and was on its way to becoming the country's second most popular religion, after Christianity. Yet I wondered how much that progress had chipped away at the ingrained, partly unconscious image of the Muslim warrior. For twelve years I had made my home in Iran, a country most Americans knew about mainly because of the hostage crisis, when images of blindfolded American captives and burning U.S. flags appeared on the news almost nightly. On top of that, I was Iraqi, and I suspected that the average citizen would be unprepared to distinguish between opponents of the Baathist regime and those party loyalists who would have cheered on Saddam's invasion of Kuwait and war with the United States in 1991.

My family and I arrived on December 6, 1992, on a British Airways flight from Dubai via London, eager to see how America would greet us. Twenty-five hours of breathing thin, sour cabin air at 35,000 feet hadn't dulled my tingling sense of anticipation and curiosity. We were reluctant to leave behind my wife's family and the life we had known in Iran, and anxious about adjusting to a country too large and complex to fathom. I knew scarcely a word of English but enough about American culture to realize that my frequent travels around the Middle East hadn't prepared me for it. I knew that each of us faced a longer and more disruptive adjustment period than I had experienced when moving to Iran. My only request for God was to be given the chance to live in peace and teach Islam.

Upon deplaning at LAX, I handed my passport to the customs official and waited with some apprehension to be waved through. He could have glanced at the previous pages and learned of my trips to Lebanon, Saudi Arabia, Syria, and elsewhere in the Middle East, and that I was arriving by way of the United Arab Emirates; he might also have noticed that I hadn't been to America before, but he applied a red stamp in the "Entries" column and ushered me past with an unexpected greeting: "Welcome home." It *was* a sort of homecoming. I hadn't seen my father, mother, brothers, and sisters in almost three years, and all of them would be waiting for me. As I waited for my wife and children to catch up, the words of Imam Ali came to me, a plea for civility and pragmatism over nationalism: "Your country does not belong to you more than any other country. The best country is the one that treats you well."[4]

MIDDLE EASTERNER IN THE WEST

Many born-and-raised Americans almost assume the disloyalty of Muslim immigrants to this country. Because we place our religion at the center of our lives, the mostly unspoken rationale goes, Muslims secretly despise America for its Christian origins and secular, commercial hype, and long for our homelands. Well into the ESL (English as a Second Language) course I enrolled in at Mt. San Antonio College in Walnut, California, my teacher surprised me by summarizing the standard American depiction of Muslim men as she was explaining the word "stereotype": When you look at Hassan, she said, you might see his Middle Eastern appearance and beard and think he's a fanatic. But as soon as you talk to him, you'll find that he's a normal, outgoing person.

I can't speak for every Muslim American, but I imagine that, given the opportunity, those who have immigrated from the Middle East over the past several generations would voice an outlook similar to mine: we don't always agree with the U.S. government's policies, and our multiple identities might not be neatly definable and harmonious, but more so than many citizens, Middle Eastern immigrants can appreciate the freedoms and personal protections we enjoy as Americans because we have lived under systems that lack them. In Iraq, one would tremble at the mere mention of the Mukhabarat. By the time you received a letter or phone call requesting your presence at the station, it would be too late to flee. You were already under surveillance, and you would have to look right and left before your every move. Freedom, religious or otherwise, was limited to whatever the government didn't find threatening. By contrast, I often tell my American audiences, if you're Jewish, you can build the largest synagogue, and no one can forbid it. If you're Christian, you can build the largest church. If you're Muslim, you can build the largest mosque and no one can bother you. And if you're an atheist, I joke, you can build the largest casino!

In my early years here, the media were covering Paula Jones's sexual harassment case against President Clinton and publishing details about his "distinguishing characteristic." The furor over President Clinton only grew during the Monica Lewinsky phase. I saw that in America, even the most powerful citizens could be called to account, fairly or unfairly, for their actions. The same applied to President Bush's daughters, Barbara and Jenna, who were cited for underage drinking in 2001, and Florida governor Jeb Bush's daughter, Noelle, charged with prescription fraud in Tallahassee in 2002.[5] Despite an imperfect justice system, no one is above the law in this country. I love that.

By and large, the people of the Middle East love America, too. They wear American jeans, watch American movies, and value American education. In Saudi Arabia, surely the strictest and most anti-western of Middle Eastern countries, a weary pilgrim just blocks from the Grand Mosque in Mecca can eat at McDonald's, Pizza Hut, or Kentucky Fried Chicken. Never have I seen so many signs and billboards for Marlboro cigarettes, or so many people smoking them, as I have in countries like Kuwait, Lebanon, and Saudi Arabia. The surest sign of goodwill among Middle Easterners is the rate at which they have immigrated to western countries. Europe has 15 million to 20 million Muslims, not counting Russia's share, and Islam is the fastest-growing religion on that continent.[6] Islamic groups in the United States estimate the country's Muslim population at 6 million to 7 million.[7] Texas, New Jersey, and New York attract South Asians. Detroit and Dearborn are known for their Lebanese, Iraqi, and Palestinian populations. And Los Angeles boasts the largest Iranian community outside of Tehran. Demographers and locals sometimes refer to its central neighborhood, located south of the UCLA campus, as "Irangeles."

That striking diversity is completely consistent with America's identity as a nation of immigrants. The United States has no superior race, just arrivals who are newer or older. (If anyone were to have a claim of superiority, it would be indigenous Indians.) In Los Angeles residents come from 180 different countries, an in-

credible range that is likely found nowhere else on earth and that
breeds a tolerance and broader perspective similar to Islam's own
colorblind creed. From its first days, Islam has championed a
world without distinctions between race, class, color, or national-
ity. Among the Prophet Muhammad's companions were Africans,
Persians, and Europeans. In America I saw a country with the
greatest potential of anywhere I had been—a potential to truly
put Islam's egalitarian principles into practice.

At the same time, the mishmash of traditions and perspectives in Los Angeles overwhelmed me, and I now realize that
Americans everywhere probably reach some variation of the
same conclusion when they first visit California: the state is full
of crazies!

The first Islamic center my father started in Pomona, called
Pomona Center, doubled as his home and sat in a tightly clustered
residential area. All seven of the Qazwinis who had immigrated
to California initially lived in the house, located on Old Settler's
Lane, the oldest part of Pomona, where fruit growers had put
down their roots in the 1800s. Now our family had made "New
Settler's Lane" seem like a more appropriate name for the street.
Early on at Pomona Center, my father held a service for Ashura,
the most passionate and emotional Shia holiday and one that
often elicits tears from those gathered. Out of respect, mosques
usually turn out the lights at the peak of the service, when the
weeping is widespread. Concerned neighbors who knew little
about the center but noticed that the darkened house was full of
sobbing people called the police and said something to the effect
of "I think the people next door are killing each other." They assumed their strange neighbors were part of a cult. Police arrived
in force. Six patrol cars pulled up in front of the house as if in a
TV drama. Overhead, two helicopters hovered as a precaution. At
least one mosque member heard the commotion outside and
stepped out to see officers coming up the walk.

"What's going on?" the lead officer wanted to know. "Why

are these people in here crying?" He summarized the complaint they had received.

The member had to think fast but didn't want to complicate things. "No one's hitting each other," he said. "No one's killing each other. They're crying because a man died."

"What?" the officer said. "Someone died? When?"

". . . Fourteen hundred years ago."

REDRAWING CULTURAL BOUNDARIES

The difference between Middle Eastern culture and American culture is striking, like the difference between night and day. Muslim countries around the Arabian Gulf use the Islamic calendar, which is lunar (the origin of the crescent symbol seen atop the domes and minarets of many mosques). The first year of the Islamic calendar coincides with the Prophet Muhammad's exile to Medina in the Christian year 622. Like the solar Gregorian calendar, the Islamic calendar consists of twelve months, but because the moon's cycles run about twenty-nine days, Islamic years are roughly eleven days shorter than the standard 365. So, deriving exact years in the Islamic calendar using Christian dates and vice versa isn't a simple matter of addition or subtraction but an operation akin to converting Fahrenheit temperatures to Celsius. To complicate things a bit further, a minority of Muslims require sighting of the new moon before a new month can officially begin, so their printed calendars are merely estimates; when an observer identifies the new moon can depend on his location, the weather, and atmospheric anomalies.

One of the biggest adjustments for me was interacting with women. At twenty-eight, after almost ten years of marriage, I had never spoken to a woman outside my family in a social setting. Even in a professional context, conversation was kept to a minimum, only what was necessary to carry out the business at hand. Women in Qum did not enter the streets without wearing the *hijab,* the traditional dress of Muslim women and usually associated with the head scarf. Wrists and ankles were always covered. You could see only women's faces. Now, in Los Angeles, I was careful to look nowhere else. In my first ESL class at Mt. San Antonio College, I stammered out phrases alongside half-dressed young Hispanic women. To prevent them from clustering together and speaking Spanish, the instructor would send them to different areas of the room, and inevitably I would end up interacting with them, using tentative English and sweaty-palmed gestures while trying to suppress my embarrassment at their dress.

Probably no aspect of Islam better symbolizes the western misunderstanding of Muslim culture than hijab ("covering" or "concealing" in English), women's conservative dress and head covering. Some non-Muslims call it oppressive and backward. In 2004 the French government identified the head scarf as such a potent religious symbol that it banned female students from wearing it in public schools. (Other prominent religious symbols, such as large crosses and Jewish skullcaps, also were banned.) The decision disturbed me so much that I wrote a letter to President Jacques Chirac. The head of Presidential Protocol responded, "We do not mean to crack down on Muslims. This is a conspicuous violation of our secular system." But secularism is supposed to be neutral toward religion, not antireligion.

The idea behind hijab, and one of Islam's core values, is modesty. The Qur'an addresses it directly: "And say to the believing women that they cast down their looks and guard their private parts and do not display their ornaments except what appears thereof, and let them wear their head-coverings over their bosoms . . ."[8] Both men and women must dress and behave modestly. A woman's beauty especially ought to be protected because of the risk of her exploitation. Magazines and billboards in the West routinely show pictures of nearly naked, or strategically naked, young women that have nothing to do with the products they sell. Pornography generates $3 billion to $12 billion a year in U.S. sales, depending on whom you ask, and the industry is growing.[9] In the Middle East, immodesty in advertising is becoming more commonplace, and I'm sure there is underground pornography and prostitution in many places, but it's nothing compared to what I encountered in America. Wherever they take place, these ventures come at the expense of women's dignity and morality.

Not long after I came to America, I happened across a cable channel showing female professional wrestlers. The idea that such a show might exist had never occurred to me: exploitation not of the female nature but of its opposite. I didn't know what to make of such a spectacle. Women radiate kindness, mercy, and affection, not aggression. Imam Ali said as much in a hadith: "A woman is a flower, not a wrestler."[10] Living in America meant interacting with women who could be wrestlers, flowers, and everything in between.

For Muslims, however, hijab is not a custom forced upon recalcitrant wives and daughters. Our women wear hijab willingly and proudly. Covering in public proclaims their deference to God, not their subjugation to men, and signifies their membership in the Muslim community. The imperative for women to cover comes from passages in the Qur'an, but the concept of hijab long predates Muslims. Paintings and sculptures often depict Mary in a head covering. Up until a hundred years ago, Christian women commonly wore head scarves. And in the Catholic world, many of the most pious women, nuns, still don their habits.

Personal introductions to women in class and elsewhere presented another dilemma. Physical contact with members of the opposite sex other than immediate relatives is not common in Muslim society. What was I to do if they extended their hands to shake? I didn't wish to offend my classmates, and yet acquiescing would entail crossing a line I didn't feel comfortable crossing. Though there were a few other Muslims in the class with me, their presence only heightened my anxiety. My compromise was a common Muslim gesture. Before a woman had a chance to offer her hand in greeting, I would put my right hand to the left side of my chest and lower my head to show respect. Sometimes it worked and sometimes it didn't, but I have since used the technique effectively in meetings with Michigan's U.S. senator Debbie Stabenow and the state's governor, Jennifer Granholm.

In writing I had to address the same cultural differences, but with a twist. "Dear," the customary salutation for even the most formal letters in English, is much too affectionate to use with someone of the opposite sex in Muslim culture. When writing letters to women, I found myself asking whether they would be familiar with the western approach. If not, I would begin the letter with a courtesy title and the recipient's name. Usually my rule of thumb was to use "dear" for letters in English and a title and name only for Arabic letters, but when I felt a respectful distance was called for, I avoided using "dear" in English letters as well.

THE FREEDOM TO REFRAIN

During my first months here, American culture felt just as backward to me as Middle Eastern culture must seem to my American neighbors. But as I traveled around the country as extensively as my time and budget would allow, my assumptions were continually corrected. The United States is the most religious democracy in the western world. Something like 96 percent of American adults say they believe in God, a figure consistent with surveys forty years ago, and three-quarters of American adults are Christian, whether Protestant or Catholic.[11] Behind those statistics lie tens of thousands of churches teeming with members, the opposite of the museum cathedrals I've visited in Europe. This strong faith in God reassures me of America's continued eminence. I know of a charismatic preacher who, in response to Friedrich Nietzsche's pronouncement that God is dead and the Communist Soviet state that followed, said, "The empire that denies God and believes He has died shall sooner or later die." My new country appeared safe in this respect.

Yet as I took in more American TV and visited cities from the West Coast to the East, I was shocked at the disrespect for Jesus. On souvenir T-shirts, in throwaway sitcom lines, on gift shop ephemera and glib bumper stickers, the casual degradation of Christians' savior shocked me. I spotted a book titled *Jesus: The Illegitimate Son of Mary,* a work that would never be printed in the Middle East. More recently we have seen the hip-hop artist Kanye West posing as Jesus on the cover of *Rolling Stone* and Madonna staging her own mock crucifixion on her "Confessions" tour. I relish the personal liberties and freedom of speech America allows, but the freedom to mock religion is one I do not condone. Even in America, freedom of speech has its limits. Law enforcement can restrict where and when protestors are permitted to organize. Speech that endangers public safety is illegal. Libel and slander are not protected. I don't wish to set off alarm bells by drawing arbitrary lines around specific religious figures, and the American people through their government are charged with defining free speech, but the idea of protecting prophets of God from slurs isn't incompatible with democracy, and, indeed, any democracy that arises in the Middle East will establish some measure that bars insulting God and all of the prophets.

(If one religious group in northern Iraq had its way, such a rule would also apply to Satan. When Prime Minister Ibrahim al-Jaafari offered the traditional statement "I seek refuge with God from the accursed devil" to open a parliamentary address early in his term, one representative identified himself as part of a devil-worshipping church and took exception to the prime minister's phrasing. The man argued that humans have nothing to fear from a compassionate God but should inoculate themselves by praising the doer of supreme evil. This, I should say, takes the argument for religious-based free speech restrictions to its illogical conclusion. The Satanists, as far as I am concerned, are on their own.)

Critics of Islam argue that a truly open society cannot safeguard religion, any more than it can prevent criticism of government, the media, or business. If the idea of restrictions on religious criticism sounds undemocratic, consider the case of David Irving, a revisionist historian banned from entering Austria in 1989 for his inflammatory statements denying aspects of the Holocaust. He later revised his outlandish views, but after he traveled to Austria late in 2005, he was arrested, tried, and sentenced to three years in prison for violating the ban. Australia, Canada, Germany, and New Zealand also have banned him for his controversial views. Muslims chafe at the idea that some countries in Europe take crass insults to Islam in stride, while questioning the Holocaust, however irresponsible, warrants a three-year prison sentence.

Again, the disagreement over insults to religion boils down to our cultures, not our religions, being fundamentally different. Middle Easterners do not make jokes about religion or deal casually with religious symbols. This also goes for Christians in the Middle East, as well as for cultures in the Far East. You won't find Tibetans lampooning the Buddha. Islam condones religious and scientific inquiry and invites discussion of varying religious principles, but it differentiates between criticism and insults. Insults for their own sake are offensive and inherently unenlightening. Some Muslims reacted viscerally to the Danish newspaper *Jyllands-Posten*'s 2005 cartoons of the Prophet Muhammad because the drawings did not constitute an intellectual critique. Their purpose was to inflame, and they succeeded.

Far from promoting a double standard, Muslims have great reverence for Jesus and in speech or writing follow his name with "peace be upon him," just as they do with the Prophet Muhammad. "The prophets are paternal brothers," the Prophet Muhammad said. "Their mothers are different, but their religion is one." One cannot be a Muslim without believing in Jesus. For Muslims, he is the Word of God, the Spirit of God, and one of five messengers of God, alongside Noah, Abraham, Moses, and the Prophet Muhammad, but not the son of God or God himself. We also believe in his virgin birth. The Qur'an devotes an entire chapter to Mary, Chapter 19, and the description of her physical and emotional pain during Jesus' birth, not in a manger but in the countryside under a palm tree, never fails to move me:

Relate in the Book
[The story of] Mary,
When she withdrew
From her family
To a place in the East

She placed a screen
[To screen herself] from them;
Then We sent to her
Our angel, and he appeared
Before her as a man
In all respects.

She said: "I seek refuge
From thee to [God]
Most Gracious: [come not near]
If thou dost fear God."

He said: "Nay, I am only
A messenger from thy Lord,
[To announce] to thee
The gift of a holy son."

She said: "How shall I
Have a son, seeing that
No man has touched me,
And I am not unchaste?"

He said: "So [it will be]:
Thy Lord saith, "That is
Easy for Me: and [We
Wish] to appoint him
As a Sign unto men
And a Mercy from Us":

It is a matter
[So] decreed."

So she conceived him,
And she retired with him
To a remote place.

And the pains of childbirth
Drove her to the trunk
Of a palm tree:
She cried [in her anguish]:
"Ah! would that I had
Died before this! would that
I had been a thing
Forgotten and out of sight!"

But [a voice] cried to her
From beneath the [palm tree]:
"Grieve not! for thy Lord
Hath provided a rivulet
Beneath thee;

"And shake towards thyself
The trunk of the palm tree;
It will let fall
Fresh ripe dates upon thee. . . ."

At length she brought
The [babe] to her people,
Carrying him [in her arms].
They said: "O Mary!
Truly an amazing thing
Hast thou brought!

"O sister of Aaron!
Thy father was not
A man of evil, nor thy
Mother a woman unchaste!"

But she pointed to the babe.
They said: "How can we
Talk to one who is
A child in the cradle?"

He said: "I am indeed
A servant of God:
He hath given me
Revelation and made me
A prophet;

"And He hath made me
Blessed wheresoever I be,
And hath enjoined on me
Prayer and Charity as long
As I live:

"[He] hath made me kind
To my mother, and not
Overbearing or miserable;

"So Peace is on me
The day I was born,
The day that I die,
And the Day that I
Shall be raised up
To life [again]"!

Such [was] Jesus the son
Of Mary: [it is] a statement
Of truth, about which
They [vainly] dispute.[12]

The Qur'an refers to Jesus 124 times, as Issa ("Jesus" in Arabic), as the Maseeh (Messiah), or as the Son of Mary. The name of the Prophet Muhammad, by comparison, is mentioned only four times in the Qur'an. Not long ago, I discovered a book called *The*

Muslim Jesus, featuring four hundred pages of quotations on Jesus as narrated by the Prophet Muhammad, a treasury of sayings most Christians are not aware even exists.

As the third and last of the divinely revealed religions, Islam has an embedded tolerance for Judaism and Christianity. The Holy Qur'an called Jews and Christians "People of the Book" since they followed the Torah or the Christian Gospels that Muslims also accept. As the Qur'an says, "O People of the Book! Come to common terms as between us and you: that we worship none but God; that we associate no partners with Him; that we erect not, from among ourselves, lords and patrons other than God."[13] To question the originality of Judaism and Christianity would undermine the foundations of our own faith. Our traditions of eating halal food and fasting follow in the Jewish tradition and, in the case of fasting, also the Christian tradition of Lent. At Christmas I celebrate Jesus' birth with my congregation by reading from the chapter of Mary in the Qur'an and sharing lessons from Jesus' life.

ISLAM UP TO THE MINUTE

Whereas Christian doctrine focuses on correct belief, or orthodoxy, Islamic doctrine focuses on correct actions, or orthopraxy. In this way Islam resembles Judaism. Even the dynamic, sweeping lines of Arabic script and the name of the religion connote action. "Islam" means "submission" in Arabic. In the *Peak of Eloquence,* Imam Ali defines Islam this way: "Islam is submission, submission is conviction, conviction is affirmation, affirmation is acknowledgment, acknowledgment is discharge [of obligations], and discharge of obligations is action." Over time this emphasis on outcome molded a structured world in which every practice represented a choice, a chance to submit to God's will. The Qur'an could not begin to cover every situation, so where it said nothing, Shia Muslims turned to the Sunna, the traditions and sayings of the Prophet Muhammad and the Shia Imams as passed down through their followers. Because the Qur'an and Sunna combined still left so much open to interpretation, and because Al-Mahdi, the last Imam, is in occultation and guides the Shia community indirectly, Shia also rely on the most learned scholars' legalistic interpretations of the existing code, a practice known as ijtihad. "Ijtihad," meaning "intellectual striving," comes from the same root word as "jihad," which refers to personal striving, and it has become an essential tool for understanding what Muslims should do. The Qur'an, Sunna, and record of ijtihad, the collective body of law established in the past fourteen centuries, is called the Sharia and covers everything from charity and ritual purification before prayers to divorce, inheritance, and warfare.

Though most Muslim countries also have a separate set of civil laws and regulations that supplement and temper the Sharia, the legacy of Islam is that of a legal tradition, not just a religious tradition. In the West it has a reputation for being out of touch with modern realities, but Islam's grounding in jurisprudence and logic and, in Shia Islam, continual reinterpretation of existing law to address societal changes, makes it much more dynamic than many realize. Muslim banking forbids the charging of interest, which would make purchasing a home difficult for Muslims in the West, where the mortgage system prevails. But scholars have determined that taking mortgages is acceptable where there is no other option. They also now permit organ donation and autopsy, two practices previously outlawed for violating the sanctity of bodies, a serious transgression in Islam. In contemporary interpretations, the social benefit of saving another's life through organ donation, or advancing science or catching a criminal through autopsy, outweighs the obligation to bury a body intact.

The combination of independent commitment and common practice lends momentum and synchronicity to Islam. Each day, all over the world, Muslims are participating in the same rites and openly professing their faith to one another. The grand stage of the annual hajj reinforces what Muslims see every day on a smaller scale: a true worldwide community that transcends national and ethnic identities, united in submission to God.

As a result, one cannot easily separate culture from religion in the Islamic world, which is what first baffled me about living in the United States, where culture bears so little relation to religion. Thousands of noisy, mismatched viewpoints converge and somehow justify their own place in the social order as a de facto culture. In my formative years, commonalities and shared history had brought people together. Here the opposite was true: the complete lack of bonds required a leap of faith that yielded a strong sense of community because of that leap, because we were forced to commit to others so different from ourselves. President Clinton touched on the topic in his first inaugural address, less than two months after I came to America. I watched the broadcast on CNN with great interest as he promoted the idea of volunteer service. "In serving, we recognize a simple but powerful truth—we need each other. And we must care for one another. Today, we do more than celebrate America; we rededicate ourselves to the very idea of America."

The idea, surely, is that the whole is stronger than the parts, however disparate those parts might be. But I didn't know what he was talking about at the time. I was still learning English, and my brothers and sisters were too busy listening to President Clinton's speech to interpret for me.

CHAPTER 5

Bridge Building

Islam has still the power to reconcile apparently irreconcilable elements of race and tradition. If ever the opposition of the great societies of East and West is to be replaced by cooperation, the mediation of Islam is an indispensable condition.[1]
—*H.A.R. Gibb (1932)*

I HAD BEEN assisting my father at Al-Azzahra, a second Los Angeles–area Islamic center he founded, for a few months when a female police officer, six feet tall and blond, entered with a slight Iraqi man in tow. He might have stood five foot six, and he spoke no English. My father and I exchanged glances at this sight, wondering what sort of trouble he could be in. Did she want us to interpret, or provide some information for a case?

"We want to get married," he announced in Arabic.

I would have been less surprised if he had claimed to be working undercover. In Arabic, he explained that she had pulled him over on the interstate for speeding the day before. She had let him off with a warning, and he was so touched by her courtesy that he proposed. I looked at the two of them. The officer smiled expectantly. I looked to my father on how to proceed. Should we consent to such an impetuous plan? My father considered the idea for a moment and finally agreed to perform the marriage while I served as a witness. And off they went.

Working as an imam in America is very different from doing

so in the Middle East. The position requires endless ability to adapt and take the unexpected in stride. My father presided over a funeral at Al-Azzahra where the deceased was a young Iranian who had left behind his American, non-Muslim wife. Mostly the husband's family and friends attended the service, which was spiritual and dignified. Afterward, however, people began noticing that his wife had disappeared. The neighborhood around Al-Azzahra was compact and incredibly diverse, so, as mourners congregated outside in preparation for the trip to the cemetery, the Latin music drifting over the fence from the party next door wasn't unusual. What caught us off guard was the widow's behavior. She had drifted away after the service, wandered into the neighboring courtyard behind the mosque, and begun dancing to the music alongside two Hispanic men. In the Middle East, a woman mourns for a minimum of four months; one year of mourning is standard. Such unconventional behavior shocked many of us and likely offended a few, but her husband's family did not protest the scene; she was not Muslim, they reasoned, and perhaps the American way was to celebrate in the face of death.

Middle Eastern imams who come here often fail or become discouraged because they cannot interpret Islam for an American audience. The traditional cultures of their homelands call for traditional rules. In the United States and Canada, imams must adjust their methods of introducing the Middle East's majority faith to the realities of a minority population. I once sat through a tedious half hour in a Los Angeles mosque as the imam used his Friday sermon to discuss the proper use of the Islamically prescribed toothpick. In this imam's homeland, where baseline Islamic knowledge is more robust, the sermon could have been appropriate, but here it was trivial. American Muslims must make sacrifices to get to midday prayer on Friday (a holy day when businesses are closed in Muslim countries), squeezing in time during work and often driving across town for services. The imam bears responsibility for preparing a sermon relevant to them: life direction, right and wrong, love, family, and politics. American Muslims have questions alien to the experience of a Middle Eastern imam. *"What if my manager won't let me pray at work?" "May I, as a woman, remove my hijab if I feel threatened for being a Muslim?" "Is it acceptable for a Muslim waiter to serve alcohol?" "As a convert, how should I behave toward my non-Muslim relatives?" "Is it acceptable to attend the wedding of my non-Muslim friends?"* One of the biggest and most common questions in America deals with mortgages. One reason the mortgage system is not used in the Middle East is a Qur'anic verse in which God tells us, "Fear God, and give up what remains of your demand for usury [lending money at interest], if ye are indeed believers."[2] Historically, usury made the rich richer and the poor poorer; debtors could be enslaved if unable to pay. In the United States, however, buying houses outside the mortgage system is not a practical possibility, and the benefits of home ownership are such that some Muslim scholars here often condone the taking of fair mortgages, and should.

Tellingly, American mosques are usually called societies or centers because their scope is broader than their Middle Eastern counterparts'. In the Middle East, imams have specific responsibilities. Most work either as preachers, or as prayer leaders, or as officiants in marriage and divorce. The most respected imams might teach in a seminary. The imam in America wears all these hats and a few dozen others. He is as much a cultural touchstone as a religious one: a leader, counselor, uncle, community liaison, and judge. The large-mosque imam fills the vacuum of all the aspects of Muslim society that Middle Eastern imams take for granted. Reporters call him for opinions and information about the Muslim community. Parents, ordinarily the stewards of matrimony, seek his help finding suitable partners for their sons and daughters. And in the post-9/11 world, law enforcement officials look to him for cooperation in investigations and the monitoring of suspected militants. My father succeeded in making the transition from East to West, but he was one of the rare imams who had already filled a multitude of roles prior to immigrating— seminary teacher, preacher, prayer leader, family court judge—

and possessed an ingrained flexibility that served him especially well once he arrived in the States. He impressed me with his mastery of Arabic, Persian, and English, a language he began learning at age fifty-six.

An imam's responsibilities can be all-consuming: As imam at the Islamic Center of America (ICOFA) in Dearborn, I get forty to fifty e-mails a day with questions on everything under the sun: Islamic rules, family problems, and social issues. Calls come at all hours of the day and night. Phone messages and appointment requests pile up. A woman finds her loyalties divided between her parents and her husband, all of whom are engaged in an icy stalemate. "It's him or us," her parents tell her. The old adage that a couple marries their spouse's entire family is nowhere truer than in Arab culture. A serious rift could spell disaster. I must sit them down all together and address each grievance individually if the marriage is to be saved. Another man wants to know whether he should stop taking his medication and opt for the doctor's surgical alternative. (I recommend that he follow his doctor's advice.) All the questions are serious and deserve thoughtful answers; mine is not a nine-to-five job, and I recall that Imam Ali, on his deathbed, encouraged visitors to come and ask religious questions of him while they still had the chance. I believe they took him at his word.

For decades, Islam languished in America in communities with no Muslim infrastructure, no mosques, cultural events, or charities. Practicing immigrants arrived well before the advent of the Internet, and there were no electronic resources, no online lectures or chat rooms, for exchanging ideas; many people gradually drifted away from the faith. Worse, some early immigrants found it difficult as Muslims to compete for jobs and so, like other minorities before them, began Americanizing their names to get ahead. Ali became Alex; Sami, Sam; Jafar, Jeff. From time to time I glimpsed how bereft of understanding the acculturation machine had left subsequent generations. In one counseling session I had with an estranged young man, he confessed more than he realized: "The only thing I know about Islam," he said, "is the Ten Commandments."

I call these lost souls "hummus Muslims" for their sole connection to Middle Eastern culture: the tabbouleh, fatoush, hummus, and other old-country foods they've often grown up with. There are varying degrees of distance from the faith: some have simply lost touch with a majority of our traditions, while others are almost wholly removed, nominal Muslims. Several years ago I presided over a funeral in Illinois; many of the attendees came dressed as if for a cocktail party and traded jokes. The son who delivered the eulogy, a professor, said he was saddened by his mother's death but also pleased because it was his wife's birthday. At the cemetery, I found that his mother would not be buried facing Mecca and in a separate section for Muslims, as is customary. "Imam," the deceased's daughter told me, "God does not care whether the grave is facing Mecca." I believe that God does care, and I believe in doing things the right way. The family's rejection of that way signaled to me a larger apathy toward their religion.

Some have edged so far onto shifting sands that they've lost their way entirely. A woman once stopped by my office to pick up a few documents that her out-of-state relatives had left with me for safekeeping. As an afterthought, she asked if I might perform an Islamic marriage for her and her partner. I was flabbergasted when I learned that she had been with this man for twenty-eight years and had seven kids and many more grandchildren, yet the two had never married. "Where have you been all these years?" I asked. "Imam," she said, "I have lived in a society where there was no Islamic guidance, and I didn't know what I was supposed to do. I didn't know."

I mention these stories not to belittle the people involved, but to illustrate how different and elemental the needs of American Muslims are. An imam in Karbala would never have a woman come into his office and profess ignorance that cohabitating with a man and raising children together should not occur outside marriage. American Muslim leaders cannot serve their communities without confronting these basic challenges head-on. We cannot talk of toothpicks when our communities are in spiritual decay. One of my favorite Bible passages comes from the Gospel of Mark:

> And it came to pass, that, as Jesus sat at meat in his house, many publicans [tax collectors] and sinners sat also together with Jesus and his disciples: for there were many, and they followed him.
>
> And when the scribes and Pharisees ["separated ones"] saw him eat with publicans and sinners, they said unto his disciples, How is it that he eateth and drinketh with publicans and sinners?
>
> When Jesus heard [it], he saith unto them, They that are whole have no need of the physician, but they that are sick: I came not to call the righteous, but sinners to repentance.[3]

I want all Muslims to feel comfortable coming to our mosque to attend prayers, even if—especially if—they have not been to a mosque in a long time or don't otherwise feel "qualified" to participate. Every year the Islamic Center of America holds open houses, community forums, fund-raisers, and various special events to which everyone is invited, a chance for people from all backgrounds to find out more about our center and about Islam. I also speak to neighboring congregations, Muslim and non-Muslim, and appear on TV and radio shows to talk about Islam and Muslim issues. Beyond a certain point, however, getting people through the doors depends on their own outlook and upbringing. Family makes the preservation of religious and cultural traditions possible, and I believe these hummus Muslims have fallen victim to America's cult of individualism. Since the country's rise to affluence after World War II, its citizens have increasingly equated success with self-sufficiency and isolation, as if they misinterpreted Henry Thoreau's famous quote that "a man is rich in proportion to the number of things which he can afford to let alone."[4] Living with parents past adolescence signals failure or apathy, while withdrawal—to the suburbs, to gated communities, to country clubs, to the privacy of one's own four walls—is the hallmark of upward mobility. The most luxurious cars are the ones that, through noise insulation and tinting, best shut out the outside world.

After living in California for a few years, I rented an apartment at a complex in Claremont near my extended family and met a man in his late sixties. I saw him walking his two dogs regularly, and as I got to know him better, I would ask about his family. (He always walked alone.) One of his children was in the Navy and was stationed in Guam. Another lived in Maine. He spoke to them every few months. His wife had left him years before, after revealing that she was a lesbian and moving in with her partner. I felt sorry knowing that half of what makes life worth living, our loved ones, was not available to him.

We are rich in proportion to the number of people we are able to engage. Muslims, like Hispanics, take great pride in their families and rely on family connections throughout their lives. Relationships in my family are passionate and are reaffirmed regularly over the dinner table or, from a distance, over the phone. My mother has been known to call me in the middle of the night from Iraq, miscalculating the time, and then express alarm at hearing my groggy voice. Am I sick? Has something happened? Even today, in my forties, I do not make a major life decision without consulting my father, and the same goes for my grown children with me.

Muslims are disinclined to place their parents in nursing homes. In a nod to standard American ways, some Muslim communities have begun building elder-care facilities, near their mosques, serving halal meals and featuring prayer rooms and same-sex caregivers, but the response from Muslims appears muted. After one year of operation, a six-bed, Muslim assisted-living facility in Hawthorne, California, had only two Christians and a Buddhist in its care.[5] I predict a similar reception for a much larger complex now open in the Minneapolis suburbs. "I could never do it," one Muslim from Minnesota told *The New York Times*. "It just is not in our culture."[6] The Qur'an makes the matter clear: "Thy Lord hath decreed . . . that ye be kind to parents. Whether one or both of them attain old age in thy life, say not to them a word of contempt, nor repel them, but address them in terms of honour."[7]

It used to be that American families took better care of one another. Now that responsibility increasingly falls to the government. At a White House prayer breakfast in 1999, President Clinton informed those of us in the audience that the number of teen deaths and suicides involving guns, while down in recent years, was twelve times higher than it was in twenty-five other industrialized countries *combined,* a travesty surely tied to family dysfunction.[8] We still expect the public schools rather than parents to educate children about sex, even as women have more and more babies out of wedlock (29 percent nationally based on data from 2000 to 2003 versus 11 percent in 1970).[9]

Some years ago, a man in his early twenties met with me in counseling. He had grown close to a girl and would spend nights with her and her friends, taking drugs in her basement. After a while she disappeared, her cell phone number was disconnected, and her divorced mother's house put up for sale. He became pale and lost weight; doctors analyzed a blood sample and diagnosed him with HIV. With six months to live, he decided to leave Michigan and spend the rest of his life in the Middle East, where this most likely would not have happened to him.

I do not pretend that Middle Eastern society is perfect. It is not and has its own problems. There, families are in good shape; it is governments at all levels that need help. Colleges and universities struggle to compete globally, public revenues rise and fall with oil prices and outside aid, and water is in perpetually short supply. But with the exception of Iraq, which I'll give a free pass under the circumstances, the difficulty of day-to-day life has not significantly eroded family life. So it can be done. Military boosters are fond of saying that freedom isn't free, and I would add that too much freedom can have a very high cost as well.

ISLAMIC SCHOOLS, AMERICAN LESSONS

By the 1990s, American Muslims were seeing encouraging signs of their own cultural and religious renewal. English-speaking imams were reaching people who had long forgotten about Islam. Mosques regrouped, new immigrants brought fresh energy, and Islam became much more visible to the average citizen. No longer did young adults have to deny their heritage in order to succeed economically. Nationwide, the Muslim community was breaking the cycle of indifference. The Council on American-Islamic Relations (CAIR) reported a 25 percent increase in the number of mosques between 1994 and 2000 and noted in a 2001 report that two thirds of all existing mosques had been founded in either the 1980s or 1990s.[10] While conducting a marriage ceremony in San Diego in 1993, I observed a surprisingly large Shia Muslim community that had no mosque and no imam, but did seem to have a genuine interest in worshipping together. I volunteered to drive down for weekly lectures if they were able to find a mosque, and they succeeded in leasing an African American mosque called Attaqwa for six months, during which time I spoke there and met some wonderful people. After six months, Attaqwa did not renew their contract, but through my father a Kuwaiti philanthropist donated funds to purchase a San Diego church, and my brother Imam Moustafa Qazwini moved from London to serve the new congregation full-time. Imam Mohammed Qazwini, the older brother I spent so much time with as a child, now runs the mosque, called Imam Ali Mosque, as well as the Islamic Educational Center of San Diego, which he opened in 2006. Imam Moustafa Qazwini directs the Islamic Educational Center of Orange County in Costa Mesa, California.

With Al-Azzahra Mosque up and running, our top priority

was to open a Muslim elementary school. At the time we arrived, hundreds of thousands of Muslims called southern California home, yet we had no private schools in which to teach Islamic principles—public schools say nothing about ethics. With family and volunteer help, we began by serving just a few dozen students, several of them my children and my brothers', at the City of Knowledge Academy in 1994. In time, through donations and fund-raisers, we added a secondary school. I would teach at least one class on the Qur'an to the higher grades. Today more than two hundred students from kindergarten to twelfth grade attend the schools, a statistic I remain proud of more than a dozen years later. Since the earliest days, we have had graduates accepted at UCLA, UC-Davis, UC-Berkeley, and other top schools. These students have the best of both worlds—the freedoms, integration, and opportunities of the larger society and a grounding in the principles of Islam: balance, integrity, and dignity.

My own children's embrace of each proves that the differences we think of as religious are, rather, cultural. They're the ones who will help forge the unique spirit of American Islam. They speak English more fluently than I do and of course are savvier about pop culture and contemporary lingo, expertise they remind me of readily. "C'mon, dude," they say. "Get real." I once delivered a sermon to a young audience on the importance of timely prayer. If President Clinton invited you to the White House for dinner, I said, you wouldn't tell him to call later because you were too busy playing soccer. Afterward, my sons critiqued my message: Kids don't care about being invited to the White House, they told me. You should have used Michael Jordan as an example.

DESTINATION DEARBORN

One of my primary duties as assistant imam at Al-Azzahra was to take on whatever my father was unable to do, such as leading Friday prayers and speaking at mosques that didn't have a full-time imam. I also led Friday prayers at Pico Rivera Mosque, a small Shia mosque in the town of the same name. Just a few months after I arrived in America, in February 1993, my father was invited by the Islamic Center of America (ICOFA), once known as the Islamic Center of Detroit, to give a guest lecture during Ramadan, the holy month during which the Qur'an was first revealed. My father had other commitments, so I readily accepted this weighty responsibility in his stead. ICOFA's leader was Imam Chirri, the impressive man I had read about and whose book *The Brother of the Prophet* a visiting student of my father's had given me in my formative years in Kuwait. Imam Chirri would turn eighty that year, and his health and abilities had declined sharply; the month-long series of lectures had become too much for him.

In this way I came to know the Muslim community in Dearborn, on the southwest edge of Detroit, which has the largest concentration of Arab Americans in the United States. That first trip opened my eyes to the prominence of American Muslims. Southern California Muslims numbered in the hundreds of thousands, but they were scattered across thousands of square miles and attended scores of mosques, just one of many subcultures. Whereas Islam in the Los Angeles area impressed me with its diversity, with Iranians, Pakistanis, Lebanese, Afghanis, African Americans, and people of European ancestry all worshipping at Al-Azzahra, Dearborn's stature came from its concentrated Muslim presence. In Pomona, surrounded by orange groves on the outskirts of Los Angeles County, I felt as if I were living in the countryside. Dearborn, with its Arabic signage, thriving halal restaurants, and myriad women in hijab making their way around town, could have been a city in Lebanon or Syria. (Indeed, one angry blogger refers to it as "Dearbornistan.") New immigrants who didn't speak English could manage with relative ease. Greater Detroit boasts 300,000 Arab Americans and also a wide-ranging diversity: Lebanese and Iraqis are most common, but there are also Palestinians, Syrians, Egyptians, and many others.

ICOFA's entire congregation welcomed me when I visited for those early lectures, but I had difficulty communicating in English, which often left me feeling isolated and frustrated at dinners and in other social settings. When I first arrived in America, my ESL teacher told the class that in order to learn English, a new speaker has to make a million mistakes, literally. More than that, the speaker has to be *willing* to make all those mistakes so that he can recognize them. I would stash an electronic Arabic-English dictionary in my robes so that I could hear English pronunciations, and for two years my most frequent request to those around me was "Spell it." In America, Muslims can be divided into two groups: those who speak English, and those who don't. The second, consisting of older parents and grandparents, is the easier to reach spiritually. They're generally immigrants who grew up with Islam and attend services regularly. For them, the mosque provides a lifeline and a sense of community. The first group is more challenging. American-born Muslims often have broader interests and social networks that extend far beyond the traditional Muslim community. At the time I began traveling to Dearborn, these adolescents and younger adults saw the mosque as stuffy and outmoded. An imam who spoke only in Arabic would reinforce that perception. They had sports, movies, and video games to attend to.

In part, this generation gap stemmed from a lack of sufficient ties to the religion for youth. They were curious about the faith but lacked the proper setting to explore it. No youth organization catered to their tastes or showed them how Islam could apply to their lives. At Dearborn's Fordson High School, 90 percent of the students were Arab or Muslim, but the Islamic Center of America had no alternative school for them to attend. My first lectures in Dearborn went over so well that the center invited me back later that year to lecture during Ashura, and for the next four years, I traveled to Dearborn twice a year to speak.

Starting in 1995, each time I did, I held nightly question-and-answer sessions for the English speakers, the younger Muslims, or I went to their homes to lecture. This challenged me as much as it did them. Until then, I had spoken about Islam mainly in Arabic; trying to explain various aspects in English in a straightforward and engaging manner tested me. The groups fired questions at me as fast as I was able to answer them. Fortunately, they were patient with my explanations as we learned together. Many had never had the chance to speak to an imam one on one.

In those days, I gave all my lectures in Arabic, but not everyone attending was fluent, and sometimes audience members would spontaneously stand up and interpret for those who couldn't understand. These impromptu translations distracted and occasionally irritated me, but the real reason I disliked them lay in my desire to carry the message directly to the people. In Arabic I could claim to be a skilled and compelling orator. I hated the idea that I had to depend on others to help fulfill my essential obligations.

Those initial visits to Dearborn motivated me more than ever to master English and reach a larger audience for Islam. Older Muslims would carry the message to their families and no further. I accepted corrections of my grammar unashamedly and read the *Los Angeles Times* every day to practice reading and pick up new vocabulary. (I also owe *The New York Times* a great deal for my improved English since I later read it daily.) Early on I had a young engineer friend who spoke a little Arabic and with whom I struck a bargain: I would teach him about Islamic jurisprudence if in exchange he would help me with my English.

After six months, I dropped my basic ESL course and enrolled in advanced-level English at Mt. San Antonio College. Then, in 1994, I enrolled in California Polytechnic University–Pomona and majored in sociology. Besides ministering to Muslims and learning English, I wanted to better understand American culture, and I found its educational system to be a crown jewel. America's colleges and universities attract thousands of students from abroad every year. Americans themselves bemoan the state of their schools, but the rest of the world envies their higher education curricula and research programs. I forged good relationships with my instructors and remember those years of study as among the happiest of my life. Historically, Islam has emphasized education, too. The Prophet Muhammad said, "The seeking of knowledge is obligatory upon every Muslim," and the Qur'an says, "Whoever is granted wisdom, he indeed is given a great good."[11] For years during the Middle Ages, doctors in Europe relied on books written by Muslim physicians, who had interpreted the learning of the Greeks and incorporated their own advances. Today the Middle East produces well-educated professionals but lacks the friendly research environments necessary for supreme scientific achievement. Once those countries start retaining scientists and engineers on par with their western and eastern counterparts, stability and a high, sustained standard of living will follow.

THE LITMUS TEST

Learning English happened more slowly than I would have liked. Without it, I was just an imam in America, no different than if I had opted to preach in Lebanon or Syria or anywhere else. I could speak to the Muslims here, but I couldn't really reach them. English required patience, but also a kind of surrender and humility, a willingness to feel vulnerable but not helpless.

The feeling reminded me of a traumatic injury I sustained as a child in Kuwait. When I was ten, a boy with a slingshot and poor aim hit my left eye, and I spent forty days in the hospital. The doctor found internal bleeding in my eye and performed surgery a week later. (My mother, who had returned to Iraq before the incident to visit her family for two weeks, was convinced that my father was sheltering her from the truth in an attempt to soften the blow, and that in fact I was dead.) For a month I lay still, eyes closed and unmoving, in order to prevent a reoccurrence of bleeding. Only sustained concentration saved my sight. By the time I recovered, I had been confined to bed for so long that I had poor circulation in my legs and required two weeks of hot water and massages to regain my mobility. My father hailed my recovery as a miracle. I was just relieved that I would again have full and independent use of my faculties. The ordeal put me hopelessly behind in my classwork, and my teacher held me back for another year of fifth grade, an affront that left me depressed. I had always taken pride in my good grades and didn't want to be branded as a failure. If I had to repeat the fifth grade, I would much rather have moved to a new school than see my old peers move on without me; with my parents' permission, that's just what I did.

After a few years of practice and continued classwork, I could lecture in English with Arabic notes. In late 1996, I chose a small Shia mosque in Claremont, California, to lecture in English for the first time without any notes, to celebrate the birth of Fatima, the Prophet Muhammad's daughter. Though I had confidence, my English was still far from perfect. I recall one early lecture in which I spoke to adolescents and young adults about cleansing their souls by overcoming their animalistic urges. "You must mate your beast," I called to them several times to smiles and giggles before a young man spoke up and said the word I wanted was "tame." In Claremont, I was reciting my first lecture in English by heart, and I'm sure I made a few mistakes, but everyone was encouraging and, most important, understood my message. No one stood to translate specific points or ask questions. Two more years would pass before I became a naturalized citizen, but that night, shaking hands with the appreciative congregants lined up in front of the lectern afterward, I joined the able ranks of those who have fulfilled the only real requirement for acceptance and success as an American.

CHAPTER 6

The Muslim Capital
of the West

Freedom consists not in doing what we like, but in having
the right to do what we ought.[1]
—*Pope John Paul II*

ON ONE OF my early trips to speak at the Islamic Center of
America, I was staying at a host's home and preparing for my lecture when I heard a knock at the door one morning. This was
in early February, when the weather in Dearborn is harsh enough
to make a person seriously consider moving south. Snowflakes
swirled in tunnels of their own making and collected thickly on
the windowsills.

I answered and greeted a man in his fifties carrying a brief-
case. I was still young and new to the country and did not recognize the hallmarks of a door-to-door evangelist. Not speaking
English (and, as it wasn't my house, after all), I didn't invite him
in to talk, but I did accept a beautiful brochure written in Arabic
as he thanked me and headed to the next house. For a minute I
stood at the window and watched, with a mixture of admiration
and disappointment, as he pressed on through the snow. On the
bitterest of days, when most people wouldn't care to linger between their car and front door, this man was calling on dozens of
his neighbors to talk about the importance of Christianity. And

he had come with literature in an array of languages, prepared for any eventuality.

I admit to disappointment because I could see right in front of me what others were willing to do for their cause, and I wondered what we as Muslims were willing to do for ours. The sixth Imam, Imam Jafar al-Sadiq, said, "Invite people to [Islam] through other than your tongue."[2] In the Islamic tradition, the best way to bring others to the faith is by demonstrating honorable qualities. But I couldn't help thinking that there might be additional ways to somehow sacrifice for the greater good and come to understand our neighbors better.

DELIVERING THE MESSAGE

Dearborn's Arab American community began in earnest in 1927, when Henry Ford opened his River Rouge plant in the city. Lebanese immigrants had been coming to the Detroit area in small numbers for a decade to take advantage of Ford's unprecedented five-dollar-a-day wage for assembly line work. By the time World War II was over, Dearborn had about two hundred families of Arab origin. The renaissance took place from the mid-1960s into the 1970s, after immigration reforms changed the focus of admission criteria from national origin quotas to societal contributions and family reunification. Palestinians, Yemenis, Iraqis, and other Middle Easterners began settling in places where Arab Americans already lived, such as Dearborn. The post-reform immigrants were generally much better off than previous generations. They opened their own businesses, taught at universities, practiced law, and quickly began leading the community.

With the larger numbers and imported tastes of more recent waves of immigrants, a new pan-Arab identity emerged. Storefront mosques, neat shops, and Muslim bakeries began appearing alongside liquor stores and nightclubs. Inspired by Iran's Islamic Revolution, thousands of women began wearing hijab. (Before 1979, only a handful of women in Dearborn had.) Imam Chirri grew out his beard and regularly donned a turban; in the past, he had often worn suits under his religious attire, but he phased them out. In the mid-1990s, the Karbala Islamic Educational Center on Warren Avenue, a Shia Iraqi social center, replaced a gay nightclub damaged by fire. Muslims began speaking more about their common issues and identities, and with that critical mass of Arab Americans, the larger community took notice as well.

Today Dearborn has restaurants that stay open all night during the holy month of Ramadan to accommodate families who fast during the day. The public schools close for Ashura, the Eid al-Fitr feast during Ramadan, and Eid al-Adha, the Feast of Sacrifice during the hajj to Mecca, and when schools are in session, hundreds of young female students stream out each afternoon with hijabs fluttering like doves in the breeze. You can order halal Chicken McNuggets at some Dearborn McDonald's. On a percentage basis, Dearborn has a higher Arab American population than any other city in the country. We call it the Muslim capital of the West.

Every time I spoke in Dearborn in the mid-1990s, I was swept away by the energy of the community. There was too much to know, too many people to talk to. I would speak at eight o'clock to an audience of eight hundred or nine hundred, and afterward, I would circulate, answer questions, and catch up with new friends until ten or eleven. I traveled alone, my wife and children remaining in Pomona for practical reasons, so I had no need to rush home at an appointed time. Inevitably, our spiritual rap sessions would continue at someone's home until one or two in the morning.

I started meeting Muslims who never would have set foot in the Islamic center. Once outside the mosque, an imam becomes less intimidating. Word gets out that the visiting imam is going to be at so-and-so's house, and the devout and the merely curious show up to ask questions. Traditionally, in most places, the clear but unwritten rule is, if you have a problem, you go to the imam—he doesn't come to you. You make an appointment, you sit in the office on the other side of a desk or table, and you listen to the imam dictate a solution. You come when you are called, and you leave when you are dismissed. I instinctively adopted a more collegial approach that grew out of my circumstances and a sense that solving problems requires dialogue, and dialogue flows better on a level playing field. I was young. As a visiting speaker, I had no office, so I had to interact with members of the congregation on neutral turf, or their turf, which allowed for more extensive exchanges and thus also gave me the chance to improve my English.

People in Dearborn, especially adolescents and young adults, were surprised by my openness. Often they would preface their questions by apologizing for bothering me or for their lack of knowledge, and I would have to assure them that it was no trouble, that there were no silly questions. Some nights I answered questions, no matter how basic, for hours and delighted in the exchanges and expressions of understanding that flashed when I found the proper explanation. In December 1996, I came to speak for Ramadan. By now, I was used to the routine and didn't mind the rigorous schedule and late nights. I had given my first sermon in English a few months before, and word was spreading among the center's board members that the young visiting imam could communicate with their youth in fluent English.

On that trip, the board formally invited me to join the Islamic Center of America as the imam. Since Imam Chirri had passed in 1994, the mosque had had no permanent, full-time imam, and their searches had not turned up the right candidate. I knew intuitively that accepting the offer was the right move. It was a chance to be the imam of my own congregation. At that time, the board had voted to start a school, but nothing tangible had been undertaken. It would need a strong hand to shepherd the project to completion, and the work held great appeal for me. My father had been a stalwart advocate for Muslim education in California.

I moved to Dearborn in March 1997, six months ahead of my family, to allow the children to finish the school year in Pomona. I set about the task of organizing a school with a relish I had rarely known before. The primary challenge was cost, a hurdle I had encountered in Pomona when we attempted to raise funds for school facilities there with bake sales and dinners. In Dearborn, as in Pomona, we held open houses and fund-raising dinners, and requested donations from the congregation. I began overseeing construction and also interviewed candidates for teaching positions. Every day brought a new crisis: a building delay, insufficient candidates, funding problems. The Dearborn public schools were on a hiring binge at the time and offered high starting salaries, which limited our options. Two weeks before school was to start, I had no principal. Even some board members were hesitant to enroll their children. I lay awake the entire night and prayed for a solution. The next day, a well-qualified principal called me and told me her contract at another school had fallen through.

Meanwhile, although the builder was assuring me that construction would be completed in time for the start of school, we did not have enough money to furnish and equip the new building. At the next Friday prayer, I passionately exhorted those in the congregation to contribute the $40,000 necessary to get the school ready. A friend of mine approached me after the sermon and asked me to repeat the number. He promised I would have a check in hand the following morning. He made good on his word, and he did so anonymously. That August, we opened the Muslim American Youth Academy (MAYA) with thirty-five students. Within a year, we had 220 students in kindergarten through sixth grade, and by 2006 we had 340.

My other priority upon arrival was to bring young Muslims back to the center. I knew from my frequent visits that they had a seed of interest in the faith and could benefit greatly, but they had no incentive to come to the center regularly. Doing so was a task, not a desire. Changing that proved to be a greater challenge than establishing the school. We started Young Muslim Association (YMA) chapters at Fordson High and Dearborn High and watched as momentum built.

Knowing that adolescents thought of mosques as old and

stuffy, I moved meetings to the gymnasium adjacent to MAYA, then a distance away, and started each meeting with basketball games. During Ramadan in 1999, we introduced a Friday-night lecture series, given in English and addressing topics relevant to young people's everyday lives. The editor of the *Detroit Free Press*'s editorial page, Ron Dzwonkowski, spoke at the Friday program on careers in journalism and said, "Imam, this is a miracle. Two or two hundred and fifty young men and women at a Friday-night religious session in America? This is unheard of." Before long, we didn't have to allot half the meeting to basketball. Members were coming to listen and learn. We have held a Friday-night program year-round ever since. The 2005 Ramadan programs brought out twelve hundred youth.

RELIGION AND POLITICS

Jesus described the role of the imam as a doctor of the spirit, but there's a major difference between doctors and religious leaders that has nothing to do with metaphysics. The doctor works deductively, analyzing symptoms and recommending tests to rule out possibilities and make diagnoses. The imam must work inductively. He takes disparate elements—a Qur'anic code, Muslim tradition, and an individual's particular circumstances—and draws from each to produce a cogent solution. Wherever he goes, the imam is making connections, trying to make sense of the larger world.

For six months or a year after I became imam of ICOFA, I devoted my time to internal matters in the congregation: lectures, prayers, staffing, the school, the YMA. As those concerns turned routine, I began directing some of my energy to a mission beyond the Muslim community. In California, the municipalities were so fragmented that very little interfaith dialogue was taking place. In Dearborn, our prominence almost required it. Our own Muslims had many questions about the faith, so I knew that people raised in other religions must wonder about Islam, too. Islam was and is the fastest-growing religion in the United States; media coverage of it seemed a daily event. And regrettably, terrorist attacks such as those on the World Trade Center in 1993 and the U.S. Embassy in Kenya in 1998 had heightened sensitivity to all things Muslim.

Just as the country's citizens were paying more attention to Islam, if for negative reasons, politicians were more interested, too. The large number of Muslims living in the Detroit area put us on the map with the state's political leaders, and one thing led to another. My remarks at a brief meeting with Vice President Al Gore in Detroit caught the attention of one of his assistants, and she invited me to a prayer breakfast with President Clinton a few months later, in September 1999. There, as I stood asking him how he could help us correct the pernicious stereotypes of Muslims as radicals or reactionaries, I watched a smile spread across his face. I think he liked the idea of a relatively new immigrant advocating for his people at the White House, a reminder of the American ideals that longtime citizens take for granted. Six years earlier, visiting the White House on a public tour, I had contemplated the history and power the building represented. Since then, I had learned English, traveled the country, studied the culture, and accepted a major leadership role in the Muslim community.

At the prayer breakfast, President Clinton said he had learned much about Islam through his daughter, Chelsea, when she took a world religions class in college. The average American, he said, lacks basic knowledge about Islam. Not many Americans know that Islam is the third monotheistic religion, after Judaism and Christianity. Muslims had a priceless opportunity to give Americans an accurate understanding of Islam, he went on. Why not take advantage of it?

I resolved to promote fair media coverage for Islam wherever I could. News can be such a potent influencer of public opinion that no group can afford inaccurate depictions. Misinformation uttered at a church picnic might reach a few hundred people when all is said and done. If Headline News blows a story, millions internalize it immediately, with video clips and a ticker to drive home the point.

I didn't have to travel far to follow through on my resolution. As the leader of the country's largest mosque in the country's "Muslim capital," I had automatically become a media source by the rules of daily journalism. Before long, I was receiving calls from as far away as London and Australia. CNN, *The New York Times, The Washington Post,* and the major networks started consulting me for their stories.

I quickly discovered, however, that the national media doesn't work like community media. Some exceptional event or activity must take place to justify coverage; positive news generally doesn't make the cut. Journalists call this standard "newsworthiness." I called it reactive. I could suggest stories about Muslim communities to reporters for months with no success, but if terrorists in some far corner of the globe bombed something, I would be deluged with phone calls asking for comments, reactions from the Muslim community, and explanations of the nature of Islam. I was always happy to offer my thoughts, but I wondered whether the archbishop of Detroit received calls when someone from the IRA attacked Protestants in Northern Ireland.

That example brings to mind another shortcoming I noticed as I worked more with reporters: subjectivity. Most professional news operations do an admirable job of presenting both sides of a story. They track down sources with opposite opinions and offer them equal chances to present their views. This translates into evenhandedness, but not necessarily into objectivity. How many times have you watched a newscast and heard the anchor or reporter use the term "Muslim terrorists" or "Muslim extremists"? By comparison, the terms "Christian terrorist" and "Hindu terrorist" ring false for Americans and are heard much less frequently, even though both now and in the past we have seen terrorists who self-identify with both of these religions. Sometimes "Muslim" and "terrorist" aren't used in conjunction but in close proximity with one another, still making a subtle connection. When a story has more than two sides, or when the moral center of an issue doesn't align with the rhetorical center, standard news reporting loses objectivity. (Imagine striving for objectivity by dutifully and neutrally reporting both sides of a child rape case.)

I watched a 1994 CNN segment in which a reporter covered an Egyptian barber's "circumcision" of a ten-year-old village girl.[3] Before they ran the story, the anchor cautioned that the images to come might be graphic or disturbing. The mother ululated with her tongue to cheer on the rite; clearly the girl was in intense pain. Afterward, the barber said the mutilation was done in the name of Islam, and that God condones it. CNN didn't question its legitimacy as an Islamic practice or interview a mujtahid to provide context for it. It simply taped a man professing his beliefs in a vacuum, as the *National Enquirer* might with a source claiming garden gnomes have taken up residence under her bathroom vanity. The truth, left unstated in the report, is that female circumcision, while very common at the time in Egypt, is an African custom and is rarely seen in Muslim countries outside the continent. The practice did not originate with Islam.

The CNN report reveals a weakness particularly endemic to TV news—the lure of the sensational story. News shows are expected not only to inform but also to entertain. They must compete for ratings: the teaser leading into the evening newscast; the coiffed, powdered anchors ready for their close-ups; the clever but inaccurate headline. All are concessions to competition, a battle sometimes won not with timely, accurate stories but with slick packaging and the softest stories with the broadest appeal: this is the Hollywoodification of corporate news.

Television news producers learned their tricks from the masters of mass entertainment, but compared with Hollywood depictions of Muslims, standard news broadcasts are a delight. In Hollywood, the sole governing principle is *Will people pay to see it?* There is no pretense of objectivity or fairness. My problem with most movies, aside from their lowbrow content, has been their static portrayal of Muslims as terrorists, and only terrorists. We rarely see Muslim characters in movies unless they're needed to advance the plot as diabolical, fatalistic antagonists. The device is repeated time and again: *Delta Force* (Chuck Norris), *Executive Decision* (Kurt Russell), *The Siege* (Denzel Washington, Bruce Willis), *Not Without My Daughter* (Sally Field). The expectations are so ingrained that the 2005 movie *Flight Plan,* starring Jodie Foster, played on them by implying that four ominous-looking Muslims aboard the protagonist's plane were the suspected terrorists—no great stretch given the deep stock of movies in which that's the case—and later revealed their innocence. That's good news, of course, but the movie doesn't work unless it can make us believe that Arab Muslims are inherently cause for suspicion. I had a different sort of problem with *United 93,* which, while based on the 9/11 attacks, depicts the terrorists as devout Muslims, only serving to strengthen the connection between Islam and their maniacal ideology.

As mere escapism, these movies might seem to do little harm, but repeated and reinforced over time through many points of contact in our personal worlds, such messages add up to a frightening, monstrous view of Muslims that explain the frowns and glares I occasionally get at airports and stoplights.

When *The Siege* came out, in 1998, I spoke out against its portrayal of Muslims as terrorists and launched an awareness campaign to offset the negative publicity. The movie has the U.S. military apprehending a suspected terrorist and then safeguarding New York City under martial law after related terrorists target the city in retaliation. Images of violent Muslims had become one of Hollywood's favorite premises for high-adventure films, and Muslims had grown tired of the cliché. As I say, we rarely see recognizably Muslim characters depicted positively in movies. They scarcely appear at all, so when their only roles are as murderous fanatics, the effect is all the more damaging. In Dearborn, we held an open house at ICOFA to give non-Muslims better access to and information on Muslim life. We handed out fliers at theaters to explain the truth about Islam.

As I often tell non-Muslim audiences in my interfaith work, if you want to learn about Islam, turn off your TV. In the first few years after I came to lead the Islamic Center of America, I spoke to thousands of people, most frequently Christians, about Islam and common misconceptions concerning it. The questions were not difficult to answer. More than one person wanted to know the difference between the two religions "Islam" and "Muslim." (Islam is the religion, and Muslims follow Islam, just as Christians follow Christianity.) I would talk about similarities between our faiths, the origins of Islamic beliefs and customs, and where Muslims fit into the larger American society. Islam and Christianity share the universal values of charity, honesty, sincerity, and hard work. Followers of both religions can agree on love for God and respect for parents, neighbors, and ourselves. We differ on only a relatively small number of issues.

Perhaps the most effective part of my talks was simply showing up. People see a bearded, turbaned Muslim, and they think *Terrorist*. Their minds fill with visions of burning American flags and chants of "Death to America!" A few months after 9/11, as I took my seat on an airplane, the woman next to me wordlessly got up and moved. Meeting face to face and staking out common ground worked against those fears. In my talks I had fun tossing wrenches into the machinery of stereotyping and eliciting spontaneous grins. When someone asked why women aren't allowed to drive in Saudi Arabia, I started my answer by saying, "The Qur'an doesn't say anything about prohibiting women from driving." A Muslim imam telling jokes and seeing things their way elicited reactions close to relief. When people approached me afterward, they were enthusiastic and grateful. "I never knew that's what Islam was," I heard again and again. People were too polite to speak frankly, but in their eyes and gestures I read their meaning: *We thought you Muslims had horns.*

A question I fielded frequently, especially as the 2000 election drew near, was "Are you a Democrat or a Republican?" Leading ICOFA has given me the chance to meet several leaders in the federal government and raise awareness of issues important to Muslim Americans.

My answer, as usual, was not what audiences might expect.

Late in the 2000 race, the Muslim community decided to support Governor Bush, and Vice President Gore had trouble finding traction—though, in fairness, he didn't spend a lot of time courting the Muslim vote.

My first brush with national politics came in April 1999, when Vice President Gore invited me, twelve other Arab Americans, and leaders of the AFL-CIO to meet with him in the executive wing of the Detroit airport, just two months before he officially announced his candidacy for the presidency. Politicians know that domestic policy wins elections, but for Muslim Americans, especially more recent immigrants, foreign policy is a make-or-break factor. By the time of the meeting, UN economic sanctions that the United States advocated had led to the deaths of an estimated 700,000 children in Iraq, while Saddam still had all his palaces and, we now know, liberal access to world markets through the corrupt UN Oil-for-Food program.[4] He had flouted innumerable post–Gulf War UN resolutions restricting the country in everything from air traffic to border crossings. Diplomacy had failed in every sense. Mr. Vice President, I asked, instead of punishing Saddam's own people, why don't we help them get rid of him? Gore was receptive but pessimistic: The only way we could get rid of him would be to use a bullet, he said—and that would be immoral. (Since the administration of Gerald Ford, presidents have substantially upheld Ford's executive order forbidding the assassination of foreign officials, so such an action could also be illegal. But the order could easily be repealed or suspended.)

Everyone laughed.

Gore asked for other ideas.

I spoke up. I am no expert on war or foreign affairs, I said, but in the 1980s, the U.S. pulled Manuel Noriega out of Panama and tried him in Miami for his crimes. Couldn't you do something similar with Saddam? Gore felt the idea was risky.

I had to disagree. For Iraqis, the risk was in doing nothing. The first President Bush was infamous in Iraq, but not so much in the United States, for taking the "safe" route. He encouraged Iraqis to turn against Saddam Hussein during the 1991 Gulf War, after the American bombing campaign dispatched Iraq's military infrastructure in a matter of days. Fifteen of Iraq's eighteen provinces, including Karbala, responded. Bush reneged when he saw that Iraqis were revolting against the government and not only against Saddam; he actually gave the order for U.S. forces to allow the Republican Guard and Baathist police through the battle lines to quell the revolt. Karbala held out for twelve days before the Baathists retook the city, massacring thousands and perpetrating the bloodbath at the Shrine of Imam Husayn, where Hussein Kamel issued his infamous challenge to Imam Husayn to "get up and see who's winning." Three of my cousins who joined the rebellion were killed, along with 1.7 million other Iraqis who rose up.

I got the chance to meet the younger George Bush in 2000 as he made his bid for the presidency. On a campaign visit to Lawrence Tech University in the Detroit area, Governor Bush invited five or six Muslims to meet with him privately for a brief question-and-answer session and photo op. My brother Imam Moustafa Qazwini attended and asked him about the prospects of getting rid of Saddam.

I'd love to see Saddam removed, Governor Bush said, but I don't think I can make it part of my official policy.

Over the next few years, meetings with President Bush would become a regular event. The presidential election that fall promised to be close. Polls before the October debates showed Governor Bush up slightly over Vice President Gore. Muslim leaders had not made any official endorsements. That spring, however, during our meeting at Lawrence Tech, I had asked Bush about his position on racial and religious profiling of Muslims in terrorism investigations of American citizens, and about the use of so-called secret evidence to detain suspects indefinitely. Bush was not familiar with the term "racial profiling" and said he would ask Spencer Abraham, a Republican of Arab descent who was then a U.S. senator from Michigan, to brief him on the issue. Days before Bush returned to the Detroit area and a few weeks before the election, he issued a written statement denouncing the use of secret evidence and racial profiling in domestic terrorism investigations.

As a community of issue voters, we were impressed. No mainstream politician had voiced strong support for Muslims so explicitly before. When we met with Bush during his visit, I commended him on his stand. But, I told him, I have something else to ask you, Governor. We Muslims have not had a chance to participate directly in executive affairs. We would like to have an Arab or Muslim in the White House to be our liaison to you, to be our voice in Washington. If you become president, will you include some Muslims on your staff?

His response was encouraging: If I am elected president—and I will be—Spencer Abraham will be close to me. He will be your key to the White House. He will brief me about your issues and needs.

He spoke of the Lebanese friends he associated with in college and his love of Lebanese food. You are Muslims, and I am Christian, but there is not a division between us, he said. I see no difference between Muslims and Christians. They are both children of God. There are some Muslims who create trouble, but the majority are good people, just as there are some Christians who create trouble even though most are good. People talk of Muslim extremists? Come with me to Texas, and I'll show you the Christian extremists.

He had promised just what we had hoped for. Bush finished by shaking hands with everyone in the room.

For most of us in Dearborn, his answers sealed the deal. There was a feeling in the community that the Clinton administration had sided too much with Israel in the Mideast peace process and that, whatever his role, Vice President Gore was tied to that policy. His nomination of Senator Joseph Lieberman, a Jew, as his vice presidential candidate made swaying Muslims all the more challenging. Muslims didn't object to Senator Lieberman's Jewishness but rather to his unconditional support for the pro-Israeli lobby. For Vice President Gore, it was too little too late.

Vice President Gore's handlers scheduled a meeting at the same hotel Bush had used, the Hyatt Regency Dearborn, with many of the same invitees a few days later. Dr. James Zogby of the Arab-American Institute accompanied him. If Gore hadn't realized Muslims' support for Bush was a fait accompli before he arrived, he did soon after. To date, he had done nothing to assuage Muslims' feelings of betrayal, and he had missed the opportunity to define the issue of secret evidence against Muslims and Arabs, a policy that had begun on his watch. Instead, Gore echoed Bush's promises. One audience member stood up and said, "We are bothered by your unconditional support for Israel." I could see the discomfort in his face, the tightened jaw. The vice president trotted out a few talking points: He spoke of his tempering of Clinton's Middle East policy and of how he had broken bread with Yassir Arafat, King Hussein of Jordan, and the president of Yemen. He called Bush an insider whose support for Israel well exceeded Gore's own, which arguably was true.

I rose to speak next and thanked the vice president for taking time to meet with the Muslim community. We are not pleased with your support for Israel, I told him, but it is not a matter of Muslims hating Jews. We do not. It is an issue of policy, of the Israeli government persecuting and attacking innocent Palestinians. Just a few weeks ago, I said, we had a rally in Washington protesting the Israeli strikes—the Second Intifada had just begun—and some Jewish rabbis joined us in condemning Israel's actions.

Vice President Gore survived his "trial," but no one exonerated him. Governor Bush might have been an insider, but he didn't have a governing record on the federal level for voters to scrutinize. His views were unclear and less publicized, and he had the benefit of the doubt. Vice President Gore was left trying to satisfy voters on both sides of an issue for which common ground can be shaped like a wedge. I felt bad for him and offered a few encouraging words as we shook hands.

Yet he could have done more. Had he come out earlier and met with Muslim leaders, he would have better understood our sentiments and could have taken more effective positions. He never really took his message to the people. Days later, a coalition of Arab American organizations in Michigan and the American Muslim Political Coordinating Council endorsed Bush for president.[5]

My next contact with then President-elect Bush came quickly, just after the Supreme Court handed down its decision on the election, in December 2000. The invitation fell during the holy month of Ramadan, an imam's busiest time of year. I flew down to Austin on two days' notice, not to meet the Christian extremists Bush had promised me, but to stump for Muslim inclusion in the new administration. Fifteen other faith leaders took part in the meeting, at a United Methodist church. After the formalities were complete, as he passed by, I whispered, Mr. President, you won the election, but Senator Abraham lost. He was one of your closest friends. I hope you will consider him for a Cabinet post. (I also stressed the importance of fighting moral decay and cited the rampant gun violence among American teenagers as evidence of our collective shortcomings.)

I hadn't forgotten that Bush had promised to make Senator Abraham his informal liaison to the Muslim community in Dearborn, and without him in office, we had lost our voice. I also knew that Senator Abraham was crestfallen at losing his Senate race by 1 percent of the vote, and I wanted to see his talents put to work.

Bush laughed and said, I know you are campaigning for your friend. Don't worry, I am considering him for something.

I passed the word to Randa Fahmy, an assistant to Senator Abraham, that the senator was down but not yet out and that President Bush had plans for him. Fahmy said that the senator had been depressed since the loss and had heard nothing from Bush officials, and she promised to tell him the news immediately. Five days later she called to tell me that Abraham was being named secretary of energy. The president had kept his word.

At a fourth meeting with Bush, a week after his inauguration, this one an announcement of his plan for faith-based initiatives, I was the only Muslim leader invited. About twenty Jewish and Christian religious leaders, some of them very prominent, also attended, as did senior adviser Karl Rove. In the meeting, President Bush spoke at length about the important work that religious organizations do on behalf of society: health care, food banks, addiction recovery, counseling, and much else. If these organizations can effectively perform the same functions as secular ones, he asked, why shouldn't they be funded as well? I and most of the other leaders there agreed, and I advocated the idea in a CNN interview opposite a rabbi who argued against it. The rabbi said this would allow the government to control religious institutions and jeopardize their ability to serve people in their own fashion.

Looking back, I regret supporting the plan because the main beneficiaries of the initiative have been evangelicals and organizational leaders who support the Bush administration, such as Pat Robertson and Jerry Falwell.

The day after the faith-based initiatives summit, a photograph that ran in newspapers nationwide had me standing right behind the president, and stories speculated that I had become an inside consultant.

COMMUNITY FIRST

Those who know me and my history with President Bush know that I'm no Svengali. I never was a formal consultant to the president. Though I would prefer it were otherwise, there is no way for me to fulfill my obligation to my religious community without engaging in politics. Dearborn's Muslims knew that there was no ideal candidate for us in 2000. We looked for the person closer to us on the issues and voted for him—such are the vexing limitations of a two-party system. The truth is, I do not have allegiance to either party. I am not a Republican, and I am not a Democrat. I prefer to look at issues and candidates, not labels. I am not interested in buying into a system. Sufficiently motivated, both parties can govern with our cause in mind. Unfortunately, pre-election promises are not always kept, and then you feel as if you have been deceived.

To vote on the basis of issues requires diligent analysis of platforms and issues and frequent engagement with candidates to communicate our needs. My responsibility is to my congregation—to preach, to counsel, and to protect their interests and those of our more distant Muslim brothers and sisters. In every meeting I attended with Clinton, Gore, and Bush, I could pick out the guests who were happy just to be there. They were content to rub elbows with power players, eat at tables with $200 centerpieces, and tour Air Force Two. At my first meeting with Vice President Gore, at the Detroit airport, one attendee requested an American visa for a friend who lived abroad. At that moment, he breached a trust, with Gore and with his community.

I don't attend the prayer breakfasts, the DC conferences, and the campaign stops for the pricey meals and the brushes with fame. The closest most Americans get to participating in democracy is punching a ballot or taking a survey, maybe writing a letter to a congressman. As the country's population continues to grow, direct access for everyone will shrink proportionally. Those of us who manage to get it are as much in the driver's seat as anyone in such a democracy. We are on the most envied side of politics in Washington—the demand side. But we have a responsibility to make the right demands.

CHAPTER 7

Paranoid America and "Islamofascists"

They that can give up essential liberty to obtain a little
temporary safety deserve neither liberty nor safety.[1]
—Benjamin Franklin

IN THE SUMMER of 2001, at the behest of a contact in the U.S.
State Department, I agreed to host a contingent of about twenty
students from the Gulf countries, including some princes from
the Saudi royal family, who wanted to visit the Islamic Center of
America. They were passing through Detroit from Washington,
D.C., on a formal U.S. tour and wanted to worship at a local
mosque. They would pray, and then there would be a reception,
at which I would speak to them about Islam in America. I had
asked the center's custodian to prepare some light refreshment
and was anticipating the students' arrival when I heard a commotion near the entrance. Confused, I strode out to the lobby,
but my guests had left. The receptionist said she had heard one
student yell, *"Mushrik! Mushrik!"* and instantly I knew.

In Arabic, *mushrik* means "polytheists," or "idol worshippers."
These students were Wahhabis. They must have spotted the bas-
kets near the entrance doors containing pieces of clay for prayer
and realized they were in a Shia mosque. I looked out the win-

dow and didn't know whether to laugh or cry. These future leaders of their countries were prostrating on the center's front lawn.

A Christian faith leader once asked me with indignation why the United States should allow Muslims to build mosques and worship freely when Muslim-dominated countries ban churches. I responded that of the approximately forty-six countries in which Muslims constitute a majority, only one has no churches: Saudi Arabia. Wahhabis, who self-identify as Salafis, follow an extreme form of Islam that transcends the four Sunni schools of thought. The sect's eighteenth-century founder, Mohammad ibn Abd al-Wahhab, preached an ultraconservative interpretation of Islam that regarded many traditions, such as visiting the Prophet Muhammad's grave in Medina and celebrating his birthday, as apostasy. Even during the days of the first caliphs, there had been multiple interpretations of Islam, but al-Wahhab's movement illogically attempted to winnow those forms to a singular, authentic religion. His ideology stems from a fourteenth-century scholar named Ibn Taymiyya, who wrote a book called *The Path of Islam* in which he labeled Shia Muslims infidels and dogs. Ibn Taymiyya followed up with another work called *The Necessity for Eliminating the Rejectors,* which resulted in thousands of Shia being killed in Syria and Lebanon and many more converting to Christianity to avoid persecution. Their Christian descendants live in those countries to this day.

Al-Wahhab's zealous speeches received only passing notice from the Muslims of the Arabian Peninsula until he formed an alliance with Muhammad ibn Saud, a tribal leader in Najd, the central region of the peninsula that includes the present-day Saudi capital, Riyadh. Ibn Saud was struggling to expand his domain through raids and warfare. By lending his religious authority to Ibn Saud's violent political efforts, al-Wahhab enlarged his influence, and Ibn Saud in turn gained moral legitimacy from the association. During World War I, the Saud family gained power with help from the British government, and in the twenties they conquered Mecca and Medina. The family's methods were notoriously gruesome, with women and children massacred, entire tribes executed after surrendering, and public beheadings personally carried out by members of the royal family. Before they had declared their domain the Kingdom of Saudi Arabia in the early 1930s, the family had amputated limbs on 350,000 people—this in a country of only 4 million.[2]

Not everyone in Saudi Arabia today is Wahhabi—estimates for the number of adherents to the sect range from 20 percent to 40 percent of the population—but the state's suppression of every other form of religious expression makes accurate estimates difficult. As I told the minister who asked about churches in Muslim countries, Saudi Arabia isn't intolerant only of Christianity. Ibn Taymiyya's *Path of Islam* is used in every academic institution in the country. Shia, about 15 percent of the country's population, live as second-class citizens and are not allowed to have their own mosques. Shia ideas and rituals are passed down through secret texts and tapes. I am told that punishments are not as harsh as they used to be, but the minimum penalty for possessing Shia materials would have to be imprisonment.

Wahhabi fundamentalists have perverted the tenets of Islam for the sake of their own ideology many times. In 2002, during a fire at an all-girls school in Mecca, the Committee for the Promotion of Virtue and the Prevention of Vice prevented students from escaping the building because they weren't dressed appropriately to be outdoors and did not have male relatives present to attend to them. Fifteen girls died, and many more were injured.[3] The Prophet Muhammad, who spoke up for women's rights at a time when they were regarded as property, would be appalled at the warped standards Saudi Arabia maintains in his name.

The modern Saudi royal family has leveraged its oil reserves, the largest in the world, to seed Wahhabi ideology in Muslim communities worldwide. About 20 to 25 percent of Saudi oil revenues, which totaled $163 billion in 2005, go to Wahhabi propaganda—meaning that, depending on the price of a barrel of oil, the Saudi state has in excess of $110 million *per day* to spend on religious proliferation programs. Many Muslims live in poverty, and Wahhabi philanthropies fund run-down mosques and religious schools where no one else will. In exchange, grateful, impressionable youth with few prospects champion the Wahhabi ideology as foot soldiers. With contributions from wealthy Saudis and cash-flush Wahhabi mosques, the Saudi state's philanthropy has fueled a worldwide campaign of extremism. The notorious Taliban regime, the terrorist organization Sepahe Sahaba in Pakistan, hard-line European clerics, and most of the Iraqi insurgency have seen funding from one Wahhabi group or another.

No one is immune. In Baghdad, a city where 75 percent of residents are Shia, Wahhabi extremists in 2003 renamed the famous Um-Attoboul Mosque for Ibn Taymiyya, the rabid forerunner of Wahhabi ideology. And some of the most prominent mosques in the United States distribute Wahhabi publications.

Growing up in a family that, from the top down, has the world's most powerful government—the United States'—in its pocket must produce a strong sense of entitlement. The students who rejected praying in the Islamic Center of America in favor of the lawn outside were violating the protocol for proper prayer by doing so without the mosque's permission. I told the State Department employee who organized the trip, "The next time you send students to pray at my center, make sure you send civilized students. These people insulted my employees, they insulted my religion, and they insulted me."

THE DAY THE WORLD CHANGED

I was at home on the morning of September 11, 2001, when a friend called and told me to turn on my TV. All the channels were broadcasting the same thing. I didn't know what to think. At first I thought it must be a new movie. When the second plane hit, I shuddered. This was no hoax or accident. Our country was under attack. I turned to my wife and said, "I really hope it wasn't Muslims who did this." After Timothy McVeigh bombed Oklahoma City's Alfred P. Murrah Federal Building in 1995, some media and politicians swiftly concluded that "Muslim extremists" were behind the attack. Human Rights Watch reported that one pregnant Muslim woman in Oklahoma City miscarried out of fear after someone threw a brick through her window. Hundreds of mosques and Muslim-owned businesses received threatening phone calls. If McVeigh hadn't been arrested, many other Muslims could have been hurt or killed. After the second plane hit the World Trade Center, I called the Islamic Center of America and ordered everyone to evacuate immediately. We couldn't afford to take chances at such a turbulent time. As it turned out, my fears proved correct. The next day, when staff returned and school resumed, someone phoned in an anonymous bomb threat to the Muslim American Youth Academy adjacent to the mosque. My daughter, Maryam, came home terrified.

Muslims have been as appalled by the 9/11 attacks as any other Americans in this country. Thousands of Muslims attended candlelight vigils held at ICOFA and other Islamic centers commemorating the victims. I heard regrets from many Detroit-area Muslims that the terrorists were associated with Islam. Their shock and anger even led some of them to deny that the terrorists could be Muslim at all.

They were right.

The men who carried out these acts were not Muslims. Their rationale for war has no basis in the Qur'an or the message of the Prophet Muhammad. The Qur'an says, "Whoever slays a soul, unless it be for manslaughter [murder] or for mischief in the land [genocide], it is as though he slew all men; and whoever keeps it alive, it is as though he kept alive all men."[4] Imam Ali said, "By Allah, if I am given the seven skies and all that they contain at the expense of oppressing an ant by stripping it away from a grain of barley, I would not!"[5] The Prophet Muhammad also articulated an elaborate framework for just war. He ruled that warfare is permissible under only two circumstances: for self-defense, and to correct injustice or oppression. His mandates for conduct in war included not starting wars; excluding women, children, and the elderly; treating prisoners humanely; and respecting monks, priests, and houses of worship.

The hijackers of 9/11 and the insurgents in Iraq have ignored these rules and cannot claim to be followers of the Prophet. The best evidence for their abandonment of Islam lay at the World Trade Center and the Pentagon on September 11. Of the 2,937 men and women killed that day, 358 were Muslims.[6]

The same applies to terrorist acts abroad. In 2005, Abu Musab al-Zarqawi's bombing of the Grand Hyatt hotel in Amman, Jordan, killed the Syrian American Moustapha Akkad, director of the first American feature film about Islam, *The Message*. The movie starred Anthony Quinn and reportedly was responsible for eighteen hundred Americans' converting to Islam. After the Hyatt bombing, al-Zarqawi's family took out ads in three Jordanian newspapers denouncing his actions and severing ties with him for all time. (In June 2006, he was killed in a targeted U.S. Air Force attack north of Baqubah, Iraq.)

AN ASSIGNMENT FROM OSAMA

Regardless of their true affiliation, the terrorists tagged every American Muslim with two mammoth responsibilities in the wake of their suicide attacks: to speak out immediately and strenuously against the violence; and, at the same time, to distinguish between the vast majority of moderate, peaceful Muslims and the madding fringe that claimed to speak for us all. I had spent years talking about Islam in churches and synagogues before 9/11, but back then I had the luxury of time, adding my words to the mountain of positive discussions about Islam. The faith was then earning broader acceptance despite the occasional attacks by extremists that popped into the headlines. Osama bin Laden created a new full-time job for me. "The terrorists have hijacked your faith, and it is up to you now to reclaim it," one rabbi exhorted Muslims just after 9/11.

On September 19, rain depressed the turnout for a candlelight vigil at the Henry Ford Museum in Dearborn, but it still drew twenty-five hundred people, among them Dearborn's then mayor, Michael Guido; U.S. Congressmen John Conyers (D-Michigan) and John Dingell (D-Michigan), both friends of mine; and Jacques Nasser, the CEO of Ford at the time. "I want you to hear this loud and clear from a Muslim imam," I announced when it was my turn to speak. "Islam does not condone terrorism, and those who committed the attacks against our nation on 9/11 are indeed terrorists. Islam disowns them, and the Muslim community abhors their actions." The crowd applauded robustly, clearly heartened to see a Muslim leader publicly condemn the attacks and stand with them in fighting the terrorists. The next day, many from the mosque said that their coworkers had listened to my speech, and they reported that tensions had eased once the Muslim stance was clear.

I compare bin Laden and his supporters to the Kharijites, an early group of Islamic extremists. Neither Sunni nor Shia, the Kharijites followed an absolutist interpretation of the Qur'an and continually attacked those who did not agree, especially other Muslims, whom they labeled unbelievers. The Kharijites are best known for abandoning Imam Ali's army in a battle against Mu'awiyah, the rogue governor of Syria who would later rule as caliph from Damascus. Despite nearing a victory in the battle, Imam Ali agreed to an Islamically mandated arbitration with Mu'awiyah's army; the Kharijites protested that Imam Ali had no right, that only God now could intervene on Mu'awiyah's behalf. Three years later, a Kharijite responded by assassinating Imam Ali in a mosque in Kufa, Iraq.

After 9/11, I began attending four or five events a day, meeting with any group interested in knowing more about Islam. I lectured, gave interviews, held teach-ins, and visited open houses all over Michigan. From my previous talks, I knew that main-stream Americans felt far removed from anything they knew as Islam. They knew Islam as the faith of extremist militants, or of separatist black Americans from the Nation of Islam, or, at best, as an obscure faith practiced mostly on the other side of the world and out of touch with modern realities. President Bush and Michigan's then governor, John Engler, helped quell impulsive reprisals against Muslims with timely public statements. "The terrorists are traitors to their own faith. . . . The enemy of Amer-ica is not our many Muslim friends; it is not our many Arab friends," President Bush said.[7] He also visited the Islamic Center of Washington, D.C., around that time.

In a February 2002 CBS News poll, the country appeared evenly divided in its opinion of Islam: 30 percent had a favorable impression, 33 percent had an unfavorable impression, and 37 per-cent were unsure.[8] In almost every case, the intelligent, well-meaning people I engaged with had learned about Islam through the lens of the media, politics, or another religion, and the opin-ions they formed depended heavily on how the messenger felt about Islam. The questions they asked me were much the same as the ones I heard before 9/11—questions about democracy and Islam, women and Islam, jihad and Islam. But now the stakes were higher, and misunderstanding could prove dangerous to all of us, a point driven home to me as the Bush administration was drawing up war plans in the fall of 2001, on the eve of Ramadan. Newspapers and TV broadcasts were abuzz with debate about whether to bomb in Afghanistan during Ramadan, which would begin on November 16. Ron Dzwonkowski of the *Detroit Free Press* told me about an e-mail he received from one reader who confused the Islamic holy month with a motel chain: "What's this hellish controversy about bombing a Ramada Inn?" he wanted to know.

That was one of the biggest paradoxes of America for me, the disparity between its cultural diversity and its insularity. A 2006 geographic literacy study found that 60 percent of eighteen- to twenty-four-year-olds could not locate Iraq on a map of the Middle East. Seventy-five percent could not find Israel.[9] Americans truly do not realize how different their pace of life is from that in less developed countries. In the Middle East, we measure life in years. In the United States it's measured in workweeks. We run ourselves into the ground with our jobs and take the few spare minutes we have each day to watch sports, TV shows, and twenty-four-hour news updates on JonBenét Ramsey, Michael Jackson, Scott Peterson, and Anna Nicole Smith. Paying attention to our political leaders, our communities, and what's going on in the world becomes an afterthought reserved for election days. Ramadan becomes Ramada Inn.

Requests for trustworthy information—from invitations to speak to calls from the media and interfaith councils—quickly outstripped my individual capacity. I began formulating an outreach program with a team of seasoned, knowledgeable speakers who could respond to invitations from the Red Cross, Rotary Clubs, the Kiwanis, the Eagles, universities, military colleges, and legions of churches. I received tremendous help from a member of the congregation whom I had known previously but grew to value even more when I was stretched the thinnest. Eide Alawan, a second-generation Muslim American, volunteered to drive me to engagements all over the state, usually rearranging his own work schedule to accommodate mine and performing triple duty as my scheduler, navigator, and companion.

As time passed, reactions from the larger community encouraged me that what we were doing was making a difference. One woman sent a flower arrangement anonymously and offered her and her family's prayers in a time of persecution. "We love you Muslims," she wrote. A few months later, a man e-mailed me at the center begging for forgiveness. He confessed to sending letters to his congressman right after 9/11 calling for the government to "nuke" Muslim cities around the world and launch a campaign to wipe out all Muslims. To underscore the sincerity of his forgiveness, he made a $100 donation to our Islamic center. Such changes of heart are at the core of our mission, and Islam venerates them. "God expects two traits/qualities from the people," a hadith from Imam Mohammad al-Baqir, the fifth Imam, says. "To acknowledge His favors so He would increase them, and to admit their mistakes so He forgives them."[10]

Anecdotal evidence suggests the number of Americans converting to Islam after 9/11 quadrupled, with perhaps 25,000 people a year converting before that.[11] The post-9/11 trend toward home and family in the United States is well known, and I believe that the many conversions to Islam were part of it. People were seeking spiritual guidance, clear directions of right and wrong, and the comfort that comes from accepting the power and knowledge of God. Some, no doubt, started on a quest to better understand the motivations of the terrorists and ended up discovering a faith that defies the facile characterizations of our mainstream culture and aligns closely with values they already embraced.

In October 2001, *The New York Times* reported on a woman named Shannon Staloch, who was looking for answers after hearing news of the attacks. A middle-school teacher, Staloch instinctively opened a book she had on Islam and repeated the *shahada,* the declaration of faith: "I bear witness that there is no god but God and that Muhammad is the messenger of God." Twelve days later she converted.[12] Her story and the stories of thousands of others who converted after 9/11 are part of Islam's rich legacy. They came to Islam in a spirit of intellectual curiosity and openness diametrically opposed to the dogma and hatred displayed by the 9/11 hijackers. That knowledge brings me peace when I consider that such unspeakable acts might have indirectly moved someone to convert. No one, no matter how powerful or violent, can force conversion to Islam. A Muslim can facilitate a conversion, but the final decision rests with God and His subject. As the Qur'an says, "Thou art truly a warner, and to every people a guide."[13]

At ICOFA, one or two converts a month became several a week. The process is not complicated. I provide potential converts with a primer on Islam, its origins, principles, prayer, and responsibilities, and then send them home with a copy of the Qur'an, some cassette tapes, and a few other books to study and contemplate. Once they feel ready to profess their faith, I ask that they come to the Friday-night lecture to perform the *shahada* before the assembled congregation. One woman, a wary Christian whose son had decided to become a Muslim, attended our Friday-night lecture to see what Islam is all about. After my sermon on the Prophet Muhammad's charisma and morality, she told me she didn't see any difference between the values I espoused and what her own reverend preached. "Of course!" I told her. "Islam is simply an updated version of Christianity."

INTERFAITH ODYSSEY

In December 2001 I received a call from the archbishop of Detroit, Adam Cardinal Maida. Cardinal Maida is highly respected and has been a priest for more than fifty years. I had first met him two years earlier, when the church promoted him from the Archdiocese of Green Bay. Knowing that the Detroit area had a large Muslim population, he set about researching Islam, a religion he confessed he knew little of. I gave him a copy of *Psalms of Islam,* a powerful collection of supplications written by Imam Ali ibn Husayn, the fourth Imam, and as the cardinal read through, he said he found much that could apply to his own sermons. We agreed to meet twice a year under the umbrella of the local Religious Leaders Forum to brief each other on our work and our communities. Now Cardinal Maida had called to ask whether he might attend the Islamic Center of America during Ramadan, and I agreed. The proximity of that year's Ramadan holiday to Christmas, the need for an elevated post-9/11 dialogue, and an escalation of the war between Palestinians and Israelis made the occasion especially opportune. We decided to hold a joint press conference and a private meeting on the final Friday of Ramadan and then have Cardinal Maida address the congregation inside the mosque—within the actual prayer room: the first time ever a non-Muslim would do so at ICOFA. Well before 9/11, we had hosted non-Muslim speakers, but they always addressed the congregation in the banquet hall, where I give my own lectures. By welcoming Cardinal Maida into the mosque, we followed in the tradition of the Prophet Muhammad, who used to receive dignitaries and foreign ambassadors in his mosque, his religious, political, and social headquarters. Our publicity efforts brought numerous local and national TV stations. In front of the three hundred Muslims gathered there, Cardinal Maida apologized on behalf of 1.4 million Detroit Catholics for the hostility Muslims suffered in the wake of the 9/11 attacks and pledged to raise money for the poor in Afghanistan, who were then caught between the Taliban and the U.S. campaign to overthrow them. "It's time for us to go forward, hand in hand, to build a community of peace," he said.[14] Afterward, students from the Muslim American Youth Academy presented him with a plaque inscribed with verses from the Qur'an.

Growing up in the Middle East, I did not interact with people of other faiths. One of the greatest advantages of coming to America for me was the opportunity to begin a dialogue with them, and it opened my eyes to the substantial tolerance Islam has for other religions. The Qur'an says

And dispute ye not
With the People of the Book,
Except with means better
[Than mere disputation], unless
It be with those of them
Who inflict wrong [and injury];
But say, "We believe
In the revelation which has
Come down to us and in that

Which came down to you;
Our God and your God
Is one; and it is to Him
We bow [in submission].

Where we share common ground, it makes sense to unite on
those issues, and where we differ, we can explore the reasons behind it. Around the same time as Cardinal Maida's visit, I joined
a new local television program called *Interfaith Odyssey,* featuring
faith leaders from an array of world religions: Jewish, Catholic,
Muslim, Baha'i, Hindu, Sikh, Buddhist, and Native American. As
important for me as the weekly discussions of religious issues
was the chance to meet representatives from so many backgrounds and come to know them as people. We bond over jokes
and share ideas. I'm convinced that dialogue is the essential starting point to reconciling our differences, and we still don't do it
enough.

One of Cardinal Maida's major accomplishments was overseeing the funding and construction of the $65 million Pope John
Paul II Cultural Center in Washington, D.C. Four years in the
making, the center opened in March 2001, at a ribbon cutting that
President Bush attended. I was surprised to learn, however, that
the center includes a department for Christian-Jewish dialogue
but not one for Christian-Muslim dialogue. When I asked Cardinal Maida about the possibility, he agreed there should be one, but
said that these ideas take time to digest. Unfortunately, America
is not yet accustomed to having Muslims on the religious landscape. Dialogue between Jews and Christians is understood. Dialogue among Jews, Christians, and Muslims seems unusual. But
the rewards are worth it. At our core we find that we are one people, with more similarities than differences. When the archbishop
of Syria, Laham III, attended a reception at ICOFA while visiting
Detroit, I quoted Imam Ali to him: "People are of two types: either
a brother in faith, or equal in humanity." Upon hearing this, Archbishop Laham descended from the podium and hugged me.

MY TROUBLE WITH THE PATRIOT ACT

In the course of three days in late October 2001, the USA Patriot Act sailed through both houses of Congress and went straight to the president's desk for a well-publicized signing ceremony at the White House. "These terrorists must be pursued, they must be defeated, and they must be brought to justice," President Bush said before the cameras. In the House, the act passed 357 to 66, a landslide by any measure. In the Senate, only Russ Feingold, a Democrat from Wisconsin, voted against it. Votes that lopsided are usually reserved for legislation on naming memorials or declaring holidays. But the Patriot Act had the potential to vastly overhaul the way law enforcement works in America, and not just in the beneficial ways President Bush continually touted at press conferences.

The act's Orwellian name is actually an acronym—in full, the Uniting and Strengthening America by Providing Appropriate Tools Required to Intercept and Obstruct Terrorism Act of 2001. As opaque as that language is, in the law proper it's even worse. The act is a legislative overlay: rather than create new rules, it changed the way many existing laws, such as those governing search and seizure, wiretapping, and monitoring of bank transactions, are interpreted and enforced. Unless you know the particulars of all the laws the Patriot Act affects, it's almost impossible to extract any meaning from the text of the legislation. I can't speculate on how familiar most members of Congress were with it, but given the speed with which it passed and the pressure on them to do something about terrorism, I would be amazed if most of them appreciated the scope of what they approved.

In a nutshell, what the act has done is roll back a raft of privacy protections to make it easier for police and federal agents to monitor all manner of personal activities and grant law enforcement more latitude in its handling of suspects—in detention, trial procedure, interrogations, and much else. Some sections of

the Patriot Act draw on laws designed for racketeering and organized crime suspects, and also for foreign intelligence targets, and
apply them to suspected terrorists. Analyzed in a vacuum, the
law is not bad, but in streamlining the checks and balances nor-
mally called for in an investigation, it leaves too much room for
individual discretion, as I would learn firsthand in the coming
months and years.

The drafters of the legislation did take pains not to single out
Muslims: section 102 says, "Arab Americans, Muslim Americans,
and Americans from South Asia play a vital role in our Nation and
are entitled to nothing less than the full rights of every American."
But that didn't allay the fears of Muslims who believed they
would be targets of random raids and searches. Indeed, more than
eleven thousand Muslims were stopped and interrogated on the
basis only of their appearance, and none was found guilty of terrorism.

For months after the 9/11 attacks, I dreaded flying because of
the heightened suspicion directed toward just about anyone who
appeared foreign and had darker skin and features. Security per-
sonnel always selected me to step aside for the random searches.
A friend from Florida who had traveled to Dearborn two weeks
after 9/11 decided to rent a car for the return trip. I told him it
would take two long days to drive home, but he was adamant.
His name is Ahmed Moussaoui, and two days earlier the FBI had
detained him before his flight out of Miami and questioned him
about his relationship to Zacharias Moussaoui. Ahmed denied
any connection, unsuccessfully. How does one easily disprove
a connection that doesn't exist? Agents interrogated him for
twelve hours. (By comparison, twelve days earlier, officials at the
highest levels of the U.S. government had approved direct flights
to Saudi Arabia for members of Osama bin Laden's family, whose
identities were well known, without any questioning whatso-
ever, before even former president Clinton and former vice president Gore were permitted to fly.)[15] Ahmed has never had any
connection with Zacarias Moussaoui; had the FBI, evidently

lacking any additional grounds for detaining him, possessed even a basic understanding of Arabic culture, they could have directed their resources toward legitimate threats and spared Ahmed considerable anguish and embarrassment. The Moussaoui surname is the Arab equivalent of Johnson here, and, as Ahmed pointed out to the FBI, he is a Shia Iraqi and Zacharias Moussaoui is a Sunni Moroccan.

Another friend, this one in southern California, saw his son caught up in a similar web, this one woven at the grassroots level. A few days after 9/11, concerned neighbors phoned the DMV after noticing that my friend's son had the vanity license plate "Jihad." The DMV suspended the plate. Upset, the son challenged the suspension in court, arguing that the plate had been taken out of context. The court did rule in his favor, thankfully. After all, his name was Jihad. Like Moussaoui, it is a very common Arab name.

We all remember the anger and panic we felt in those days. Our picture-perfect world, where the biggest domestic concerns were economic recession and corporate scandals, seemed lost forever. A visceral response to that loss was understandable. What grew out of that gut-level impulse, however, was a three-headed serpent that ensnared Muslims wherever they went. The first head was cultural ignorance, as illustrated in the above stories. So many headaches for officers and Muslims could have been avoided if law enforcement had elementary cultural training. For someone with the power and responsibility of an FBI agent, it is unprofessional not to obtain that training.

On a return trip from Windsor, Ontario, in 2003, the customs official looked annoyed that I had a lot of stamps from Middle Eastern countries. Why so much travel? she wanted to know. I ended up waiting in the immigration office for forty minutes before four different agents wearing gloves called me into a room where they were looking at a chalky substance under a high-powered light. The agents appeared concerned that the substance could be raw material for explosives. I took a closer look and realized they had recovered a clay Karbala prayer tablet from my luggage.

Routine inconveniences like this, which take place daily across the country, become dangerous and form a second serpent head when irresponsible media magnify misinformation, either in their quest for the scoop or out of willful prejudice. These distortions are not unique to Muslims, nor are they new. After the bombing of the U.S. embassy in Beirut in 1983, one network put an "expert on Shia terrorism" on the air. These people, he said, have a tendency to kill. He defined Shia as a fringe group and said that if they could not kill their opponents, they try to kill themselves. The camera then cut to images of self-flagellating Shia during Ashura celebrations. A friend of mine who saw the broadcast, a neurologist and a Shia, fumed at the portrayal. The next day, his receptionist missed work for the first time in six years, and he suspected the reason. "I knew you were Shia," she said when he called her, "but you didn't tell me you were inclined to kill people. I'm afraid you might try to kill me one day."

Having given scores of interviews over the past ten years, I have noticed a marked difference between media outlets and even between journalists within the same company. You almost have to consider them on a case-by-case basis and then be careful to make clear points and read between the lines of reporters' questions to infer what the real story is. The more you talk, the greater the chance your comments can be taken out of context. A month after the attacks, I met with a writer from *Rolling Stone,* Jeff Goodell, who was covering the dynamics of the Dearborn community in this new environment. For a week he shadowed me at sermons, lectures about Islam, and media appearances. When the story came out that December, there were many inaccuracies and negative shadings. The worst was his insinuation that, despite my unqualified statements against terrorism, I hoped the acts would teach our country a lesson: "Qazwini would never put it this way in a million years," he wrote, "but if you listen to him long enough, you might get the sense that, in some awful way, America is now getting what it deserves."

I felt Goodell had taken advantage of my openness and hospitality and twisted what I said for his own ends. His approach was of a piece with the behavior of those overzealous law enforcement officers who ensnare many innocents in order to catch one criminal: set your agenda, presume guilt from the outset, ignore evidence and statements to the contrary, and chalk up any disagreement to anti-American fervor.

In summer 2006, two young Dearborn men made national headlines for buying hundreds of discount cell phones in Marietta, Ohio, for resale in Michigan with the goal of defraying their tuition expenses that fall. The specter of two young Arab-looking men buying cell phones, which can be used as bomb detonators, in bulk raised suspicions at Wal-Mart, and the store notified local authorities. The pair also had the misfortune to be driving a car that belonged to the mother of one of them. The mother worked at an airport, and the car contained a Royal Jordanian Airlines manual with passenger lists. Injustice was swift. One of the accused recalled seeing the ticker headline on jailhouse TV soon after their arrest: "Is This an Act of Terrorism at Work?" The father of one of the two men came to me crying while his son was in jail and asked me to pray for him. "Your son is innocent," I told him, "and I am sure he will be freed soon." The charges were soon dismissed for lack of evidence, and I saw the father with his accused son at Friday prayer the next week, but in the interim the two young friends had their names and pictures on TV and in papers linked to terrorism. "The media made us into animals," one of them said. "This is going to stick to us the rest of our lives."[16]

Cultural ignorance and the media's ambition are not the only factors in unfair targeting of Muslim Americans. Ambition in law enforcement contributes, too. Federal agents are expected to make arrests and foil plots. With high-profile arrests come promotions, raises, and prestige. If those are not causes, perhaps the

Type A personality required in police work is. Either way, I continually attract attention from Patriot Act–era operations that have no reason to suspect me beyond my ethnicity. On October 28, 2001, I was waiting near the gate before boarding a flight to New York when an FBI agent sat down next to me and flashed his badge. He sat close, as if attempting to rattle me by dominating our interpersonal space, and the questioning commenced. What's your name? When were you born? Why are you flying to New York?

I must have looked uncomfortable. Why are you nervous? he asked.

I said that after nine years in the United States, I had never been confronted this way by law enforcement before. I was wearing a suit in preparation for my trip and had packed my robes and turban away in hopes of looking less suspicious—clearly an ineffective technique. Then an answer hit me: *The Detroit News* had profiled me the day before. I fished the paper out of my carry-on. With its pictures of me and descriptions of my stand on terrorism, I was sure it would clear up any confusion about my identity or intentions. "We cannot be an isolated community," I had said in the *News* story. "We are part of this great society. We have to work at being proactive American citizens."

The agent set the paper aside without a glance. How much do you weigh? he asked. At one point he felt sure he had me pegged: "You were born in Lebanon, right?" he asked. "No, I was born in Iraq," I said. No one answer led him to back off, but after several more minutes and a few more attempts to gauge my weight, he satisfied himself that I didn't represent a threat. Other than the high-alert atmosphere of the time, I have no idea what caused him to suspect me.

Five years later, the fervor had yet to die down. On the way back from a 2006 youth retreat in Port Huron, Michigan, I made a wrong turn and ended up in Canada by accident. I knew even as I crossed the bridge into Canada that this spelled trouble, and I tried persuading an attendant to allow me through a gate to the

U.S.-bound lanes before I joined the flow of traffic at the border crossing station on the Canadian side. My answer to the agent's standard question "What were you doing in Canada?" ("But I wasn't in Canada") sounded unconvincing, of course, and my son Mohamed, who was riding with me, did not have his passport. Two customs agents split up Mohamed and me to search out inconsistencies in our stories. We had arrived at the station immediately before a shift change, so the first staffers soon disappeared, and we waited thirty minutes while the next shift got settled in. I took advantage of the wait to tap out an SOS text message to my friend Eide Alawan urging him to call anyone he knew. The new officer who called us in identified himself as Agent Brown and reprimanded me for using my cell phone. They had a "no phone calls" rule but no signage to that effect. Agent Brown seemed sure I was a big fish, perhaps a ringleader for a terrorist cell bringing underlings or materials into the United States. Others searched my car several times but could find nothing. With each passing hour, I grew angrier. We had arrived at 1:30. It was now 6:30, with no hint of a conclusion. Just then Brown motioned us into an office with his finger and said I had a phone call. An agent from the Department of Homeland Security who was on the line told me Eide had called and explained the situation. On his word, Customs would have to let us go. Brown handed me my keys with a terse dismissal.

In his quest to make tangible the United States' enemies in the war on terror, President Bush began deploying the terms "Islamofascists" and "Islamic fascists" in August 2006, first to describe the perpetrators of a plot to blow up U.S.-bound planes from the UK. Though Bush has stressed for years that he does not blame Islam for today's terrorism and counts Muslims as valuable American citizens, that stance hasn't kept him from using language that pulls an entire religion into this uneven, ill-defined conflict. In reality, only the smallest fraction of American Muslims, or any Muslims for that matter, are responsible for the bombings, kidnappings, and videotaped boasting that make the evening news. The rest react with the same chills and butterflies that any American has. Sometimes I wish we Muslims had signs that explained those sentiments in a phrase or two. We could hold them up behind the wheel for the glaring driver in the next lane, near airline check-ins while the recorded "Report suspicious activity" message plays, or at the store while buying cell phones. "Don't worry," the signs would say. "We're on the same side."

One day America will wake up and feel ashamed that Congress ever passed the Patriot Act, just as we now feel ashamed of the internment camps in which Japanese Americans were confined during World War II. I call it the Unpatriotic Act for Patriotic Americans. The details and enforcement have become a stain on America's legacy. Those who love America do not sacrifice it for the sake of their political agenda or a misguided sense of security. The arguments advanced to pass the act were the same used by Kim Jong Il and Saddam Hussein in enforcing their tyrannical restrictions, namely that they were ensuring their citizens' safety by apprehending dangerous rebels. I have no tolerance for terrorism, but we should be humane no matter what.

CHAPTER 8

Carrying the Mission to the Halls of Power

We are not afraid to follow truth wherever it may lead,
nor to tolerate any error so long as reason is left free to
combat it.[1]
—*Thomas Jefferson*

THE MUSLIM STUDENT Association at the University of
Michigan–Dearborn invited me to address its students before the
2000 presidential election to encourage voter participation and po-
litical activism. Afterward, as I left the auditorium, I noticed some
Muslim students outside passing out fliers and took one. "Don't
lend support to the Zionist regime," it read, "support" meaning
American political participation and "regime" referring to Israel.
These students were advocating a boycott of the election.

There is a small segment of Muslim Americans that resists
any attempt at integration and regards with disgust anything
American. They have no constructive agenda or hope for the future. Their sole interest lies in railing against U.S. policy and pushing the Muslim community to the sidelines. They are ashamed of
the American flag. They criticize imams who encourage participation in American society. Can't you see that this country is run by
Zionists? they say, in language peppered with insults. Why would
you voluntarily participate in such a system? Yet they don't offer
any solutions. I heard from some of these people when we hosted

President Clinton's former secretary of state Madeleine Albright at the center for a community forum in spring 2006. Albright is notorious in the Muslim community for an interview she gave Lesley Stahl on *60 Minutes* in 1996, speaking then as ambassador to the United Nations. In it she defended the UN sanctions against Iraq, which exacted a terrible toll on hundreds of thousands of its citizens in the 1990s, particularly young children; Albright argued that this was a steep price to pay, but worth it.[2] In an op-ed piece published in the *Arab American News,* I tried to explain to Muslims angered by Albright's visit that an invitation to ICOFA did not translate into an endorsement. Sometimes it means we are trying to break through a wall and replace it with a bridge.[3]

Forty-six percent of the American people now have negative views of Islam, I pointed out. What would you have us do? Sit in the mosque, close the door, bark at everyone, and not do anything about our situation? Like it or not, you already are participating in this society, regardless of whether you cast a ballot or talk to your non-Muslim neighbors. Your job is part of the country's economy, governed by the Federal Reserve and U.S. trade policies and treaties. You also pay taxes, thousands of dollars every year. Don't you want to have a say in how those are spent? Lighting one small candle is better than cursing the darkness a thousand times.

CLAIMING A SEAT AT THE TABLE

Though I reject these isolationist Muslims' approach, I do empathize with their frustration over U.S. foreign policy. In America, news stations routinely ignore violence against Palestinians in favor of attacks against Israel, though Palestinians' deaths outnumber Israelis' ten to one, and most are children and teenagers. The feeling among many Muslims, and especially Palestinians, is that Israel usurped what for hundreds of years had been part of Syria and the larger Ottoman Empire. In 1967 it took additional territory, Syria's Golan Heights and the West Bank and Gaza

Strip, in the Six-Day War with Egypt, Jordan, Syria, and Iraq. Except for Gaza, from which Israel withdrew in 2005, that land remains under Israeli control. The Israeli occupation of these territories over decades has turned millions of Palestinians into refugees with little recourse against Israel's military might, which is reinforced by copious U.S. aid. The Apache helicopters and F-16s that kill Palestinians in the West Bank and Gaza come courtesy of America's defense budget. President Bush's 2008 budget calls for $2.4 billion in military aid to Israel, with a mandate that 75 percent of that be spent in the United States. We are fooling no one but ourselves when we ship cluster bombs, ordnance internationally prohibited in heavily populated areas, to Israel and ask its leaders to "be careful." The segment of Palestinians that has responded by attacking civilians is labeled terrorist, but the same media say nothing when Israelis carry out grisly state-supported attacks.

In November 2002, the then treasury secretary, Paul O'Neill, and the homeland security director, Tom Ridge, traveled to Dearborn and requested a meeting with local Arab American leaders to discuss the erosion of Muslims' civil liberties after 9/11. I was honored to give the invocation. As they spoke of the measures they were taking to defeat terrorism, I asked Secretary O'Neill how he defined the term. A terrorist is anyone who intentionally takes the lives of innocent civilians, O'Neill said.

That's a good definition, I told him, but it also makes Israeli prime minister Ariel Sharon a terrorist.

Sharon was Israel's defense minister in September 1982, during the Lebanon War, when Christian Phalangists, members of a Lebanese political faction aligned with Israel at the time, slaughtered somewhere between 700 and 3,500 Palestinians and Lebanese in the refugee camps Sabra and Shatila in southwest Beirut. Lebanon's Israel-friendly president-elect, Bachir Gemayel, had been assassinated just days before, and Israeli leaders feared that the PLO would take advantage of the consequent instability to regroup in Muslim West Beirut, though the PLO was not responsible for the killing. The Israeli military, after disarming opposing factions in West Beirut, ushered Phalangist militias into Sabra and Shatila to eliminate PLO combatants and infrastructure, but in practice the operation was an indiscriminate bloodbath of unarmed civilians. With knowledge of what was taking place in the camps, and on Sharon's orders, Israeli soldiers blockaded the camp exits for a day and a half, preventing the refugees' escape. Outraged Palestinians and Lebanese Muslims began calling Sharon the Butcher of Beirut, and the Kahan Commission, established by the Israeli government and chaired by the country's president of the Supreme Court at the time, found Sharon personally responsible.

The massacre has not been the only one committed in the Middle East, but it did happen, and it was preventable. Most remarkably, less than twenty years after being dismissed as defense minister for his role at Sabra and Shatila, Sharon won election as prime minister of Israel.

In 2002, during the second Palestinian uprising, Sharon authorized Israeli troops to enter and demolish another Palestinian camp, Jenin, in the northern part of the West Bank, citing its harboring of Palestinian militants there. Dozens of innocent civilians, and possibly many more, were killed in the Battle of Jenin, and most of the city destroyed. President Bush didn't bolster opinions of U.S. government in the Arab world when, that very same week, he praised Sharon as "a man of peace" for responding to U.S. calls to withdraw from Palestinian cities.

Confronted with Sharon's crimes, O'Neill spoke frankly. Look, he said, all the presidents before President Bush couldn't do anything about the Israeli-Palestinian conflict, and Bush won't be able to either. If Sharon does this—here O'Neill put his thumb to his nose and waved his hand like a rooster's comb—there's nothing Bush can do.

There's little Palestinians can do, at least. Those who dare to speak out see their homes razed and their children jailed. But the claim that President Bush has no leverage rings false. If not Bush, who? If he cannot wean Israel from its privileged status, he could start by dealing with other states more equitably. Israel has refused to sign the nuclear nonproliferation treaty. India and Pakistan are given free passes to ramp up nuclear arsenals. But the United States won't even consider talks with Iran until it closes down its civilian nuclear program. Only European parties will conduct talks. At a forum of Muslim leaders with the National Security Council in February 2006, I questioned NSC member Michael Doran about eschewing confrontation in favor of diplomacy. The suggestion had barely left my mouth before he ruled it out, saying that talks with Iran only buy its leaders time and that the nuclear program warrants a more aggressive response. Iran and the United States have some competing interests, but there is no reason they cannot improve relations.

In April 2002, I held a council of Muslims and Christians at the Islamic Center of America during the Jenin attacks in an attempt to induce Muslim and Christian leaders to take a public position on the issue. I asked that they ignore the fact that most Israelis are Jewish and most Palestinians are Muslim. If Jesus were alive today, I said, whom would he stand with? The occupiers or the occupied? One reverend came forward and agreed that Jesus would stand with the Palestinians.

Why, then, would you not speak out about it? I asked.

Another minister said they feared losing their jobs and being publicly criticized as anti-Semitic, one of the worst accusations a critic can level. When you fear you will lose your business, he said, the risk becomes too great.

I qualify all this with a statement that too few Muslims will make: I have the utmost respect for the Jewish faith. Our dispute is not with Judaism, without which, after all, Islam would not exist, but with Israeli aggression and America's sanctioning of it. I confess, even, to envy of Jews as a whole for their ability to organize and rally behind a cause. Muslims ought to stop asking why Jews are so powerful in America. They became powerful because they earned it. The first Jews arrived in the United States in 1752; they have been working for 250 years with singular focus to secure their seat at the table. There are 4 million to 6 million Jews in this country, about 2 percent of the population, but they held thirty-seven seats in Congress, or 7 percent, as of January 2003. Two of the nine Supreme Court justices are Jewish.

I began to fully appreciate what they had accomplished after speaking to a *Detroit News* reporter about media bias in 1997, shortly after I took over as imam at ICOFA. In the past the reporter had covered Jewish community affairs and said he learned something from the Jewish community: If there is the slightest criticism of Jews in the newspaper, you'll get a box full of letters the next day condemning it. The phone lines will be busy for days. If there's positive coverage, our mail brims with complimentary letters. With Muslims, we've learned the exact opposite. When we write about you critically, nobody calls to complain, and when we write positively, nobody calls. If you don't care, why should we?

The last lines tormented me most. They went hand in hand with the reaction I got from a meeting of young Muslims not long ago at which I asked them to consider their futures. How many of you want to be doctors, I asked. Dozens of hands shot up. Engineers? Several fewer hands. When I asked how many wanted to be journalists, only a couple raised their hands. Finally, I asked how many wanted to be politicians, and it was as if I had told a bad joke. I saw expressions of dismay.

I don't expect these young Muslims to begin planning their bids for Congress yet, but I do want them to change the way they think about citizenship and to consider the differences they can make in their communities. Their futures and a better world depend on it. The Jewish community has proved that a people can overcome adversity against great odds to reach the highest rung on the sociopolitical ladder. We have an Arab expression for my dream: "There's nothing like your own nail to scratch your back"—we must, in other words, take responsibility for reaching our own goals, as we know best what they are.

America's Muslim community has adapted and begun using more advanced methods to promote its causes. The Council on

American-Islamic Relations, for example, has done yeoman's work in responding to anti-Muslim attacks and also urging all Muslims to organize and respond to public attacks the way Jews do; other groups are catching on. At an Iftar dinner the State Department hosted during Ramadan in 2002, I sat across from Secretary of State Colin Powell and asked why the United States does not make better use of American Muslims as foreign ambassadors. In our diplomatic tradition, ambassadors frequently share the predominant religion of their host country, but we had no Muslims working on our behalf in Muslim countries. Secretary Powell agreed but remarked that the Foreign Service, the government office charged with testing and training potential diplomats, does not get enough Muslim candidates. If Muslims were to encourage their youth to consider international relations as a career path, he said, they could remedy the shortfall of Muslim ambassadors in fifteen to twenty years.

His answer struck me as a stock reply. I agree that we need to push young Muslim Americans to consider diplomatic careers, but the United States desperately needs ambassadors *right now* who know the cultural terrain of the Middle East and have the credibility and trust to build allegiances with local authorities and power brokers. If there are not enough qualified Arab Muslim Americans to call on, then the Foreign Service ought to be training them. We have a broad divide to bridge in our international relations, and the more common ground we have with the parties across the table, the better our chances of closing it.

ON THE POWER TO PREVENT EXTREMISM

After the London subway bombings in 2005, *The New York Times*'s Thomas Friedman wrote a column in the form of a letter to the world's Muslim community. In it he said that it was incumbent upon Muslims to deal with the terrorist problem. If it did not, he wrote, western governments would have to take care of it themselves, and we might not like the results.[4] I admire Friedman and often agree with him, but in this case his advice was impractical. We Muslims can denounce the actions of these extremists who have hijacked our faith, and we can cooperate legally and politically with the governments and international organizations addressing terrorism, but we cannot police these groups alone, any more than the FBI could prevent U.S. bombings by Timothy McVeigh and Eric Robert Rudolph.

Arguing that we can assumes that we operate as a single unit, a monolithic culture in which all Muslims are directly connected. It also ignores a hard reality: the average Muslim fears extremists as much as anyone else. Wahhabis have sacked my hometown of Karbala several times in its history. In Iraq's Al-Anbar province, Fallujah residents have complained about terrorists who descended on the town, renting homes at ten times the going rate and drawing American troops into the city with strategic attacks. The resulting combat destroyed permanent residents' homes and left them hostages in their own town. A journalist for *Asharq Al-Awsat,* an Arabic newspaper, asked them why they didn't speak out publicly and revolt, and a source responded that the terrorists would kill his family immediately. The same fears depressed voter turnout in the first Iraqi election. Most Sunnis were not boycotting: they stayed away from the polls because foreign terrorists had intimidated people into not voting.

I think most Muslims, both here and abroad, share these feelings of being caught in the middle, if not so dramatically. Osama bin Laden revealed that his intention on September 11 was to force Muslims to choose sides, to embrace the Wahhabi school of Islam or be destroyed along with the decadent West, an ideology President Bush reinforced when he strayed from his more moderate post-9/11 position and declared on September 20, 2001, "Either you are with us, or you are with the terrorists." Though he was speaking of sovereign nations, President Bush could just as easily have been speaking to Muslim Americans.

If Muslims could have prevented the insurgents' bombings of

Samarra's Al-Askariyya, the "Golden Mosque," they would have. That was Iraq's own 9/11. The Golden Mosque is a thousand-year-old Shia holy site eighty miles north of Baghdad, the only such shrine located in a primarily Sunni area, and it contains the tombs of the tenth and eleventh Imams. In February 2006 (I was in Michigan at the time), insurgents dressed as Iraqi special forces soldiers subdued the few guards on duty and set explosives to demolish the iconic golden dome and much of the building, knowing that doing so would infuriate Shia and spark a sectarian war. Until then, Iraq's Shia had been relatively patient with the ineffectual government and lack of progress.

In August 2005, the residents of Najaf *did* intervene in a major bombing attempt, the Iraqi prime minister, Ibrahim al-Jaafari, later told our congregation on a visit to Michigan. A crowd at the shrine of Imam Ali, the holiest site in Shia Islam, spotted a suspicious-looking man—suspicious-looking probably because he didn't appear to be Iraqi—and found he had explosive strips all over his body. A mob dragged him outside and began beating him; only a security force saved his life, and once extricated from the crowd, he broke down in tears. Police asked whether he was crying because the mob had abused him. He said no. They asked whether he was crying because he was grateful to be alive. No, no, he said. I am crying because I am fasting and you just prevented me from dining with the Prophet tonight. To purify themselves, suicide bombers typically fast from sunrise onward the day of their attack, when they believe they will meet the Prophet Muhammad and get their due reward. These are the kinds of people we are dealing with. This is indeed a battle for the Islamic faith, but Muslims are so diverse in their perspectives, and its outcome holds so many implications for the world at large, that no one ought to write it off as a Muslim problem. This is especially so because Muslims alone were not responsible for creating this menace.

We like to think of the United States as traveling the moral high road. Sometimes it's true, but too often we have shown a willingness to get our hands dirty when it suits our interests, especially if government officials think the rest of us will not find out.

In the 1980s, the administration of President Ronald Reagan aligned the United States with numerous unsavory guerrilla groups that happened to be anti-Soviet, the purpose being to contain Communism in the last days of the Cold War. Reagan supported, with money, weapons, and sometimes military assistance, the Contras in Nicaragua, Renamo in Mozambique, and Unita in Angola. He supported the rightist government in El Salvador and the South African government during apartheid. The centerpiece of this "proxy war" policy was funding for rebels in Afghanistan, the mujahideen, to overthrow the pro-Soviet government, a strategy put in place not by President Reagan but by President Carter. President Reagan continued it, however, and increased funding throughout his tenure in hopes of miring the Soviets in endless wars. The charismatic figure around which the Afghan rebels rallied and who benefited richly from our aid was Osama bin Laden. We hailed him and his allies, the Taliban (the same group we have seen on television whipping women for not wearing veils and men for having beards that are too short) as freedom fighters, an expedient stance reminiscent of our mid-1980s relationship with Iraq when Donald Rumsfeld, who was then the U.S. special envoy to the Middle East, and was George W. Bush's secretary of defense until December 2006, visited Saddam and U.S. intelligence sold him weapons.

By the early 1980s, the United States had partnered with Saudi Arabia in a dollar-for-dollar match to fund the mujahideen, aid the Saudis offered readily because it pleased conservative clerics and helped channel the energies of restless Saudi militants. Saudi Arabia also was one of three U.S. allies to recognize the Taliban diplomatically, along with Pakistan and the United Arab Emirates, when it came to power in 1996.

President Carter's national security adviser, Zbigniew Brzezinski, who developed and pitched the Afghanistan plan to Carter, struck a defiant pose in 1998 in the face of militant Islam's proliferation. "What is most important to the history of the world?" Brzezinski said in an interview in the French magazine *Nouvel Observateur.* "The Taliban or the collapse of the Soviet empire? Some stirred-up Muslims or the liberation of Central Europe and the end of the Cold War?"[5] I wonder whether Brzezinski and his fellow policy-makers would think the tradeoff was worth it now.

A PRAYER FOR THE COUNTRY

U.S. Congressman John Dingell is a living treasure, known as the dean of the House of Representatives because he has served longer than any other member. The residents of Dearborn, Monroe, and Ypsilanti in Michigan's 15th District first sent him to Congress in 1955, in a special election to replace his father, John Senior, who had died in office after serving for twenty-three years. John Junior has fought to protect Michigan's auto industry, proposed a national health insurance system, taken on corporate waste and fraud, championed the Endangered Species Act, and led the passage of the law establishing the "Do Not Call" list for telemarketers. In 2001 he was one of only eleven brave congressmen and congresswomen to vote against a congressional resolution expressing solidarity with Israel in its conflicts with Palestine; 384 members voted for it.

That I deeply respect him should go without saying.

I first met Congressman Dingell, a Democrat, at a fund-raising dinner at ICOFA in 1997. In September 2003 he made history by inviting me to give the opening prayer for the 108th Congress. Few imams had had the chance before, and no Shia imam ever had. I felt as if, with this opportunity, I finally had arrived in the halls of power. I had met with President Clinton, Vice President Gore, President Bush, Vice President Cheney, Donald Rumsfeld, Colin Powell, Condoleezza Rice, and others over the past few years, in some cases several times. But those previous meetings had taken place because a politician needed me: needed my knowledge and expertise on Islam, or needed the confidence of my community. Now I was going because they wanted me.

On October 1, Congressman Dingell picked me up personally at the hotel and, after the prayer, explained the congressional voting system and hosted a lunch in my honor at the Capitol with two other representatives, Nick Rahall of West Virginia and Marcy Kaptur of Ohio, and the chaplain of the House. A few others popped in at times, among them Congresswoman Nancy Pelosi and Senators Carl Levin and Joseph Biden. I talked to the lunch guests about how partisan American politics had obscured the importance of Iraq's future. Iraqis had been living at the mercy of the Coalition Provisional Authority and the thriving insurgency, and it was time to allow the will of the Iraqi people to prevail. We hear all about the feelings of the Iraqis from everyone, I said, except the Iraqi people themselves.

Congressmen Dingell and Conyers both introduced me at the opening session of Congress. Congressman Dingell's words in particular touched me:

> Imam Qazwini has become a leading voice for Muslims in America. He has spoken movingly of the need for reconciliation, for tolerance, and for the recognition of our shared humanity. He has worked with leaders in both the Christian and the Jewish communities to help bridge the differences between us and to dispel prejudice. His work has touched Muslim and non-Muslim alike, and his devotion to our State and our community of Dearborn has been recognized by the mayor, the governor, and by President Bush.

> Mr. Speaker, as I have said before, Imam Qazwini's life is a statement on the greatness of our nation. In only a few years, he has become a leader in our nation's religious life. . . .

I told Congressman Dingell that I wanted to thank him publicly before I gave the prayer, but he discouraged my every attempt. When I finally stepped to the lectern, it was with a sense of honor and humility (further bolstered afterward when many lined up to introduce themselves and give thanks). And then I addressed the assembly:

> Respected congressmen and -women, I would like to greet you with the greeting of Islam. Peace be with you in the name of Allah, the Compassionate, the Merciful.
>
> Glory be to Allah, the Lord of Abraham, Moses, Jesus, and Muhammad. As we commence our legislative day in this 108th Congress, we ask You to bestow Your blessing upon us and help our legislators enact that which pleases You and ensures the interest of our people. Lend Your infinite wisdom to this Congress and allow them to embrace what is right, not what is popular.
>
> As our Nation faces many challenges, we beseech Your guidance. And as we pursue those who intend harm to our country, let us seek justice rather than revenge. Guide our leaders to use the influence of their power as an instrument for the betterment of all humankind and peace throughout the world.
>
> O Allah, endow the people of this great land with a growing trust in one another and an increasing faith in You. Help us all uphold our God-given rights of freedom and equality. Allow us never to evoke Your law by embracing color or creed as tools for superiority. As You say in the Holy Qur'an, "O people, We had created you from one male and one female, and made you into nations and tribes so that you may know one another. Verily, the best amongst you are those who are the most pious."
>
> Amen.

CHAPTER 9

Our American
bin Ladens

*Our prosperity does not depend on someone else's
suffering. In order for us to do well, another person
doesn't have to be discriminated against and vilified.*[1]
—*U.S. Representative Keith Ellison*

EVENTUALLY, IN PROMOTING dialogue between the faiths
and stressing commonalities, a cleric gets cornered by differences.
It happened to me when a respected Christian leader in the Detroit area requested that I speak to a group of one hundred pas-
tors on "Why I Am Not a Christian." At first I declined. The
lecture would require me to criticize another religion, something
I studiously avoid, and surely no good could come from such
comments no matter how artfully phrased.

My colleague pressed, saying his church sought exactly that:
a thoughtful, constructive critique of the shortcomings of Christianity. I reluctantly agreed to speak and resolved to present my
beliefs in a noncontroversial way. When I accepted the microphone to address the crowd at a hotel in Livonia, Michigan, I
opened with a joke. I said three things would happen if I were to
convert to Christianity: First, I would lose my job. Second, my
wife would divorce me. After that, my parents would disown me.

Someone in the audience shot up and, with a smile, replied
with three offers, ticking them off on his fingers as he spoke: "We

will provide you with a job, find you a wife, and embrace you as part of our community!"

Everyone laughed. I could see I had a delicate task before me. Discussions of competing faiths can be sensitive even when the participants are respectful and open-minded. I prefaced my comments by saying that religion is rooted in culture and upbringing. Perhaps 90 percent of religious people identify with their religion because of their parents. To tell someone that his religion is incorrect is to suggest that he was born into the wrong family.

Philosophically, two of the barriers to my being a Christian relate to the divine nature of Jesus. The Prophet Muhammad is the messenger of God, not God himself. When he died, his direct connection with God passed also. Jesus also had a physical body and lived, ate, and preached as a man. The idea that a heavenly, omniscient God would father a physical son does not square with our understanding of Jesus. We believe that the only relationship God has with mankind is that of creator and created. Similarly, the Trinity confuses the Judeo-Christian-Islamic concept of monotheism. How can three be one? we wonder. If Jesus' position as the son of God is meant to be symbolic of his miraculous birth, then all human beings are God's children because we are all created from Adam, who was also born miraculously. For Muslims, viewing Jesus as a brilliant but human prophet removes this conflict.

Finally, we do not hold with the notion of original sin. God, we believe, as just and merciful, does not penalize the son for the sins of the father, as our justice system does not hold us accountable for the crimes of our ancestors. In the Islamic tradition, Adam did not sin in the Garden of Eden: he forgot God's command, and in order to sin, willful intent must be present. One must knowingly challenge God. Yet certainly, whether one accepts original sin or not, we can agree that, as a people, we have produced more than enough sins on our own.

My talk finished with less drama than it had started. As my inviter had indicated, the audience members were not looking for a theological debate, just a candid assessment. Their reasoned consideration of my views and questions afterward are the foundation for interfaith dialogue but, regrettably, such goodwill and intellectual curiosity are not as common as they should be.

THE ANTI-MUSLIM CLAMOR

My friend John Esposito is a well-known scholar who has written numerous books about Islam and heads the Prince Alwaleed bin Talal Center for Muslim-Christian Understanding at Georgetown University. When he lectures about Islam, Americans often ask him, "Can you tell us who is an extremist and who is not?" His response is "Can you tell me which priest is a pedophile and which is not?" In other words, the answer is not so easy to discern. Imams do not have tags inside their turbans that say "progressive," "moderate," or "extreme."

The questioners are really asking about the cultural norms of Muslim communities, a measuring stick by which they can determine for themselves who the extremists are. This is a natural tendency and one that comes easily to us in our own culture. When I am asked about Al-Jazeera and its negativity toward America, I point out that we have a parallel in the West: Fox News. Everyone who has watched a Fox News broadcast knows that it presents a conservative point of view, because Americans have an innate sense of the country's political scene and have watched many other newscasts that provide points of comparison. Most of us don't consider Fox to be the voice of the nation. Similarly, those who understand Christianity know that firebrands such as Pat Robertson and Franklin Graham are stuntmen in clerics' garb, not true arbiters of the faith.

Anyone acquainted with the moral and cultural standards of East and West, however, should recognize these intolerant cultural conservatives to be as threatening as the terrorists who attacked our country on September 11. I call them our American bin Ladens.

I acknowledge that these figures are not *literally* terrorists, for they have not waged war as Osama bin Laden has; they have not trained fanatical armies and taken the lives of innocent civilians. Yet, judging by their comments, I believe that with sufficient resources and minimization of risk to self, they would. They are extremists who, like bin Laden, have the ultimate goal of forcing fellow believers to take sides and protect their religion from "invaders." In the process, they distort the principles of their professed faith and provide their opposition with more reasons to hate. The days after September 11 brought some of the ugliest sallies. Of the Al-Qaeda terrorists then identified, the *National Review* columnist Ann Coulter wrote that we should "invade their countries, kill their leaders and convert them to Christianity."[2] (Shortly afterward, Coulter and the *National Review* agreed to end their relationship, and *National Review* editor Jonah Goldberg glibly accepted responsibility for running the inflammatory column. "It was a mistake," he wrote in a follow-up. "Our bad.")[3] The Christian evangelist Franklin Graham said, "The god of Islam is not the same god. . . . It's a different god, and I believe it is a very evil and wicked religion."[4] On his television show *The 700 Club,* Pat Robertson said that Islam "is not a peaceful religion that wants to coexist. They want to coexist until they can control, dominate and then, if need be, destroy."[5]

The terrorists' attacks didn't make sense to any of us in the shock of the moment, and these public figures understandably spoke hastily and out of anger. Several years later, however, by which time such leaders had presumably had a chance to learn about Islam, study its history, and develop an informed opinion, we heard more of the same. Commenting on the massive demonstrations over the cartoons of the Prophet Muhammad run in the Danish newspaper *Jyllands-Posten* in 2006, Robertson said, "These people are crazed fanatics, and I want to say it now: I believe it's motivated by demonic power, it is satanic and it's time we recognize what we're dealing with."[6] Two days later, John Donovan of ABC News asked Franklin Graham whether his views of Islam had changed since his comments in 2001. "No," he said. "I know about Islam. I don't need an education from Islam."[7]

This air of certainty and consistent refusal to consider other points of view make dialogue impossible. In 2002 I appeared on MSNBC to offer a counterpoint to Graham's argument that Islam is a violent religion. Graham again attacked Islam as violent and said that the Qur'an "talks nonsense." The interviewer said the Bible can also be difficult to read, and Graham became angry.

Occasionally a popular outcry or demand from a moral authority will lead one of our American bin Ladens to apologize or offer clarification. Graham wrote an op-ed in *The Wall Street Journal* in 2001 in which he stressed his dislike for Islam, not Muslims as people. "I decry the evil that has been done in the name of Islam, or any other faith—including Christianity," he wrote.[8] Such clarifications, if sincere, are helpful, but the mean-spirited remarks seem to come much faster and more loudly than the retractions or apologies. Pat Robertson says the Prophet Muhammad is a "brigand." The Reverend Jerry Vines labels him a "demon-possessed pedophile." Such statements make me feel disgusted and sick. When I hear extremists calling for the president to nuke Muslim cities, I feel even sicker. Degrading insults and wild threats are not the hallmarks of legitimate religious leaders. Moreover, these are highly visible and, in some quarters, respected Christian leaders. Their conduct should be of the highest standard. But I see little connection between these men and the noble standards of Jesus himself, the prophet of forgiveness who said, "Love your enemies, bless them that curse you."[9] Pope John Paul II called for atonement and understanding between the faiths. By comparison, Franklin Graham seems to have little in common with his father, the Reverend Billy Graham, save for his name. I cannot respect men who won't respect their calling.

In trying to tear down Islam, these people ignore the respect that Muslims show for Christianity and Jesus in particular. Muslims might criticize secularism, imperialism, and American foreign policy, but not Christianity. The Christian leaders who preach violence in response to violence misrepresent Jesus through their words and behavior.

The most disheartening aspect of the theatrical gestures of these extremists is their influence among our political elite and the larger society. We expect to hear incendiary rants from the margins, not from the prominent and well-connected. Jerry Vines is the former president of the Southern Baptist Convention. Franklin Graham gave the invocation at President Bush's first inauguration in 2001. Pat Robertson, a former Republican presidential candidate, and the late Jerry Falwell, founder of the Moral Majority in 1979, have been major political players and have met frequently with presidents and lawmakers. They quietly backed George W. Bush in the 2000 election to undo his Republican primary rival John McCain. Only briefly did they surface publicly, in South Carolina, where President Bush needed to reinforce his standing among evangelicals to reverse McCain's early surge and establish himself.[10]

That crucial support must have squeezed President Bush after September 11, when Robertson and Falwell began vocal critiques of Islam that were at odds with the president's public statements. In October 2002, Falwell called the Prophet Muhammad a "terrorist." A month later, at an Iftar dinner (the meal that breaks the daily fast during Ramadan) at the White House attended by fifteen American Muslim leaders, ambassadors of Muslim countries in Washington, and senior administration officials—among them Condoleezza Rice (then the national security adviser), Andy Card (then the White House chief of staff), Colin Powell (then the secretary of state), and top adviser Karl Rove—I cautioned President Bush that Falwell's comments would have a devastating impact on his standing with Muslims. Bush assured me that Falwell did not represent his own views, nor did he sympathize with them.

But Mr. President, I told him, unless you publicly condemn these remarks and distance yourself from him, many Muslims will see you as condoning his views.

He agreed, but he felt that the chapter had closed. Falwell had issued his nonsensical comments weeks earlier. I am missing the opportunity [to say something], the president said, but we may call on you to do something.

Mr. President, it's never too late, I urged. You still can say something.

For a week there was nothing. Then, during a meeting with UN Secretary-General Kofi Annan, he did speak up. Two days earlier, Robertson had compared the world's 1.5 billion Muslims to Hitler. "Adolf Hitler was bad, but what the Muslims want to do to the Jews is worse," he said.[11] Bush took advantage of the fresh attack to make his position clear: "Some of the comments that have been uttered about Islam do not reflect the sentiments of my government or the sentiments of most Americans," he said. "Islam, as practiced by the vast majority of people, is a peaceful religion, a religion that respects others. . . . By far, the vast majority of American citizens respect the Muslim people and the Islamic faith. . . . And we're not going to let the war on terror or terrorists cause us to change our values."[12]

President Bush's statement did provide some comfort, though I knew that it wouldn't change his relationship with the Religious Right. The fact that he hadn't singled out any of the critics by name showed that he wasn't interested in burning bridges and, in addition, likely didn't want to call attention to his affiliation with them.

THE EXTREMISTS ALSO WORK IN WASHINGTON

Sometimes the religious bigots roaming Washington's halls of power aren't visiting. They're drawing federal paychecks. When President Bush defeated the Christian conservative Gary Bauer in the 2000 Republican primary and succeeded in silencing the Pat Robertsons and Jerry Falwells of the religious community in return for advancing their agenda, he became the de facto leader of that constituency. He brought evangelicals into his administration, for example appointing former U.S. senator and Missouri governor John Ashcroft, a devout member of the Assemblies of God, the country's largest Pentecostal denomination, as U.S. attorney general. In November 2001, the conservative commentator Cal Thomas quoted Ashcroft as saying, "Islam is a religion in which God requires you to send your son to die for him. Christianity is a faith in which God sends his son to die for you."[13] (Months later, when mainstream media began picking up the quote and Muslims demanded a retraction, Ashcroft issued a statement saying the quote was not accurate.)

In 2002, a Bush appointee to the U.S. Commission on Human Rights alarmed Muslim Americans by saying that the government might need to consider internment camps if another attack occurred on U.S. soil. The publisher of the *Arab American News* recalls that Attorney General Ashcroft made a similar statement in a private meeting at which Muslims were complaining about violations of civil liberties. You Muslims should be happy that we did not put you in internment camps, Ashcroft reportedly said.

In the ranks of the military, Lieutenant General William Boykin, of the Army, inflamed anti-Muslim sentiments in a series of speeches he gave to evangelicals in Oregon, Oklahoma, and Florida. Among other things, he related a tale of his combat in Somalia, where he had engaged a Muslim combatant who insisted he was under God's protection and could not be harmed. "My God is bigger than his God," General Boykin boasted. "I knew my God was a real God and his was an idol."[14] Though entitled to his private opinion, General Boykin crossed the line by making such statements publicly. He couched America's military actions as a war between Christianity and Islam. (President Bush's early reference to the war on terrorism as a crusade did not help matters.) In his role as deputy under secretary of defense for intelligence, General Boykin would be responsible for collaborating with Muslim leaders in the Middle East to share intelligence and formulate strategy, and his portrayal of

Muslims as satanic could only diminish his effectiveness. Reporting to Under Secretary of Defense Stephen Cambone and Secretary of Defense Donald Rumsfeld, Boykin also helped direct a special-access program at the Pentagon known as Copper Green, which was designed to streamline the military's handling of insurgents, and which resulted in the macabre torture scenes at Abu Ghraib—initially dismissed by the Pentagon as the work of a few renegade American soldiers.[15] I wonder how much the moral certitude indicated by comments like Boykin's influenced the military's torture program. General Boykin retired in June 2007.

Media and officials often blame extremism on the Muslim world, but the comments of government officials and media figures contribute to these problems, and the president implicitly endorses them by not speaking out. When a foreign president makes anti-Semitic remarks, our president is quick to condemn them, as he should, but the same does not go for Islam. Silence makes Muslims feel as if he doesn't care.

Even before the Abu Ghraib scandal broke, Muslims worldwide were unhappy to hear how some Americans were treating Iraqis after the fall of Baghdad—not violently, in this case, but with a twist. As U.S. soldiers streaked toward Baghdad to capture Saddam and secure the country, Christian missionaries prepared to trail them offering food and medical supplies in exchange for conversion. Some such groups were based in Jordan to avoid provoking Iraqi Muslims, but not the Southern Baptist Convention, whose eighty thousand boxes of beans and rice bore the Bible verse John 1:17 ("For the Law was given through Moses; grace and truth were realized through Jesus Christ") and the relief program Samaritan's Purse, led by Franklin Graham. Graham told the website Beliefnet, "We realize we're in an Arab country and we just can't go out and preach. . . . I believe as we work, God will always give us opportunities to tell others about his Son. We are there to reach out to love them and to save them, and as a Christian I do this in the name of Jesus Christ."[16]

As an imam who cherishes the power of conviction, I empathize with the idea of welcoming others to join my faith. There is a time and a place for everything, however, and a war-torn country where people are desperate for clean water and safe housing, where people are herded and restricted by U.S. troops on one side and harassed and abused by insurgents on the other is no place for missionary work. If Christians want to offer assistance, they should do so with no strings attached. Ultimately these attempts will fail. I cannot imagine Iraqis relinquishing their faith for twenty pounds of wheat.

When I meet with potential converts, my primary concern as an imam is the authenticity of the person's intent. The first question I ask of male converts is "Are you doing this for a girl?" which is usually met with a laugh. But I'm dead serious. Though relationships can be powerful motivators, they are a poor reason to change religions. I want people to come to Islam because of the power and purity of the faith, because they recognize the difference it can make in their lives. If someone converts when he is physically hungry, how long will his reverence continue after he is full?

I raised these issues with Secretary Rumsfeld in a meeting on April 10, 2003, at the Pentagon, one day after the fall of Baghdad, but he sidestepped my questions by labeling them irrelevant to the military mission. "These people represent themselves," he declared. "We have nothing to do with them." Other religious leaders at the meeting disputed Rumsfeld's take. A rabbi near me seconded my concern, and Theodore Cardinal McCarrick, then the archbishop of Washington, D.C., echoed our statements. Secretary Rumsfeld stressed several times, in nervous tones, that the government wasn't responsible and that it wasn't his place to intervene. "There's nothing we can do," he said. (This is as close as we got to a real answer at the time. The White House press secretary, Ari Fleischer, referred the media to the State Department, which referred them to the U.S. Agency for International Development. The USAID spokeswoman, Ellen Yount, said, "How could the U.S. government control that? We can't just say to an organization, 'You can or cannot do something,' if we don't fund them. Imagine what the United States Congress would say to us.")[17]

Well, obviously that is not the right answer. In a war zone it dominates, the United States has not only the right but the obligation to control who enters and exits, funded or no. The country certainly exercises strict control of its own borders: a friend of mine, Dr. Muhammad Habash, who came to Washington from Syria to attend a conference in 2004, saw his valid visa inexplicably rejected, and the Swiss scholar Tariq Ramadan was similarly denied entry in 2004 and again in 2005 after he had signed a contract to teach at the University of Notre Dame. Surely the United States ought to be able to muster the security needed for its campaigns abroad.

The charge of interfaith dialogue sounds like an easy cure-all, but sacred principles, cherished beliefs, and revered traditions continually confound our efforts. Islam and Christianity are both universal systems, addressing all people in all times, and as such, they don't allow for more than one true belief. Adhere to both faiths, and you reject them both. If you were to ask me what the most authentic religion is, I would say Islam. Similarly, Cardinal Maida respects Islam but would never embrace it at the expense of his Catholic beliefs. The same goes for Judaism and Rabbi David Nelson, a friend and interfaith partner of mine who is rabbi emeritus of Congregation Beth Shalom in Oak Park, Michigan.

Yet those exclusions should go without saying. In interfaith dialogue, we are seeking not converts but understanding. To do that, we must be willing to debate the controversial, but we begin and end as cousins in faith, not as opponents. For many of our prophets are the same. The God of Abraham, whether we call him Yahweh or Allah, is the same. Built from one foundation, our halls of worship cannot be so far apart. The best preachers—Billy

Graham comes to mind—know how to impassion their support-ers while simultaneously and gently reaching out to those be-yond. When people like Franklin Graham, Pat Robertson, and the late Jerry Falwell publicly air their ill-informed opinions, whose minds are they hoping to change? Whom are they speaking to? If to their rank and file, they should remember that the whole world is listening.

CHAPTER 10

Lines in the Sand

What is strength without a double share of wisdom?[1]
—*John Milton*

THE WAR IN Iraq was just as messy in my mind as it was on the ground. My Iraqi relatives had real freedom of expression for the first time in their lives—but amid the sort of turmoil where talking is of little use. Entire villages hundreds of years old were lost to gunfights between U.S. forces and insurgents as the former asserted control and the latter floated out of reach. The sanctions that had contributed to the deaths of 700,000 or more Iraqis through malnutrition and inadequate medical care were lifted after more than a decade. Some desperate, impoverished Iraqis took advantage of the chaos to loot irreplaceable ancient treasures. Saddam was gone, forced underground. Porous borders invited foreign terrorists from all over the Middle East to filter into the country and, with weapons and threats, undo the progress already made.

Muslims and non-Muslims everywhere opposed the war. Although Saddam deserved to be removed, the Bush administration was not truthful in its justifications. As we had suspected, Saddam had no weapons of mass destruction. There were no attempted uranium purchases from Niger. Saddam's criminal and inhumane reputation was well earned, but the U.S. government historically has abetted many of his crimes, no matter how savage, when the outcomes pleased the CIA or the State Department. And while it's true that Saddam violated several UN resolutions, other countries have also done so in the past and suffered no consequences at all.

I respect many of those who opposed the war. They had genuine and noble desires for peace and opposed the unilateral invasion of a sovereign country when the facts on the ground did not match the explanations coming from Washington. But some in positions of power strongly opposed the UN resolutions to invade Iraq and the U.S. plans to go in unilaterally for reasons that had nothing to do with Iraq's best interests. In 2004, the Iraqi Oil Ministry released a list of individuals who had received oil vouchers from Saddam, vouchers furnished at a discount and that holders could then resell for a handsome profit. The list of buyers included the former interior minister of France, members of the Russian parliament, and Cyprus's Benon Sevan, the UN's own director of the Oil-for-Food program, whom U.S. federal prosecutors indicted in January 2007 for bribery and conspiracy to commit wire fraud. The Russians, Chinese, French, Germans, and member countries of the Arab League profited from Saddam's illegal trading through the program.

The governments of France and Germany, in particular, were seen in the international community before the war as humanitarian advocates for the people of Iraq, countries with close ties to the Middle East that understood its problems and were defending it against U.S. aggression. I don't believe the Oil-for-Food program as it was set up ever had a chance of helping Iraq's citizens, and those who cashed in on it can only heighten Iraq's skepticism about the motives of do-gooding outsiders. Whether the gains were personal or governmental, the criminals who perpetrated the fraud should be tried fairly and publicly, with a full accounting of their acts.

At the time, I appreciated the courageous voices criticizing the war and associated human rights violations, but where were these same humanitarians when, for more than thirty years, thousands of Iraqi citizens were being raped in the bowels of Abu Ghraib? Where were they when the Mukhabarat tortured parents to death in front of their children? When my grandfather was taken away in the middle of the night?

Saddam's eldest son, Uday, whom U.S. forces killed in a July 2003 attack in Mosul, was notorious for crashing parties and plucking beautiful women off the street to rape them. A body double of Uday's, Latif Yahia, has written about a woman who resisted Uday's advances at a gathering and was shot in front of everyone. As for the women who resigned themselves to rape— that is, those who wanted to live—Uday would allow the rest of his gang to rape them as well. At one time Uday was seen as Saddam's successor, but he fell out with his father in 1988 after he beat Saddam's valet to death, in full view of guests, at a party held in honor of the wife of Egyptian president Hosni Mubarak. It was as if the rules of a civilized society didn't apply within the bubble of the Hussein clan.

In April 2003 President Bush traveled to Dearborn to meet with twelve Iraqi Americans and give a speech about the U.S. mission in Iraq. I had met him on numerous occasions and noted his generally upbeat, jocular moods, but this time outshone all. He appeared jubilant. At the private meeting, all twelve of us had a chance to speak: Kurds, Chaldeans, Shia, and Sunnis. When my turn came, I thanked the president for helping the Iraqis get rid of Saddam and said, "Mr. President, you have heard what the Kurds want, what the Chaldeans want, and what the Sunnis want. Now you should hear what the Shia majority wants. I feel I can now speak for the Shia majority, including Ayatollah Sistani. Mr. President, the Shia in Iraq are Iraqis before anything else." Before the invasion, some Arab countries had attempted to sway the Bush administration by suggesting that a Shia-dominated government in Iraq would be loyal to Iran.

Shia Iraqis' understanding of clerical rule is different from Iranians'; the latter are more accepting of it, as with Ayatollah Khomeini's "guardianship of the jurist" system, in which Iran's supreme leader and a Council of Guardians have ultimate authority over laws made by the legislature and similar panels of clerics oversee most other branches of government. Ayatollah Sistani, by contrast, resisted getting involved in politics but also has tremendous credibility in all religious and public matters and has repeatedly encouraged Iraqis to embrace the democratic process.

"Iraqi Shia don't want a theocracy," I said to President Bush. "They don't want to assemble an Islamic republic. *They want a democratic government.* Islamic theocracy does not work for Iraq because of its ethnic diversity. Iraqi Shia respect Iran, and they will not forget Iran's favors to them, because at a time when the entire world stood by Saddam Hussein, Iran was the only country that hosted more than half a million within its borders and gave them shelter. That said, this does not mean that Iraqi Shia owe their national allegiance to Iran at the expense of an independent, sovereign Iraqi government.

"Therefore, I demand from you, Mr. President, that now you push for democracy. Shia during Saddam's regime were not only denied access to power. They were denied their basic religious rituals. It is natural for us to want democracy."

President Bush agreed and said he did not send troops to die in Iraq so that we could replace a dictator with another dictator. "Of course there will be democracy in Iraq," he said. "Please convey to Ayatollah Sistani and your brothers that democracy is assured in Iraq."

We had great reason for hope coming out of that meeting. If democracy worked in Iraq, it would mark the first time in nearly *five hundred years,* since the rise of the Ottoman empire, that Iraq's Shia would have self-determination. More than that, a makeover of Iraq could inspire others to push for democratic changes in their own countries. I never advocated for war there, however. On the occasions when President Bush and I met, I spoke only of removing Saddam, not invasion. When I contemplate the Bush administration's disastrous mishandling of Iraq, from the treatment of captured enemy soldiers to widespread civil war, I despair at how things went so wrong. Iraq could have resumed its rightful place among the world's great civilizations, and now it's as if Iraqis will have to start from scratch once again, for the most part on their own.

A week after Saddam was forced out of power, my father returned to Karbala, our home, to lead prayers at the shrine of Imam Husayn. My father felt as if he had fulfilled his calling in America. In an expansion of the square surrounding Imam Husayn's shrine, our old house had been razed, but my father took up residence in my grandfather's house, which, because of the same expansion, now stood on the perimeter of the shrine. A Baathist intelligence officer had taken up residence there but fled after the invasion.

HOW IRAQ FELL APART

That U.S. intervention in Iraq has been an unmitigated disaster is hardly a news bulletin. War strategists had hoped to slip into Iraq and help set up a new government with a light, nimble, and inexpensive force. By 2004 it was readily apparent that they did not have the manpower necessary to provide security, and areas that had already been cleared of insurgents saw them spring back as soon as American troops left. Retired U.S. generals have since spoken out about having recommended at least 380,000 troops for the initial invasion, three times as many as Secretary Rumsfeld decided on. The policy research firm the RAND Corporation released a report in spring 2003 estimating that 500,000 soldiers would be needed to succeed in Iraq.[2] The unprecedented chorus of critical voices among high-ranking military officers makes it clear where responsibility lies and what has gone wrong in Iraq.

The Bush administration had a dream, but not a plan. Its officials loved the idea of sweeping change in the Middle East but had little interest in nation building. They expected to wind up

Imam Qazwini's great-great-grandfather Ayatollah Hashim Qazwini (holding book), with a few students and associates. The small child second from left in the front row with his head turned (circled) is Imam Qazwini's grandfather Ayatollah Mohammad Sadiq Qazwini. This photo was taken in Karbala, Iraq, in 1901.

Imam Qazwini's father, Ayatollah Mortadha Qazwini, addressing the former president of Iraq, Abdul Karim Qasim, in Baghdad in 1961.

Ayatollah Mortadha Qazwini speaking at the shrine of Imam Husayn in 1960.

Ayatollah Mortadha Qazwini speaking at the shrine of Imam Husayn in 2003, forty-three years later.

From left to right, the first four men are Imam Qazwini's great-uncle Ayatollah M. Salih Qazwini; his grandfather Ayatollah Mohammad Sadiq Qazwini; his father's cousin Ayatollah Kadhim Qazwini; and his father, Ayatollah Mortadha Qazwini. The little boy is Imam Qazwini's uncle Sayed Abdul-Hussein Qazwini. This photo was taken in Iraq in 1954.

Back row, from left to right: Imam Qazwini's brother Imam Moustafa Qazwini, and two of Imam Qazwini's cousins. Middle row: Imam Qazwini. Front row, from left to right: Imam Qazwini's brothers Jafar Qazwini and Imam Mohammed Qazwini. The photograph was taken in Kuwait City in 1975.

Imam Qazwini and Ayatollah Mortadha Qazwini performing the hajj in Mecca in 1994.

Vice President Al Gore and Imam Qazwini in April 1999.

Imam Qazwini and then-governor George W. Bush during the 2000 presidential campaign.

Imam Qazwini and Abdulrahman Wahid, the former president of Indonesia, in Jakarta during the Muslim Leaders Summit on World Peace in December 2001.

Imam Qazwini and Patriarch Laham III, the archbishop of the Catholic community in Syria, in Detroit in 2002.

Imam Qazwini and then–secretary of state Colin Powell during an Iftar dinner hosted by the State Department in 2002.

A candlelight vigil in Dearborn, Michigan, on the first anniversary
of the September 11 attacks.

An interfaith gathering in memory
of the victims of September 11
outside the Dearborn City Hall on
the first anniversary of the tragedy.
(Heritage Newspapers)

Imam Qazwini and
Amr Musa, secretary-
general of the Arab
League, in Dearborn
in 2002.

Congresswoman Nancy Pelosi, now the Speaker of the House; Congressman John Dingell; Ishmael Ahmad, the chairman of the Arab Community Center for Economic and Social Services (ACCESS); and Imam Qazwini in Dearborn in 2002.

Back row, from left to right: Imam Qazwini and his five brothers, Imam Mohammed Qazwini, Imam Ali Qazwini, Imam Moustafa Qazwini, Sayed Hossein Qazwini, and Dr. Jafar Qazwini. Front row, seated, from left to right: Imam Qazwini's father, Ayatollah Mortadha Qazwini, and Imam Qazwini's uncles Hashim Qazwini and Abdul-Hussein Qazwini. The photograph was taken in California in 2003.

A lunch held by Congressman John Dingell in honor of Imam Qazwini on Capitol Hill on October 1, 2003.

Imam Qazwini giving the invo-cation at a session of the 108th Congress on October 1, 2003.

Dr. Abd El Aziz Hegazy, former prime minister of Egypt; Sadiq Al-Mahdi, former prime minister of Sudan; and Imam Qazwini in Seoul, South Korea, in 2004.

Imam Qazwini and Senator John Kerry during the 2004 presidential campaign.

The new Islamic Center of America (ICOFA), completed in May 2005.

Jennifer Granholm, governor of Michigan; the late Michael A. Guido, who was then mayor of Dearborn; and Imam Qazwini (all three holding scissors) during the ribbon cutting at the ICOFA in May 2005.

Imam Qazwini and Governor Jennifer Granholm at the official reception for the grand opening of the ICOFA.

Imam Qazwini giving the first Friday sermon at the new ICOFA.

Imam Qazwini leading the first Friday congregational prayer at the new ICOFA.

From left to right, starting with the fourth from the left: Imam Qazwini; Patriarch Emmanuel Delly, the Iraqi Chaldean archbishop; and Bishop Ibrahim Ibrahim, in 2005.

Pope Benedict XVI and Imam Qazwini at the Vatican in March 2006.
(www.fotografiafelici.com)

Top row, from left to right: One of Imam Qazwini's cousins; his brother Imam Moustafa Qazwini; Imam Qazwini; and four of the Imam's cousins. Bottom row, from left to right: Imam Qazwini's son Ahmed Qazwini, three of the Imam's nephews, and his son Mohamed Qazwini. The photograph was taken in the summer of 2006.

Imam Qazwini; Theodore Cardinal McCarrick, who was then archbishop of Washington, D.C. (to the left of Imam Qazwini); and other Jewish, Christian, and Muslim leaders during an interfaith event at Georgetown University in April 2006. (Georgetown University, Charles Nailen)

Imam Qazwini receiving Shirin Ebadi, the Nobel Peace Prize winner (to his right), at the ICOFA in May 2006.

From left to right: Governor Howard Dean, chairman of the Democratic National Committee; Imam Mardini; Imam Qazwini; and Imam Hisham Husseiny, in May 2006.

Former secretary of state Madeleine Albright and Imam Qazwini at the ICOFA in May 2006.

Imam Qazwini giving the invocation at the Michigan state capitol in May 2006. Senator Irma Clark-Coleman is on the left and Lieutenant Governor John Cherry is on the right.

Adam Cardinal Maida (center), Imam Qazwini (second from left), and other Muslim leaders during Cardinal Maida's visit to the ICOFA in October 2006 after remarks made by the pope were deemed offensive to Muslims.

Imam Qazwini overlooking the Kaaba inside the Grand Mosque in Mecca in January 2007.

Iraq like a child's toy, put it in motion, and let the country run itself. That impulse predictably compounded almost every problem the invasion had been expected to solve. As Senator John
Kerry said frequently on the 2004 campaign trail, the administration knew how to win the war, but not how to win the peace.

U.S. administrators have displayed a galling political and cultural ignorance of Iraq. In 2005, their wavering (for security reasons) on holding elections endangered the fragile trust the military
had established, as war began to look more like occupation. Coalition forces train and equip police officers, some of whom funnel
weapons to the insurgents and help them carry out attacks from
the inside. Money as much as ideology can be a strong motivator
for underpaid police officers. Coalition forces have trouble telling
civilians from noncivilians, and they do not always know when to
fight, when to negotiate, and how to negotiate.

Right at the time it is trying to rebuild and reconcile competing visions, Iraq faces two monsters: Baathist loyalists and foreign
terrorists. The Baathists are determined to inflict maximum damage and casualties in order to regain control of the government.
They do not care whether Iraq's entire infrastructure is destroyed
or whether millions of its citizens are murdered, terrorized, impoverished, or humiliated. Fear and intimidation are their allies,
just as they were during Saddam's time. I have great reservations
about attempts to appease these insurgents by entertaining their
political demands. Pro-Baathist politicians argue that offering the
insurgents a seat at the table will help convert violence into constructive political discourse, but instead it shows insurgents that
the halls of power will be thrown open to any maniac who can
build a car bomb. Let us not be fooled that these groups are interested in participating in the government as it has been set up.
They will not be satisfied until they have obliterated the existing
government, and some of these pro-Baathist politicians are com-
plicit in insurgents' plans to attack Iraqi civilians.

The foreign terrorists and their Al-Qaeda-affiliated operatives
are just as ruthless but have no political agendas as we know

them. They fight with two intentions: to kill as many Americans as possible, and to kill as many Shia as possible. As U.S. forces have pulled out of cities and regions declared to be safe, insurgents filter back in and, without U.S. soldiers to kill, pursue Shia and anyone else who gets in their way. They target mosques and bakeries, funeral homes and restaurants. The Baathists and foreign terrorists have forged an unholy alliance, and they pose a lethal threat to the already weak central government because the coalition forces, not the Iraqi government, are in charge of security.

Millions of Iraqis have fled the country since 2003, most to Jordan and Syria. Those left behind get by without electricity, running water, gas, emergency services, waste disposal, and most other essentials you can think of, and despair and distrust of the U.S. mission deepen by the day. In the fall of 2006, Johns Hopkins researchers estimated that 654,000 Iraqi civilians had died as a result of conflict since the ground invasion in 2003.[3] On top of it all, the people in charge have mostly refused to own up to their errors and misdeeds. Every occupying force is fully responsible for what happens in an occupied land.

I crossed paths with Secretary of Energy Spencer Abraham on a March 2004 flight to Washington, D.C., to attend a United Institute of Peace conference. I had not spoken to Secretary Abraham since the president's election and was disappointed at his lack of advocacy on any major Muslim issue. As we discussed policy on the flight, I expressed dismay at the mismanagement of the war, the deteriorating situation in Iraq, and the rising death toll. I pushed Secretary Abraham to request a meeting with the president. "I can't promise you anything," he said. "They've told me, 'If you *want* to see the president, you can't, but if you *need* to, you can.' If I have to, I can go, but I can't promise that I can take someone with me."

That did not come to pass. The campaign season was already in full swing, which compressed the president's all-consuming schedule into another realm. Bush officials had indicated that a meeting with the president was possible, but it would be contingent on my endorsing him in 2004, something I had no backing for in the Muslim community.

A few days later someone from the Pentagon called and instead offered a one-on-one meeting with Deputy Secretary of Defense Paul Wolfowitz, the architect of the Iraq war. I did not feel Wolfowitz was in a position to address my concerns, nor did I believe he had any inclination to do so. Insiders have reported that he expressed little regard for coalitions and allies; he had few reservations about going it alone. Wolfowitz lacked a clear sense of the situation on the ground and when in Iraq stayed in the Green Zone, the downtown section of Baghdad secured with concrete blast walls that keeps its occupants suspended in a bubble. The reality of Iraq's condition must have surprised him during an official tour in October 2003 when rockets hit his hotel, the Al-Rashid, and killed an army lieutenant colonel there.[4]

Despite my misgivings about Wolfowitz, I also felt I had to do everything possible to minimize the damage in Iraq and help its people. I reluctantly accepted the appointment. My top concern was elections. There didn't seem to be a plan in place for how they would happen. At our meeting, Wolfowitz spoke of Paul Bremer, the head of the Coalition Provisional Authority, picking 270 candidates for provincial caucuses: tribal leaders, prominent people, influential clerics. They would make up the Iraqi National Assembly and then manage the election of the Iraqi Interim Government. I felt that strategy would be a disaster because it did not place enough authority in Iraqis' hands. To this point, Ayatollah Sistani had called for peace while a new Iraqi government took shape, but such meddling would force him to speak out, and the United States would lose credibility. Do not provoke Ayatollah Sistani, I advised Wolfowitz.

The second issue I spoke of was the disbanding of the Iraqi army and the reentry of Baath loyalists into the military. Out of fear of permitting Baathists to infiltrate the new military, Bremer had disbanded it, right down to the foot soldiers, and U.S. forces

already found themselves dangerously overmatched and culturally estranged from citizens who were potential allies. Meanwhile, I said, high-level Baathist officers were advising the army
in such hotspots as Falluja—information that came as a surprise
to Wolfowitz. (A year and a half later, in August 2005, I would express the same concern to Secretary Rumsfeld, who responded,
"Can we not hire a Baathist teacher at an elementary school?" I
said, "No, I'm not talking about teachers. I'm talking about commanders of security forces who coordinate with insurgency leaders to compromise their own officers.")

I also warned Wolfowitz about the futile U.S. battle with
Muqtada al-Sadr. U.S. strategists suspected al-Sadr of being responsible for the assassination of a major Shia cleric. Fierce fighting had then erupted between al-Sadr's Mahdi Army and U.S.
troops in Najaf and further angered citizens there because of the
resulting damage to holy sites. The killing had taken place a year
ago, I told Wolfowitz. Why go after Muqtada now? I urged him
to let the Iraqi government deal with the Mahdi Army and focus
on reconstruction. Wolfowitz listened and seemed understanding, but I don't know how effective any of my arguments were.
Ultimately the outcome was positive, as Ayatollah Sistani met
with al-Sadr in Najaf and persuaded him to direct his efforts politically instead of militarily. Al-Sadr declared an end to fighting
and saw thirty-three seats in Iraq's January 2005 parliamentary
elections go to his supporters.

ELECTIONS AT HOME

The 2004 campaign season didn't bring much good news for Muslim Americans either. Some law enforcement agencies and the Department of Homeland Security had compensated for their
inadequate security preparations for hard targets—ports, nuclear
facilities, airports, and military installations—with harassment
and detention of Muslims under the auspices of the Patriot Act. I
attended a campaign event in Lansing with Vice President Cheney

that May and decided to ask him about those issues myself. This time I came not as a supporter but as a concerned citizen. I was the only Arab present, sitting in the first row of seats behind a table reserved for questioners hand-picked by the campaign. I was not supposed to speak, which I did not realize at the time but which I do not regret, and the vice president must have been caught off-guard. I asked him about both the prospects for elections in Iraq the following January and the waning support the administration was receiving among Muslims. (Bush enjoyed broad Muslim support in the 2000 election, but in 2004 just 14 percent of voting Muslims cast a ballot for him.) Vice President Cheney, whom I had also met during the 2000 presidential campaign, was warm and reassuring in speech and tone. He agreed that elections in Iraq needed to move forward as scheduled to prevent momentum from shifting toward the insurgents and offered a remark about the administration doing its "level best" to avoid profiling Muslim Americans in pursuing security.

I had hoped the administration would engage more with Muslims. It had not reached out to our community in some time, particularly on the subjects of profiling and secret evidence. At the Cheney campaign stop, a reporter from the *Los Angeles Times* asked whether I had chosen a candidate yet, and when I said I had not, political strategists saw my vote as winnable.[5] Not long after, Senator Kerry's campaign called to discuss his positions.

I met with Senator Kerry in August 2004 at the airport in Flint, Michigan, where I waited in a seat next to Bill Ford, the CEO of the automobile company. A handler guided Senator Kerry toward a line of us, and I took a few moments to weigh in on the frightening domestic casualties of the Patriot Act. I also reminded him of the 6 million to 7 million Muslims who needed his representation, and Kerry promised to invite imams to the White House to brief him about our issues and community.

Exit polls indicated that a majority of the Muslim community went for Kerry in the 2004 election. President Bush's reneging on the promises he had made to Muslims in the 2000 campaign soured too many on the Republican approach, and I was among them. In the reductive two-party political system, the only other realistic choice was Senator Kerry, in whom I lacked confidence. Ralph Nader, a second-generation Lebanese American, most closely approximated the qualities I sought, but I knew any independent candidate stood only a slim chance of winning. Ultimately I endorsed no one in 2004.

MY GREATEST LOSS IN IRAQ

My father's return to Iraq magnified all the contradictory feelings I had about the war there. He had given up a pleasant, comfortable life in California. Even under the best of circumstances, Karbala's standard of living could not have matched what he had become accustomed to in the United States. With the city surrounded by war, he could take nothing for granted. Of course, without Saddam gone, he never could have returned at all. The Mukhabarat file my father received after the regime was unseated showed pictures of him and our family in Pomona, eight thousand miles away, as well as in Kuwait and Iran.

Coming back also required him to confront the old emotional scars that life under the Baathists had inflicted. Good friends, classmates, and colleagues he had once known had not survived. The sacrifices had been made for them. Iraqi authorities found documents in Abu Ghraib prison showing that fourteen members of the Qazwini family had been executed in 1985. One of my cousins, Hassan Rajaa, had been executed earlier, in 1981. Hassan had earned a Ph.D. in nuclear physics in London, where he befriended and studied alongside the well-known Iraqi nuclear physicist Hussein Shahristani. They both returned to Iraq in 1978 to work in nuclear facilities there. When it became clear that Saddam wanted to build a nuclear weapon, they resigned and faced execution. But Shahristani had spent time in Canada and married a Canadian woman. The Canadian embassy negotiated a life sentence for him, and he escaped during Gulf War bombing. Today he is the oil minister of Iraq. Hassan, who married an Iraqi woman, was not so lucky.

The hardest thing for my father was learning the fate of his own father. He had survived for several years after his arrest. A man imprisoned there recalled seeing him alive, blind and enfeebled, both surely as a result of torture. But Saddam collected political prisoners in such prodigious numbers that every few years he killed those detained earlier to make room for more. Relatives in Karbala had talked to an undertaker who recalled seeing my grandfather's body pass through his funeral home, sometime between 1983 and 1985. From the marks left on his body, the undertaker could tell that my grandfather had been beaten and executed. Friends and relatives in many countries held memorials for him.

CHAPTER 11

Return to the Cradle

To Adam, paradise was home. To the good among his
descendants, home is paradise.[1]
—*Augustus William and Julius Charles Hare*

IN THE SUMMER of 2004 I was visiting my in-laws in Iran, particularly in Qum, and was hoping to make a side trip to Karbala
to see my family. I had not been to Iraq since 1978, when I went
with my mother, and I discovered that getting into a besieged
post-Saddam Iraq would be nearly as distressing for us as our in-
voluntary exit was for my father in 1971. Iraqi military patrolled
the international border; not just anyone could pass through
checkpoints into a country still very much at war. I would need
credentials. I contacted a friend who knew someone in the Iranian government, and he obtained the necessary official papers
and set me up with two drivers who would shuttle my family
and me to the border.

Before we left, I was planning to go to Mashad, a sublimely
beautiful town in far northeastern Iran, close to the border with
Turkmenistan, to visit the shrine of the eighth Imam, Imam Ali
ar-Rida, and my friend advised me to say a prayer for safe travels
to Iraq while I was there. The shrine of Imam Ali ar-Rida is the
largest in the Muslim world; one of its courtyards can hold as

many as 200,000 people. Muslims say that the wealthy travel to Mecca, and the poor go to Mashad. Every year 16 million people visit the city—many more than visit Mecca—for its holiness and scenery, but for me the flight there was less pleasant. I flew to Mashad on an ancient Tupolev, a Russian military plane that I was reluctant to board. Iran's air fleet is notoriously outdated and its air safety record is among the world's worst. U.S. sanctions stemming from the Iran and Libya Sanctions Act of 1995 strictly limit the trade American businesses can conduct with Iran, including airplanes and parts. In 2002 the United States scuttled a French deal to sell Airbus planes to Iran because they consisted mostly of American-made parts.

A week later, without any in-air incidents, I departed from Qum with my wife, four sons, and one daughter. Nine hours later, just after dawn, we reached Iraq. Soldiers on the Iraqi side were courteous and made a point of calling me Sayed, the term of respect used for the Prophet's descendants, which I would not have expected. My father had sent a van with two guards to take us from the checkpoint directly to Karbala.

Watching the landscape scroll by was a study in dissonance. Everywhere I looked along the roads, I saw large pictures of Iraq's famed religious leaders, such as Grand Ayatollah Sistani and Grand Ayatollah Mohammad Mohammad Sadeq al-Sadr (Muqtada al-Sadr's father), which Saddam never would have allowed. At the same time, much of the scenery appeared medieval. Forsaken homes, buckled as if by earthquakes, lined rutted, trash-strewn streets. Through four hours of villages and towns, I saw not one house intact. The barefoot children, open sewers, and derelict cars reminded me of Tijuana, Mexico, and this in a country where Saddam had seventy mansions, the combined cost of which could have provided new housing for nearly the entire Iraqi population.

During the Abbasid dynasty (A.D. 750–1258), when Baghdad was the seat of the caliphate, Iraq was known as the Country of Black because from a distance the greenery looked black. Now it really was. The date farms surrounding Karbala had been destroyed, a few converted to orange groves. After the Gulf War rebellion, Saddam had cut down almost all of the 4 million palm trees in Karbala province to eliminate havens for rebel fighters and punish Karbala's date farmers economically. The richest date-producing land in the world was now desert.

My emotion welled up as we drew closer to Karbala. Within six miles of the city, I could see the dome of the shrine of Imam Husayn. From my childhood I remembered the houses, streets, and bazaars between the two shrines for Imam Husayn and his brother Abbas, but these had been demolished. Residents told me later that this happened after the 1991 uprising: Saddam ordered the city shelled, and a street battle destroyed whatever homes had survived. Four out of every five men between twenty and forty years old were arrested and ultimately executed and buried in mass graves, found near Karbala afterward. Two thirds of the city center was lost. The government cleared out the wreckage to remove any traces of rebellion and constructed a central square in their place.

The expansive new square gave the old town area a more modern feel and directly affected our family: our old home near the shrine was gone, razed in the creation of the new square, and my grandfather's two-story house, formerly a few blocks farther than ours from the shrine, now stood on the perimeter of the square, among the houses closest to the shrine of Imam Husayn. My father, who had been born in the house, now lived there with my mother and my youngest brother.

My father was waiting for us when our van arrived. From the front door of the house, one could see the shrine of Imam Husayn across the street. (My father had built a larger house on a piece of land on the new side of town before we fled, but the government had given it to a Baathist school principal who refused to vacate when my father returned.) I gave myself the shortest of breaks for a shower—the July daytime temperatures were hitting three digits—and then set out for the shrine.

What, no lunch first? my father protested. It's so hot out. Why don't you wait?

I insisted that I go at once. I had been away from my Imam and guardian for twenty-six years. As I entered the cool interior of the shrine, his presence overpowered me. Imam Husayn is not dead. Always I could feel him, but nowhere more than here. I felt a deep serenity and a rapture bordering on paralysis. For some time, I wept in peace before his tomb. I apologized to Imam Husayn for being away for so long and explained that I had had no choice.

FACE TO FACE WITH AYATOLLAH SISTANI

Karbala was not yet a safe place in July 2004, but it never crossed my mind that I might be in danger. As the center of the Shia world, Karbala and Najaf bore the brunt of Saddam's oppression, for there resided the essence of what he hated. The post–Gulf War rebellion at Karbala was the fiercest of the uprisings against Saddam, and he punished its residents correspondingly. During the U.S. military's initial ground invasion in 2003, however, Karbala and Najaf saw much less violence than such cities as strategically important Basra, the insurgent stronghold of Falluja, and Baghdad.

Acquaintances and passersby told me I had come at a good time, that things had been much worse previously. Before the war, the average university professor was earning the equivalent of six dollars a month because of the sanctions. Lebanese friends who visited here shared stories of people hunting for food in trash cans. A woman who had nothing to live on, whose husband had disappeared during the 1991 postwar fighting and who apparently feared that she and her three daughters might be forced to turn to prostitution, ranked among the most desperate. One night, she insisted they all sleep together in the same bedroom, for safety's sake. Sometime in the night, she barred the door and set them all on fire, herself included, to prevent her family's humiliation and dishonor.

In March 2004, during massive Ashura celebrations, insurgents had set off a string of explosives near the shrine of Abbas, adjacent to the shrine of Imam Husayn, that killed at least sixty people and injured more than one hundred; this was one of the deadliest attacks on civilians up to that point in the war. In April, adherents of the Shia cleric Muqtada al-Sadr had taken up arms after the Coalition Provisional Authority shut down al-Sadr's newspaper, *Al-Hawza,* in the poor Baghdad neighborhood known as Sadr City. Many Shia in the south protested the closure, and members of al-Sadr's militia, the Mahdi Army, pushed into Najaf and Karbala. After two months of heavy fighting, U.S. forces were able to drive Mahdi militiamen out of Karbala but left the city in ruins.

I spent all ten days of my return to Iraq in Karbala, save for one side trip to Baghdad to visit two aunts and Al-Kadhimiya, the shrine of the seventh and ninth Imams, and a trip to Najaf to visit the shrine of Imam Ali and meet with Grand Ayatollah Sistani. If Karbala is the emotional center of the Shia, Najaf is their academic center. In its importance to Shia scholars, it is not unlike the Vatican for Catholic clergy.

Ayatollah Sistani has lived in Najaf for more than fifty years and has been the highest Shia authority since Grand Ayatollah Abu al-Qasim Khu'i passed in 1992. For decades he has stood as a sage, reassuring voice for families torn asunder by oppression, poverty, and war. When the BBC, as Baghdad was falling, mistakenly reported that angry hordes were accosting Ayatollah Sistani at his house, alarmed Shia from around the country took up arms and hastened to Najaf. Though a Shia leader, he has been a father for all Iraqis. The ayatollah has spoken out against post-invasion looting, reprisals against former Baathist leaders, and stockpiling of gasoline for sale on the black market. In the last case, gas lines dropped by 75 percent after his fatwa. In 2005, the *New York Times* columnist Thomas Friedman recommended him for a Nobel Peace Prize: "How someone with his instincts and wisdom could have emerged from the train wreck that was Saddam Hussein's Iraq,

I will never know," he wrote. "All I have to say is: May he live to be 120."[2]

Islam does not have the fixed hierarchy of Catholicism. Through the tithing system that sends 20 percent of their discretionary income to key ayatollahs for charity, the Shia people determine the influence and prestige of any given scholar. They are free to tithe to the ayatollah they feel is the most knowledgeable. Many believe that's Ayatollah Sistani. He handles and disburses hundreds of millions of dollars, yet he rents his home, which doubles as an office, a small, tidy house on a narrow alley in the old part of Najaf where visitors, statesmen and indigents alike, line up in hopes of a few minutes in his presence.

I called on Ayatollah Sistani with my two eldest sons, Mohamed and Ahmed. His own son Sayed Mohammad Redha greeted us in the ayatollah's office, served us tea, and led us back into the residence, where Ayatollah Sistani sat alone on the floor. The only furnishings in the spotless room were two blankets folded over for visitors to sit on. No servant or aide was present. I had never before met His Holiness. He travels little, and my occasional visits to the Middle East since 1992 had never included Iraq. My father, however, had met him in 2003, after returning to Iraq permanently, and was surprised to learn that Ayatollah Sistani had attended some of his lectures when they were young men (they are the same age) and remembered him as a charismatic speaker. Today our families are joined: a cousin on my father's side is married to the ayatollah's son Mohammad Bakir.

Before my sons and I arranged ourselves in a semicircle in front of him, I hugged the ayatollah, kissed his hand, and asked after his health. He has a chronic heart condition; the month after we talked, he was transported to London for treatment. For years he has shouldered the weight of Iraq's upheavals. His resolve that clergy should refrain from political activism whenever possible spared him the worst punishments of Saddam's regime, yet he has endured frequent threats and harassment from Baathists, several assassination attempts in the 1990s, and, shortly after the Gulf

War, a brief imprisonment because of the thwarted Shia rebellion. The Baathists shut down his mosque, Khadra, in 1994, and it's said he rarely left his house again until U.S. forces arrived in 2003.

Ayatollah Sistani appraised us with his gaze and spoke quietly, in Persian with me and in formal Arabic when he spoke to all of us, but with a Persian accent. He could be loquacious or laconic, I had heard. That day he seemed deep in thought. Everyone, he told us, especially American officials, was requesting meetings with him. His moderate path and the Iraqi public's unyielding trust in him had every faction grasping for legitimacy through his approval. Abstention from politics for religion's sake was no longer possible, he had realized. Politics surrounded him.

Secretary Rumsfeld and the U.S. administrator of Iraq, Paul Bremer, had sent envoys to Ayatollah Sistani many times, and always, through emissaries, he politely declined to see them. My personal belief is that he didn't want history to show that he had met with Iraq's occupiers. His position was delicate. He wished to avoid taking sides, but his paramount objective was self-determination for Iraq. In 2004 Deputy Secretary Wolfowitz had proposed having the Coalition Provisional Authority select parliamentary candidates for presentation at Iraqi-led caucuses. American officials also had a plan to draft an Iraqi constitution and submit it to the interim parliament for ratification. Ayatollah Sistani derailed both efforts and resisted delaying elections over concerns about security. He consistently demanded only one thing: that Iraqis be permitted to choose their own leaders through free elections.

As the war dragged on and Iraqis became increasingly disenchanted with the political process, Ayatollah Sistani called on citizens for patience and a commitment to building a representative government, and frequently he got the response he asked for— but at considerable risk to himself. Before a UN discussion about nationwide elections in 2004, he escaped an assassination attempt, and not for the first time.

Ayatollah Sistani shocked me with his openness and guileless appeal for others' knowledge. Time and again his son entered the room to announce the arrival of other guests, but Ayatollah Sistani insisted we stay and talk. When I asked his advice on whom Muslim Americans should vote for in the fall presidential election, he turned the tables.

I should ask you that question, he said. Because you're well acquainted with American politics, you must tell me whom Muslims should vote for.

I told Ayatollah Sistani we had voted for Bush in 2000 because he had spent time listening to our concerns and had spoken out repeatedly against racial profiling and the use of secret evidence in cases against Muslims, but that now sustained and wanton targeting had disillusioned Muslim Americans into indecision. They felt they had no good options.

Ayatollah Sistani said, You Muslims need to vote for whichever candidate can serve the Muslim causes best. He did not say which one that was.

The ayatollah also asked about President Bush's religion, wondering whether he was Catholic, and we spoke in depth about American society and religion. Until that moment I had imagined he spent all his time reading about Islam and jurisprudence, but I could see that he knew much more than that. He had read the memoirs of President Carter and former secretary of state Henry Kissinger. When he spoke about America, he spoke so knowledgeably. It was obvious to me that he was deeply interested in probing the psyche of America and of its Muslims. At one moment he turned to my son Mohamed, only nineteen at the time, and asked him about his studies at the University of Michigan, where he majored in sociology. Mohamed hadn't expected the ayatollah to ask *him* questions, and he paused, shyly, to gather his thoughts. Ayatollah Sistani reassured him. I don't mean to put you on the spot, he said. I want to learn from you.

The key to his wisdom, I think, is meta-knowledge. He knows what he knows but also acknowledges what he does not. At times he was insistent. I had to inform him that ICOFA had not yet opened an Islamic high school and that boys and girls attended class together. I told him we would segregate classrooms by gender as the funds became available. At the time we still were finishing a new mosque, itself a major undertaking.

You must open an Islamic university, he said. You can't bring our children through twelfth grade and then leave them on their own.

He was right, of course. The difficulty of completing such a project does not make it less obligatory. Our region *should* have an Islamic university. After our meeting, I was able to see more clearly how one man, through divinely inspired knowledge and consensus-building, almost single-handedly prevented Iraq from plunging into civil war.

A SECOND VISIT TO A MORE DANGEROUS IRAQ

On that 2004 trip, a nostalgic longing for home tempered my shock at the widespread destruction of the country and the dire need of its citizens. When I returned in August 2005 to visit my family and the shrine of Imam Husayn, I observed the situation with a fresh eye. President Bush had pledged $20 billion for reconstruction, but I saw few signs of its being spent. In 2004, Iraqis were getting six hours of electricity a day—except for the hotel my family stayed in at first, where the manager would shut it off after half an hour and feign ignorance in response to my questions. We soon checked out. In 2005, people had three hours of electricity—a dangerous situation when summer daytime temperatures can hit 120 degrees. We drank only bottled water. Residents drink from their faucets, but we were told this was risky. The wait for gasoline also was worse than in 2004. Before Ayatollah Sistani's fatwa, lines would stretch for miles and could take an entire day to work through, a preposterous exercise in such an oil-rich country.

In Karbala, word spread that I had met with President Bush and senior officials on several occasions, and people on the street would approach me and ask me to pass along messages. I had to explain that I did not have a direct line to the president and that, at any rate, he did not appear to be entertaining suggestions from outside sources. Nevertheless, their resolve amazed me. With so few basics available, and work hard to come by (May 2005 estimates put the unemployment rate at 50 percent), I saw Iraqis smiling readily, their patience and optimism born from some unknown inner reserves.

In 2005 I had hoped to again visit two of my aunts in Baghdad and to pray at the nearby shrine of the seventh and ninth Imams, but I couldn't find anyone willing to make the sixty-mile trip from Karbala. The outlying areas south of Baghdad, the transitional country between the capital and the heavily Shia settlements of the south, had earned a reputation for danger. Insurgents on the main road harassed travelers, or worse. Visibly identifiable Shia received the most severe treatment. One cab driver I approached about making the journey refused on account of his last foray north, when he had attempted to take three men, one a Shia imam, to Baghdad. Gunmen who controlled the road in a village called Latifiyah, about halfway between Karbala and Baghdad, stopped the car and spat on all the passengers and cursed them. They pulled the imam out of the car and beheaded him in front of the rest. The driver said he would never make the trip again. People called this region the Triangle of Death. (This is different from what journalists often call the Sunni Triangle, a much larger area roughly defined by Baghdad in the east, Ramadi in the west, and Tikrit in the north.)

WHAT THE WAR LEAVES BEHIND

People frequently ask, "Has the war been worth it?" The question leaves me at a loss for words, a state I have seldom known. A debater could point to dozens of facts to justify answering either way, and Middle East experts have remarked how the most knowledgeable observers can spend time in Iraq just days apart and come away with entirely different impressions. During Saddam's regime, I had occasional nightmares about returning to Iraq and imagined I was being chased and hunted. *Why did I go back to Iraq?* I would think, and wake up in a sweat. Just before I visited in 2004, authorities discovered new graves near the town of Hillah where all those buried shared the same first name, Sabah. Eventually the story came out that a student at Baghdad University had been accused of plotting against the government and was interrogated and tortured day and night for eleven days to uncover his accomplices. The student stayed silent until moments before his death, when he gave the name Sabah. He did not give a last name, so Saddam ordered that every student at the university with the first name Sabah be executed. The Sabah Graveyard contains three hundred bodies.

American Muslims overwhelmingly opposed the war, not out of support for Saddam but because of its false rationale; the ill-conceived, ideologically driven planning; and the whiff of western colonialism evident in the administration's intent to remake the Middle East for its own ends. I understand this opposition and share their skepticism about the current state of affairs.

Every year we hear reaffirmations about the validity of the war on terror and the same optimistic rhetoric that the U.S. coalition is making progress. The truth is that America has run out of good options. Even the politicians who have most vocally opposed the war do not have the formula for a successful outcome. America's strength in Iraq lay in its advanced military and highly trained soldiers. The scenario now is much more an internal conflict that requires finessed relationship building and a willingness to take calculated political risks. No matter how much candy we give to the children or how many medical stations we set up, we will still be seen as outsiders, if not occupiers. Images of American soldiers patrolling streets in Humvees sting Iraq's national dignity. The role for Americans now should be to step aside and allow Iraq's political and military leaders to birth their country.

The State Department ought to be applying political pressure to Jordan, Saudi Arabia, Egypt, and other countries in the region to shut down the flow of money, soldiers, and supplies now streaming unchecked into Iraq. Foreign fighters are a tiny percentage of insurgents in Iraq, but their desire to inflict maximum damage, as with suicide bombings, and their systematic destruction of infrastructure make them dangerous far out of proportion to their numbers. The Defense Department should be devoting its resources to training and equipment for Iraqi soldiers and security forces. I believe there has been a reluctance by the U.S. government to fully equip the Iraqi military and police because of concerns about either training or their underground connections to insurgents. I agree that some security forces have been penetrated by insurgents and that American weapons will find their way into the hands of the opposition. But with careful controls and the cultural advantage Iraqi soldiers have in close-quarter patrols and exchanges on the street, the pros of that strategy outweigh the cons. Ultimately, weapons leaks are something we'll have to accept in order to return Iraq to Iraqis.

No one, regardless of his stance on the U.S. role in Iraq, can deny that a new age has arrived. Every Iraqi can see that, no matter what happens, Iraq will never be the same. Iraqi Shia have survived emperors, colonialists, monarchs, and dictators. Every Shia carries in his genes the history of this oppression and seeks its elimination through Al-Mahdi, the twelfth and Hidden Imam. Shia strive to be worthy of selection as one of the 313 companions who will appear alongside Jesus and Imam Mahdi when they launch a new campaign for justice and renewal.

We owe God thanks for our survival. We trusted that through Him justice would prevail, that the historical record of our trials would be documented and somehow brought to balance. In Arabic we frequently use the word *enshallah,* which means "God willing." Shia Islam teaches that we all are free agents whose power to choose comes from God. We can do good and earn God's praise, or do ill and earn his wrath—religion means little without the will to freely embrace or reject it—but always God lights the path. Saddam continually searched for people of principle who might oppose him, and in Iraq those were most often religious scholars, Sunnis and Shia. He launched an antireligion campaign and virtually halted visits to shrines and other expressions of religious sentiment. He suppressed, but he could not obliterate. Once his threats dissipated, people joined in public worship en masse. With suicide bombings quite possible and even likely, hundreds of thousands of Shia have flocked to Najaf and Karbala to celebrate major holidays at the shrines of Imam Ali and Imam Husayn. One day Iraqis will enjoy their freedoms to the fullest.

The people of Karbala selected my father as the leader of a reenergized congregation of three or four thousand at the shrine of Imam Husayn. At Thursday-night services, between fifteen thousand and twenty thousand attend. My father had left Karbala in 1971 an imam and returned an ayatollah, the most respected cleric in town, after founding three Islamic centers and a school in California over seventeen years. He leads the prayer every day. Imam Husayn's shrine has always been my second home. When I attend prayer there now, prostrating over the clay of Karbala, I feel a supreme sense of order and peace at worshipping behind this great man who has dedicated his life to Islam. Without the vision and dutiful actions of generations of my ancestors, from Imam Husayn down to my father, Karbala would not exist. Much has gone right for me to be here now in this place.

I am prepared to honor what Karbala has given to me. Living in America, I have witnessed the highest levels of philanthropy. As of 2005, Americans collectively were donating $248 billion per year to charity.[3] Muslim Americans have embraced the ethic as well. Prophet Muhammad said, "Be merciful with people on earth so the One in heaven shall be merciful to you."[4] I have seen volunteers at the Muslim American Youth Academy, our elementary school, who have hard, demanding jobs still come in regularly to help.

Members of the Islamic Center Women's Society Auxiliary do without sleep and bake bread late into the night to raise funds for the center. The society's cofounder, Hajji Manifeh Dakroub, did this at least twice a week for fifty years, summer and winter, baking from midnight till morning. Before she died of cancer in August 2004, she was still calling the store herself to order flour and other supplies needed for the bread. Members of the congregation continually find funds to contribute to emergencies throughout the world. They have donated to refugees in Bosnia and Kosovo, earthquake victims in Pakistan, 9/11 families in New York, tsunami survivors in Indonesia and Thailand, and Hurricane Katrina victims on the Gulf Coast.

In Karbala, 27,000 orphans, many of whom lost their parents to Saddam and the Mukhabarat, have no official guardians to care for them. Without love and guidance, these children may lose their way forever, and their families, and the community, will be twice victimized. My brothers and I have made plans to set up the largest orphanage in Karbala, and I plan to dedicate much of my efforts and energies to fulfill this dream. Already we have purchased almost two acres of land near central Karbala, a major breakthrough in a place where land is sold in square meters. In addition, my father, who flew to the United States in the fall of 2003 for heart surgery, has resolved to build the first department of cardiology in Karbala and to make sophisticated surgical technologies available to the people of southern Iraq.

Sometimes God directs money your way, and you can pass that along. Sometimes He gives you other ways to help, like the ability to fund-raise from others or the ability to identify what needs doing. To us He has given brotherhood, a bond with which to pool our unique skills and fashion some good out of what must be the city's greatest tragedy, the forsaking of its children. *Enshallah,* we will make it happen.

CHAPTER 12

The Islamic Frontier

What a difference there is between two kinds of actions:
an act whose pleasure passes away but whose consequence
remains, and the act whose hardship passes away but
whose reward stays.[1]
—*Imam Ali*

IF THE WEEKS and months after September 11 brought an unexpected solidarity with Muslim Americans, the subsequent
years have yielded the opposite. In 2002, six months after the attacks, 33 percent of Americans had an unfavorable impression of
Islam.[2] In a 2006 CBS News poll, those with an unfavorable view
composed a near majority: 45 percent.[3] Almost 40 percent in a
Gallup poll taken a few months later supported the idea that
Muslims should carry a special form of ID.[4] Survey after survey
shows the same trend: Muslims are seen as unpatriotic, as back-
ers of Al-Qaeda, and as disrespectful of western ideals. The
Council on American-Islamic Relations reports that the number
of complaints it receives of civil rights discrimination and harassment has jumped sharply, from 602 in 2002 to 1,972 in 2005.[5] Reported hate crimes against Muslims more than tripled from 2002
to 2005, from 42 to 153.[6]

These are alarming statistics for American Muslims, and they
ought to be alarming for all Americans. We look back at the internment of Japanese Americans during World War II and wonder

how a government and its citizenry could have discriminated so baldly on the basis of only appearance and ancestry. We lament that German Americans changed their names and downplayed their origins during World War I out of fear, even though more Americans had immigrated from Germany than from any other country. We know that America refused asylum to tens of thousands of Jews up to and during the Holocaust, and we say never again. Martin Luther King, Jr., charismatically reminded everyone how African Americans struggled against racism long after they supposedly had their freedom.

Now we have yet another case of blatant, widespread discrimination toward a religious and ethnic group, a new discrimination that permeates our society from common citizens to the highest levels of government. We again need to make good on our historical promise and to say, "This will not stand."

The 2006 Gallup poll did contain one encouraging figure: Americans are less likely to disapprove of Muslims if they know one. Instinctively, I know this must be true. The most basic and often unspoken mandate for Muslims is to demonstrate the highest Islamic qualities in every aspect of their lives: personal, professional, and civic. In Islam, anything you do to enhance your spiritual life is a form of worship. The Prophet Muhammad often won converts more through character and compassion than through preaching. One story tells us that the Prophet had a neighbor who didn't believe in Islam. Every day the neighbor put his trash in front of the house of the Prophet, who said nothing and disposed of the garbage himself. One day, the Prophet came out, did not see any garbage, and learned that his unlikable neighbor was sick. He went to visit the man and was met with suspicion and anger. Why did you come? the neighbor wanted to know. The Prophet said that he had two duties: to love his neighbor and to visit the sick. The man then gathered himself and bore witness that there is no god but God and that Muhammad was the messenger of God.

After September 11, I spent endless amounts of time speaking before any group that invited me and describing the Muslim experience in America. I did this in the interest of improved understanding, not conversion. By 2006 I had spoken to more than 230 churches, colleges, and community organizations. When I pick up a paper and read that almost 50 percent of Americans have a negative view of my religion, I do not understand it. For me, this disturbing trend indicates that either we have not been reaching out to enough people or that provocative, slanted reports of international events are eroding our gains. Either way, we have a long way to go.

COMMON GROUND

Muslims want the same things all other Americans do: good schools for their children, safe neighborhoods, a responsive government, clean air, water, and food, and the chance to succeed economically. Muslims embrace Americans' generosity and add to it. They value America's commitment to education and come from all over the world to take part. They accept that their neighbors won't necessarily worship the same way they do, or at all, and they appreciate the American idea of pluralism. If one were to draw a circle on a piece of paper representing Islam's values and the boundaries of what it permits, that circle would fit easily within the larger circle of what the American legal system, and its cultural standards, permit. However you wish to view Islam, nothing about it disserves the American way of life.

The question of whether Islam and democracy are compatible is no longer open. Ayatollah Sistani has shown that they are. His advocacy for an Iraqi state founded on Islamic principles, governed by democratic administrators, and shaped by the people has pointed toward a workable model for a Muslim democracy. He rejects the two extremes in Middle Eastern governments: the unelected regimes that pay just enough lip service to Islamic tradition to head off revolt, and de facto clerical rule, in which scholars become politicians.

Aside from the evidence of existing Muslim democracies such as Indonesia and Turkey, the principles of Islam argue in favor of representative government. The good of the community is paramount in Islam, with every individual equal in the eyes of God and possessing basic human rights. Just as every Muslim has personal and religious duties, he also has a responsibility to the community, which obligates him to express his views on political and social issues. This, too, is a religious duty. Likewise, although Islam did not develop amidst a culture of democracy, the Islamic tradition of *shura* requires political leaders to consult the community on important issues. A passage from the Qur'an lays out the concept: "Whatever ye are given [here] is [but] a convenience of this Life; but that which is with God is better and more lasting: [It is] for . . . those who harken to their Lord, and establish regular prayer; [and] who conduct their affairs by mutual consultation. . . ."[7] So Muslims are bound to air their views to leaders, and rulers are bound to listen, a good start for a democratic system. Ayatollah Sistani has gone further on American democracy by issuing a fatwa calling for Muslims here to vote in elections provided they have a stake in the outcome.

One reason the typical American lacks proper knowledge of the Muslim faith is that some Muslims have not integrated well into the larger society. There's a cycle at work in which some Muslims are reluctant to become more involved in community affairs, and their lack of involvement leads to further alienation. Perhaps without even realizing it, Ayatollah Sistani has illuminated a model for Muslim political organization in America. As in the ayatollah's vision for Iraq, in America, one need not approve of the current leaders or approach in order to participate in government as a voter, volunteer, or candidate.

This is the attitude American Jews adopted early in their history here, and it's one Muslims have noted and tried to learn from. As a closely knit community that did not share the majority faith, Jews worked diligently to overcome stereotypes and familiarize Christians with Jewish beliefs while also embracing American life so fully that, from Irving Berlin to Henry Kissinger—immigrants both—they have come to embody and define many aspects of America itself.

In thought, word, and deed, Muslims must begin turning the flywheel to *make* America a pro-Muslim country, as Jews made it a pro-Jewish country. As Jews did, Muslims need to transfer their political involvement from a broad following of international events to local activism: writing letters to the editor, volunteering, attending political rallies, conducting voter registration drives, and running for office. In 2005, Michigan had 350,000 Muslims and no Muslim judges. When a judicial opening came up that year, I called Governor Granholm, Michigan's first female governor, and asked her to make history by appointing the state's first female Arab Muslim judge. I recommended a highly qualified Dearborn lawyer, Charlene Mekled Elder. After much consideration and review of nine other candidates, Governor Granholm named Judge Elder to the Third Circuit Court of Wayne County. David Turfe joined her as a district court judge after winning election in 2006.

It's a start. With the number of Muslims in Michigan, they already have been accepted as part of the establishment here, and I believe that embrace will eventually extend across the entire country, in some places faster than others. A local political director tells me that the greater Detroit area now has fifty thousand registered Arab voters, which is more than I would have thought. We should have Muslims running for the school board, city council, mayor, state congress, and U.S. Congress; we should have Muslims devoting time to political action committees. They must vociferously make their love of America known and continue to tell the truth about Islam, while reserving the right to disagree on matters of policy. Once people *see* that Muslims are balanced leaders and have the country's best interests at heart, that they stand with America on its bitter days as well as its happy ones, Muslims will be recognized as an integral part of the

American fabric. This is the real meaning of loyalty: outrespecting the country that respects you.

PEACE AND CONFLICT WITH THE POPE

In March 2006, with fifty other scholars, I attended an interfaith conference at the Vatican titled "War and Peace from an Abrahamic Perspective," and sponsored by the Catholic University of America and the International Peace Research Institute in Oslo. In his reception of conference delegates, Pope Benedict XVI met with nine Muslims, including eight Shia; a handful of Jewish religious scholars; and major Christian leaders on such topics as just war, interfaith dialogue, and nuclear weapons. I was the only American Muslim present.

I had always hoped to meet Pope John Paul II but never had the chance. I especially welcomed the invitation from Pope Benedict XVI because he had earned a reputation for unfriendliness toward Muslims when he was John Paul's prefect of the Congregation for the Doctrine of the Faith: he had opposed Turkey's membership in the European Union and evinced skeptical views of Islam. As I took a seat near the pope before he addressed an enthusiastic crowd of twenty thousand in the square, I wondered whether his views had changed. The pope speaks six languages, so speeches take a fair amount of time as he orates in Italian, German, English, French, and Spanish. (He is also fluent in classical Latin.) When he finished, he took his armored cart to circulate through the crowd and returned to speak with those of us from the conference. Originally we were slated to meet with him privately, but his schedule permitted only a brief exchange. The pope was nothing but cordial when he first greeted me on the plaza in a long reception line. A handler nearby announced, "Your Holiness, [I present] Imam Hassan Qazwini, the imam of the Islamic Center of America." Knowing Americans' pride in their country, he smiled widely and called out, "Amerrrricaaa! Amerrrricaaa!" I responded warmly and took the opportunity to ask him to encourage more Muslim-Christian dialogue; he agreed it was necessary.

So I was shocked in the fall of that year when the pope quoted a fourteenth-century emperor, Manuel II Paleologos, in an address about religiously motivated violence. "Show me just what Mohammed brought that was new," Paleologos said, "and there you will find things only evil and inhuman, such as his command to spread by the sword the faith he preached." The pope's intent was to critique the use of violence for advancing religion, but most Muslims, including me, viewed his choice of quotes as poor judgment, even if he meant well and apologized. I could not believe that this was the pope I had met a few months before. Critics of the Muslim response have said Muslims are being overly sensitive by demanding retractions and apologies. I disagree, and said so. The Vatican had taken offense that summer, I pointed out, when Madonna performed in Rome on her "Confessions" tour and staged a mock crucifixion. The show was a cheap, and no doubt profitable, shot at Christianity, and I empathized with the Catholic church's response. On the same note, Muslims are right to hold their religion sacred. Others can criticize, but not insult, and that goes both ways. Cardinal Maida visited ICOFA a few weeks later to extend his sympathies and engage the Muslim community.

I was not scheduled to give a formal lecture at the Vatican conference, but the day after meeting the pope I did build on my theme of improved dialogue. At the end of one of the day's sessions, I emphasized that we must look at other faiths from their adherents' perspectives, and to illustrate, I offered an anecdote about Moses. Moses was traveling in the desert; becoming tired, he sought some relaxation under the shade of a tree. Ants started to bite, so he moved under another tree. The biting continued. He looked up and said, "God, why did you create ants?" God did not respond. He asked a second time, and still received no answer.

The third time he asked, God said, "Listen, Moses, ants have been asking me for a long time, 'Why did you create Moses?' "

A SYMBOL OF MUSLIM AMERICAN SUCCESS

The new Islamic Center of America in Dearborn, just outside Detroit, serves as an elegant ambassador along Ford Road, down the street from the Ford Motor Company's world headquarters. To its left is an Armenian Catholic church, and to its right a Greek Orthodox church. Twin minarets flank the seventy-thousand-square-foot center, built in the Arabic style with white sandstone and a grand, golden central dome. Governor Granholm called it a gem in the state of Michigan at the opening ceremony. The center, the largest in the country, is the fruit of endless fund-raisers, donor relations, and member contributions. The mosque itself holds one thousand people and the banquet hall another two thousand. The kitchen allows us to serve thirteen hundred people for special events and fund-raisers, almost twice what our old center permitted, which is fortunate because construction cost more than $15 million.

Greater Detroit's Islamic growth has mirrored the spectacular gains in the rest of the country. In the 1940s, the city's Muslim population stood at three thousand. Today it is more than 350,000. The trend led ICOFA's leaders to begin initial planning for a new mosque in the early 1990s. The old mosque on Joy Road had been in an upscale area when it was built in 1963, but the neighborhood is now downtrodden since the wealthy abandoned it after riots in the late 1960s. Our congregation, too, had moved, from southwest Detroit into Dearborn and Dearborn Heights, now the heart of Detroit's Arab community, and we needed a center that was convenient and more representative of our culture. The new site comprises the center and the Muslim American Youth Academy and incorporates materials from around the world. The hand-carved mahogany doors are from

Turkey. The Saudi-style carpet is from North Carolina. The chandeliers are from Egypt. The granite comes from Brazil and India, the porcelain from Italy, and the dome from Mexico. All in all, a fitting monument for the Muslim capital of the West.

There is only one problem with our shiny new center—it already feels small. The crowds have forced us to accommodate people in the banquet hall and link them to the mosque with audiovisual equipment. In order to keep up with the increased attendance and unflagging growth, the center, like Muslim Americans' culture and identity, will have to be a work in progress.

MUSLIM EMPOWERMENT

The mandate for dialogue does not apply only to interfaith work. I attended a panel discussion in Michigan in 1999 with two Shia scholars and two Sunni scholars. One audience member asked what Muslims are doing to build good relationships with Christians and Jews. A friend of mine, the respected Sunni leader Mahir Hathout, responded, "Don't worry about building bridges with Christians. We have been doing this. We need to build dialogue and bridges between Muslims themselves." Iraq has reached a point where which sect or faction holds power is more important than what those in power do with it, and militants are willing to die to disrupt the political process. We cannot allow those hostilities to injure our relations and progress in the rest of the world. Wherever they live, Shia and Sunnis have to work together.

That goes for men and women, too. Some time ago I spoke at another Islamic center in Detroit and noticed that the main room, the mosque itself, was divided into two sections, one for men and one for women. The divider ran parallel to my line of sight so that I could see both groups but they could not see each other. The men's section was quiet, but the women's section looked and sounded like a kitchen five minutes before dinnertime. "If I have one wish tonight," I said, "I wish to knock down this wall and have these sisters participate and listen." There was laughter and noise and clapping. Most approved of my sentiment; some didn't.

There is an entrenched belief among some Muslims that they must practice total separation of the sexes in the mosque. Some mosques even bar women from attending: services are for men only, and women must pray at home. Others welcome women but have a partitioned-off section for them, a setup that did not exist in the Prophet Muhammad's day, when men and women prayed separately but were not segregated. Occasionally these partitions engender disruptions because some men send their misbehaving sons away for their wives to supervise. Crying and tantrums break the solemn, purposeful mood, and women should not have to baby-sit during prayer. I submit that mosques with the financial means should make arrangements for a separate child-care room during services or ask that families hire baby-sitters for their youngest children while attending prayer.

If Muslims are to meet the challenges that lie ahead, they will need the full weight and measure of all. The Prophet Muhammad knew that. His first wife, Khadija, gave away her entire wealth for Islam, and in an early battle against the Meccans, a courageous woman named Nusaybah bint Kaab was one of ten loyal Muslims who encircled the Prophet Muhammad, swords in hand, to protect him from death. She was hailed as a great warrior. Certain mosques and communities will have to discard restrictive notions about what a woman can do for Islam. Women can be at least as eloquent, articulate, and thoughtful as men, and we need those voices to carry our message. At ICOFA, women serve as trustees and board members, run campaigns, volunteer, and raise funds. We have common missions, and it is time to move ahead together.

Muslims' unique rituals and concerns call for the advent of cultural guideposts that we must construct ourselves, piece by piece. My wish list for a Muslim American subculture looks like this:

TV. As the new adage goes, five hundred stations and nothing to watch. Muslims need to take advantage of media fragmentation and new delivery technologies to establish our own satellite and cable TV channels that cater to our emotional, religious, intellectual, cultural, and social needs. The Muslims of yesteryear lost touch with their native faith in part because of isolation—nothing around them reinforced its importance. A few Islamic stations have entered the market. Comcast's Bridges TV broadcasts Islamic programs for families, such as educational cartoons and Islamic soap operas. My brother Imam Moustafa Qazwini and I have spoken on Salaam TV, an Islamic Persian- and English-language satellite station out of California. More should join the fray. I would like to see new English-language stations providing all the information and entertainment a Muslim household needs: Middle Eastern news shows, children's cartoons celebrating the lives of the prophets, and Middle Eastern cooking shows.

Radio. In the past two decades, conservatives have demonstrated the power of talk radio to reach a passionate audience and sway opinion. I get occasional calls about a Detroit radio station run by extremist Christian missionaries and intended for Muslims that broadcasts programs antagonistic toward the Prophet Muhammad and Islam. Why not have a radio program for the broader community that also appeals to Muslim Americans? If there's one corner of American culture in need of some diversity, it's mainstream radio. I have a dream to one day produce an Islamic talk show that provides airtime for the complex Islamic points of view TV does not have time for.

Islamic recreation. Muslims' adherence to modest dress and behavior makes leisure activities an area of special concern. When our center's new facilities were under construction, I suggested incorporating an indoor swimming pool. "Imam, are you serious?" someone asked. I was. We should have swimming pools segregated by gender, and sports arenas and teams that cater to Muslim interests, such as soccer and basketball—the best way to engage youth on their turf and spark an interest in Islam. As Imam Ali said, "Do not coerce your children to your own customs and habits, for they are born for a time that is different from yours."[8]

Conventions. The Islamic Society of North America (ISNA), based in Indianapolis, has been holding an annual convention for more than forty years, now usually in Chicago. Notable scholars speak on important topics like politics and family. Forty thousand Muslims attend this conference annually. The Islamic conference circuit has grown, but twenty-first-century issues such as stem cell research and euthanasia, as well as the increasing diversity of American Muslims, will make these sorts of meetings even more important in the years to come. In 2003, the Universal Muslim Association of America began holding a conference attended by Shia Muslims (ISNA is primarily Sunni) in Washington, D.C., over Memorial Day weekend. I hope to see these initiatives continue.

Retreats and youth camps. For the past seven years, ICOFA's Young Muslim Association has been holding a retreat in northern Michigan that connects members with powerful speakers on what it takes to be a good Muslim. The results are visible and dramatic. Young sisters decide to wear hijab. These young men and women start praying five times a day. Removal from the daily blitz of cultural messages allows them time for clarity and focus, qualities that we don't often see encouraged in ads and on TV. Mosques in all areas should consider offering these activities to their members.

Like women, the young will be instrumental in steering the Muslim American communities of tomorrow. All the prophets of God, including Moses, Jesus, and the Prophet Muhammad, started their missions at a young age and were mostly surrounded by young men. Although America is not the alien land to Muslims it once was, we are still adapting. Much of the Islamic literature remains untranslated and unindexed for English-speaking audiences. The new generation is the most capable of distilling Islam's widely diverse traditions from central and eastern Asia, Africa, and, of course, the Middle East into a coherent whole and figuring out how it will be carried on in the years to come. With their supple minds and intuitive understanding of the rhythms and chords of American life, they will most effectively navigate the halls of power with an Islamic compass needle and an American base. We will count on them to carry our messages and concerns to the American public in accent-free, grammatically sound English.

With my full blessing, my oldest son, Mohamed, considered attending law school after studying sociology at the University of Michigan, but ultimately he gravitated to the ancestral calling and traveled to Qum in 2004 to join the seminary. A year later Ahmed, who went to Qum after graduating from Fordson High School, did the same. Both were 4.0 students. Already they have been invited to speak in Michigan, Florida, Costa Rica, Dubai, London, and elsewhere on important holidays. After completing their studies, they plan to return enriched with the knowledge of Islam but as conversant in American ways as any native.

FRIENDS' PRAYERS, GOD'S MERCY

My youngest brother, Hossein, graduated from the University of California–Berkeley with a degree in religious studies in May 2004 and immediately left for Iraq to assist my father at the shrine of Imam Husayn and continue his academic work at the seminary in Karbala. Given our age difference—nineteen years—his experiences more closely approximate my oldest sons' upbringings than my own. He was seven when he came to the United States. In the summer of 2003, he slipped into Iraq to visit my father in Karbala. The next summer, as he began working under my father's tutelage, attending seminary, and teaching English at Karbala University, he married the daughter of one of our cousins. The bride's father, unfortunately, was not present: Hassan al-Tiaef was the cousin who had been held and beaten by the Mukhabarat for eight months in 1980 by mistake, and he had been killed along with two of his brothers by Saddam's soldiers in 1991.

My brothers and sisters and I were not happy when my father announced his intention to go back to Karbala in March 2003. We knew the risks involved, however much my father tried to downplay them. One day after U.S. troops took control of Baghdad, the London-based cleric Sayed Abdul Majid Khu'i, a friend of our family's whose father, an ayatollah, had passed the mantle of Shia leadership to Grand Ayatollah Sistani in 1992, was attacked by a mob and brutally slain outside the shrine of Imam Ali in Najaf. Iraqi and U.S. authorities never proved conclusively who was behind the attack, or even whether Sayed Khu'i was the intended target. For my father, assuming leadership of the shrine of Imam Husayn raised the stakes further. He would be the most visible cleric in Karbala, speaking before thousands of Muslims every day. My grandfather, before he was arrested, had led prayers at the shrine of Imam Husayn but stepped down in 1980, in part to deflect government attention from himself. None of this deterred my father. "I have lived my life," he told us. "I need to go serve my people."

A friend of mine from Europe was visiting Karbala recently and hailed a cab from the airport. As they loaded luggage and settled into the car, they began talking about Karbala's scholars of Islam and whose messages resonated with them. "There's one in particular I like most," the taxi driver said. "Which one?" my friend asked. "This guy Qazwini. Ever hear of him?" My friend smiled. "Do you know where I want you to take me now? . . . I'm going to visit him."

Although he does not consider himself a political leader, my father speaks readily about the problems of the Iraqi people regardless of those problems' origins. He has repeatedly condemned the insurgents' tactics and their crimes, and he also has criticized American and coalition forces for their negligence and mistreatment of Iraqis. A new Middle Eastern television station, Al-Anwar, broadcasts his speeches daily throughout the Arab world and this, combined with his populist stance, has made him an unwitting celebrity—and a target of the insurgency. At age seventy-seven, he is indefatigable. The older he gets, the more duties he takes on. He teaches at the seminary in Karbala, lectures every day, leads prayer every day, and works on the orphanage and heart hospital initiatives. He will continue as an ayatollah and an imam to his last breath. In America, I talk to elder religious leaders of other faiths who tell me they are retired. I can comprehend a retired engineer, doctor, or official, but not a retired religious leader. Laboring for God is not a career; it is a responsibility.

On June 16, 2006, two gunmen on motorcycles drove up alongside my father's car about ten P.M. and shot him twice. He had finished delivering his nightly speech at the shrine of Imam Husayn, and a driver was taking him home. My sister sat in the backseat and conversed with him as they approached a checkpoint and slowed. All she heard was the sound of bullets firing and then my father uttering *"Lah illah ella Allah"* over and over— "There is no god but God." He had been shot in the left arm and right thigh. My brother Hossein followed at some distance in a second car with armed guards. They had not seen what happened and did not realize that the reason my father's car had turned around was that it was now headed to the hospital. During the ten-minute ride to the hospital, he was completely calm.

I had just finished leading Friday prayer at the Islamic Center of America when the caretaker approached me and said, "Your father got hit in Karbala." I took that to mean he had been killed and that the caretaker was speaking euphemistically. Ordinarily I would greet each member of the congregation one by one, but that day I went straight to my office and called Hossein, who had stayed with our father in the emergency room. He's fine, Hossein said. My father had the bullets removed and returned home the next day. The former Iraqi prime minister Ibrahim al-Jaafari visited him. Muqtada al-Sadr stopped by. Tribal leaders and thousands of others came. I personally got calls, letters, and e-mails of support and sympathy from thousands of people. Governor Granholm called me. A week later, a contact in the State Department called and said, "We were shocked to hear about your father. How come nobody told us?" (The State Department—always the last to know!) The contact pledged to write a report and include it in the daily briefing for the president.

Four men were arrested in the case. They appeared to be insurgents, though it wasn't clear what group they belonged to. I don't know what their motives were, but there has been a trend of targeting religious leaders in Iraq. Hundreds of them, including Sunnis and Christians, have been killed since the invasion.

Three and a half weeks later, I met my father in Iran, where he was receiving a month-long follow-up treatment to prevent a bone infection. He left for Karbala the same night his treatment was complete. We begged him to stay a few more days and recuperate, but to no avail. He had to go serve his people.

Apparently my father's will of steel can stop bullets. That trait has seen him through a life of adversity as he stood up for what is right, no matter how unpopular. He is living and leading as we all should—for others, and especially for the young. Strong will alone could not account for his narrow escape and quick recovery from the insurgents' attack, however. In the Islamic tradition, God has ninety-nine names: the Originator, the Just, the Protector. Christians emphasize God's love. Muslims stress his mercy, referenced in the first lines of the Qur'an and frequently in daily prayers: "In the name of God, the Compassionate, the Merciful." As Muslims in search of the straight path, we submit ourselves to a gracious, benevolent God and in turn seek his protection. As people, Muslims and non-Muslims alike deserve refuge from the earthly horrors we regularly inflict upon each other.

Our stay here is short; pleasures and victories mean little if we don't guide and support the next generation. The convergence of cultures, ideas, and religions around the world is already under way and will beget new cultures, new breakthroughs, and, if history's pattern holds true, new conflicts. In all of our dealings, we must surrender our enmity, open our hearts, and indulge, as Abraham Lincoln said in his first inaugural address, the better angels of our nature.

Epilogue

I WAS IN SAUDI Arabia for the hajj when I heard about Saddam's hanging. We were three days out from Mecca and traveling to Jamarat that day for the ritual stoning of the devil. After I finished my prayer in the morning chill, some celebrating pilgrims from Dearborn approached me to share the news. It was all over the Arab media, and with 2.3 million people collected in one place, it didn't take long for word to spread.

The jubilation was contagious. So finally it was over. At a Mukhabarat facility renamed Camp Justice by the U.S. military, on the same spot where his operatives had executed thousands of innocent people, Saddam was dispatched to face the ultimate authority. My first thought was of God's punishment of Pharaoh for his enslavement of the Israelites. Saddam loved to compare himself to the great Arab statesmen of history; I rank him among the worst leaders the Arab world has ever suffered. I've often considered him to be a contemporary version of Yazid, the imperial caliph who had Imam Husayn and his companions murdered at Karbala, but Yazid did not have to answer for his crimes in this life. Saddam's fate reminded me more of the fate of Pharaoh, upon whom God unleashed the waters of the Red Sea. The Qur'an tells us that God dispensed divine justice in designing Pharaoh's end:

> And We made the children of Israel to pass through the sea, then Pharaoh and his hosts followed them for oppression and tyranny; until when drowning overtook him, he said: I believe that there is no god but He in Whom the children of Israel believe and I am of those who submit.
>
> What! now! and indeed you disobeyed before and you were of the mischief-makers. But We will this day deliver you with your body that you may be a sign to those after you, and most surely the majority of the people are heedless to Our communications.[1]

For decades I have prayed for justice for my family and for those whose lives have been torn apart by Saddam's actions. I needed to be reassured that God would not ignore the cries of the innocent and the oppressed—and, though reparation was a long time in coming, He did not. As my father's Mukhabarat file with pictures of us in America showed, we could never completely escape his grasp while Saddam lived. He was the dark matter around which millions of Middle Easterners revolved, and with his death it was as if we were all released from an orbit of fear. If not for Saddam, I would probably still be living in Karbala right now.

Yet in the absence of his terror-enforced order, chaos has taken hold. I would like to think that Saddam's execution marked a new age for Iraq beyond holding him accountable for his violent reign. Instead we have seen the rise of a thousand would-be Saddams who are destroying Iraq just as wantonly as Saddam himself did when he was alive. They do not care about the innocence of their human targets or the sanctity of the mosques they bomb. With the array of insurgent groups all pursuing different agendas, it is unlikely, were any of them able to overthrow Iraq's elected government, that they could institute a stable, viable government regardless of its nature. The civil war they wage will cause only more heartache for suffering Iraqis.

Unfortunately, Iraqis who have looked to their Arab brethren for help in quelling the violence have received little support. Many Arabs, surprisingly, actually mourned Saddam's execution and hailed him as a martyr. The pro-Saddamists in the streets of the Middle East identified with his defiance of the West at any cost. Pro-Saddamist Arab governments feared that praising Saddam's fate would invite more active scrutiny of their own similarly corrupt regimes. The Arabic satellite TV station Al-Jazeera had its anchors wear black for three days, and the female anchor who broke the news about Saddam's execution actually choked up on camera. In Libya, leader Muammar Gaddafi declared three days of national mourning and erected a statue of Saddam in Tripoli. Such gestures ignore Saddam's true legacy in favor of expedient posturing at a time when Iraq needs border security and solidarity, not rhetoric. Once again, justice awaits.

★   ★   ★

America is constantly changing. Its values change, its economy changes, and what it means to be an American changes. Those dynamics are inevitable. They can be shaped or controlled by movements or policies, but they cannot be stopped. They are part of what makes America great. The evolution of the American identity is one reason I have such high hopes for the future, despite the current political climate and opinion of American Muslims.

The early Muslim arrivals to U.S. shores, mostly men, trickled in alongside much larger waves of Middle Eastern Christians. Those Muslims, referred to as "Mohammedans" at the time, worked in the lowest economic strata as peddlers and laborers to send money to their families back home, or they saved to bring them here. In Dearborn, thousands of Arab immigrants flocked to Henry Ford's automobile assembly lines in the first half of the twentieth century, the foundation for the thriving Muslim community to come. Forty years ago, the United States had only a handful of mosques. Thirty Americans made the pilgrimage to Mecca each year.

Today there are more than four thousand mosques for the 6 to 7 million Muslims who call America home, and 12,000 of them go to Mecca annually for the pilgrimage. A UCLA survey reports that from 1974 to 2000 the percentage of first-year Muslim students at American universities rose from .1 percent to 9 percent.[2] The per-capita income of Muslims is above the national average; many of them are professionals. If you don't already have a Muslim neighbor, you surely will before long: an estimated 25,000 Americans convert to Islam every year.[3] As Islam here progresses from curiosity to phenomenon to establishment, I believe that Muslims increasingly will be seen as valuable community leaders and as essentially American. The 2006 election of Keith Ellison, the first Muslim elected to the U.S. Congress, signaled the leading edge of that transition. (Ellison, a Democrat from Minnesota, took his ceremonial oath of office on a copy of the Qur'an once owned by Thomas Jefferson.)

This is not a new pattern. Since the country's founding, most every immigrant group has undergone harsh trials of initiation—accusations of ineptitude, inferiority, disloyalty, and cultural contamination, and the marginalization that goes along with those perceptions. As time wears on, those prejudices fade, but not without hard work and dedication to proving them wrong. There is no question that the fallout of September 11's terrorist attacks set Muslims, particularly Arab Muslims, back decades, possibly a generation. In our quest to clear our names and move forward, we have drawn strength, inspiration, and wisdom from the African Americans who have campaigned so long for justice themselves. They have learned from hard-fought battles, some of them centuries old, how to protect their civil liberties and spread the truth about their cause. New Muslim immigrants especially owe a debt of gratitude to the African American

Muslims who have paved the way for the mainstreaming of Islam in this country.

I remember that at President Clinton's 1999 prayer breakfast at the White House, he told me, "You Muslims have a priceless opportunity to give Americans an accurate understanding of Islam. Why not take advantage of this opportunity?" I hope that all Muslims will take a cue from other minorities, religious and ethnic, who have long organized themselves, and take advantage of the opportunity.

Acknowledgments

I received help and support from many people in my work on *American Crescent*, and I would like to thank the following individuals for their invaluable contributions in helping me bring it to fruition:

Will Murphy
Lea Beresford
Brad Crawford
Geneive Abdo
Eide Alawan
Dan Mekled
Hiba Hassan
Najah Bazzy
Atef Elsayed
Congressman John Dingell and his staff
Jeff Kleinman
Alex Kronemer

The full list of those whom I have relied on and gained perspective from in developing the book is much longer. To those who fall into the second category, know that your help has not gone unnoticed or unappreciated. May God bestow His blessings on all of you.

Americans Ask About Islam: 20 Questions

FROM THE MOMENT I set foot in America, I have been answering questions about Islam for Muslims and non-Muslims alike. I actually honed my English skills by finding the proper words to explain Islamic concepts to American audiences! Since taking over as imam of the Islamic Center of America in Dearborn, Michigan, and especially since September 11, 2001, I have spoken to hundreds of American civic and religious groups—230 at last count—and the same thoughtful questions tend to surface again and again. Islam's outlook on war, peace, women, and other religions are the most popular topics, and I have addressed them all here.

1. IS ISLAM PEACEFUL?

Islam is undoubtedly a peaceful religion. In formal settings, the first words Muslims exchange are *"As-salaamu alaikum"* ("Peace be with you") and *"Wa alaykum as-salaam"* ("And with you, peace"). Indeed, one of the ninety-nine names for God in Islam is "The Peace." In chapter 5, verse 32, the Qur'an says, "Whoever slays a soul, unless it be for manslaughter or for mischief in the land [genocide], it is as though he slew all men; and whoever keeps it alive, it is as though he kept alive all men." Chapter 60, verse 8, says, "God does not forbid you respecting"—meaning he compels us to respect—"those who have not made war against you on account of [your] religion, and have not driven you forth from your homes, that you show them kindness and deal with them justly; surely God loves the doers of justice."

But the best proof of Islam's peaceful message is the Prophet Muhammad himself. He fought many battles in his life, but he did so to defend his people and community, and he established an elaborate framework for just war in Islam. (See Question 4.) The Prophet Muhammad received God's message in seventh-century Arabia, at a time of frequent warfare, instability, and, for many, deprivation. Tribes routinely raided neighboring tribes to obtain life's necessities while ignoring society's underprivileged and en-slaved. One reason the Prophet Muhammad met with such vio-lent resistance in Mecca upon the revelation of Islam was his advocacy for a new social order. He stressed people's essential equality, called on the rich to help take care of the poor, and preached that violence should be avoided wherever possible. He condemned female infanticide. He purchased slaves and set them free. As he developed the means, he adopted many orphaned chil-dren and raised them in his household. Many of the earliest con-verts to Islam were from this underclass.

Critics of Islam cite other passages from the Qur'an to justify an opinion of Islam as violent. Those verses that seem to condone aggression or warfare are taken out of context and are not more shocking than line-by-line quotes from other holy books, includ-ing the Bible. In the faith's early years, Muslims were a small band of vulnerable and controversial followers nearly engulfed by bru-tal adversaries. The real threat those adversaries posed, whether in Mecca or Medina, required the Prophet Muhammad to set the boundaries of defense without expanding war. Numerous passages in the Qur'an make that clear, and the rule is summarized in chapter 8, verse 61: "If the enemy incline toward peace, do thou [also] incline toward peace, and trust in God: for He is the One that heareth and knoweth [all things]." Other examples in the Qur'an include 2:190, 2:194, and 4:90.

Islam's peaceful nature also has been manipulated historically by schemers and extremists. There are no membership requirements to be a Muslim. One must only profess faith and perform obligatory duties, such as prayers, charity, and fasting. Today, we still have violent extremists who exploit Islam as a religious rationale for their acts, but they cannot and should not speak for true Muslims.

2. DIDN'T ISLAM SPREAD BY THE SWORD?

The history of early Islam shows that nations and tribes accepted Islam wholeheartedly and converted voluntarily. Undoubtedly Muslims fought wars in those years: with the Persian Sassanid empire, the Byzantine (Roman) empire, and neighboring tribes of the Arabian Peninsula; among the clashes were the famous battles against Meccans in the Prophet Muhammad's lifetime. But these battles were not about forcing other peoples to convert to Islam. Early on, they were about preserving Muslims' own rights to worship; later, during the Umayyad and Abbasid empires, they involved political goals: trade, land, and control.

When the Prophet Muhammad entered Mecca unarmed in A.D. 630 and accepted the surrender of its inhabitants, he not only granted them amnesty for their crimes during war, he also left them free to worship as they wished. Many, in awe of his ideals and fairness, converted to Islam. In a verse revealed during the Prophet Muhammad's early years in Medina, the Qur'an reinforces his actions: "There is no compulsion in religion," chapter 2, verse 256 says. "Truly the right way has become clearly distinct from error."

The *Peak of Eloquence,* a collection of Imam Ali's writings and sayings, relates a story of the Muslim attitude toward freedom and justice. During the period of Imam Ali's caliphate in Kufa, Iraq, a bold man took Imam Ali's shield and claimed it as his own. The witnesses who could have refuted the man's claims were traveling, yet Imam Ali asked a judge to hear the case and render a decision. In the course of the hearing, the judge honored Imam Ali and tried to address him as "Commander of the Believers," but Imam Ali insisted on absolute neutrality in the case, and he lost the dispute—and his shield—because of it. Afterward, the man caught up with Imam Ali and returned the shield. "Imam, teach me Islam," he said. "I am a Christian, and I want to be converted."

"Did anybody force you to do that?" Imam Ali asked.

"No, Imam," he said, "but your behavior of treating even a non-Muslim subject as your equal, the prestige you granted to justice and fair play . . . made me feel that Islam is a great religion. . . . You could have easily ordered me to be killed and my property looted, and nobody would have dared ask reasons for your actions. . . . I have never heard of such a ruler before you."

Certainly Muslims in the course of history have encouraged others to convert, and at the peak of Islamic political strength, there would have been financial incentives for poorer civilizations to do so. But ultimately one's religion must be a personal decision. Of the importance in recognizing the majesty of creation, God told the Prophet Muhammad in chapter 88, verse 21, "Therefore do remind, for you are only a reminder. You are not a watcher over them."

3. WHAT IS JIHAD?

"Jihad" might be the most misunderstood word in Islam. Jihad, often cited on newscasts and in terrorists' propaganda videos, is most important in Islam as personal reckoning, a concept Christians and Jews know well: the daily struggle to overcome one's base desires and fulfill the call of the higher spirit. Imam Ali said God created three kinds of entities: one with intellect but without desire, the angels; one with desire but not intellect, the animals; and one with both, human beings. A person whose intellect overwhelms his desires, Imam Ali said, stands above angels. One whose desire overcomes his intellect is worse than animals. This personal reckoning is called the greater jihad, and almost anything a Muslim does to improve himself or herself and follow God's law qualifies: getting an education, praying, donating to a philanthropy, and helping others are but a few examples.

The definition most non-Muslims know is that of Islamic holy war. The Prophet Muhammad called that the *lesser* jihad. Like the greater jihad, it is also about struggle and striving, but externally. It is a defensive jihad, meant to correct injustice or protect Muslim communities and practices. Jesus said that he who denies a wounded person should be treated the same as the one who wounds him. In the early Muslim community in Medina, the sense of societal obligation was very real. The city constantly came under attack by Meccans who felt threatened by Islam, and Muslims had a civic and religious duty to defend themselves and help fellow Muslims.

However, not just anyone can declare a lesser jihad. Only the highest Islamic scholars are qualified to interpret the circumstances. Osama bin Laden, for example, is not qualified to declare a jihad. Muslim scholars agree that the violent acts committed in Islam's name against innocent people around the world are not legitimate jihad. These scholars have news for the perpetrators: they are sinners and criminals, not heroes, and they will not end up in heaven as they might think.

4. WHAT DO MUSLIMS CONSIDER "JUST WAR"?

The Prophet Muhammad held what might be the two most difficult societal roles to reconcile: he was both head of state and the messenger of God, the moral conscience of his community. From the time he ascended to the leadership of Medina, he had to unite a fractured society (the two native tribes of Medina, the Aws and the Khazraj, had been warring for a century before his arrival) and defend against outside attack while simultaneously instituting the high philosophical principles he had preached so fervently in Mecca before his exile. He established a strict code for just war at a time when the rules of war were mostly governed loosely by tradition or expediency. Midnight raids, enslavement, mutilation, torture, and assassination were common, so the Prophet Muhammad's new standards were far more humane than what the clashing tribes were accustomed to.

The Prophet Muhammad identified two contexts in which warfare is permissible: for self-defense and to correct an injustice or resist oppression. In these cases, he said, war may become mandatory. He put his prescriptions into practice at the Battle of Badr, a brief but decisive fight between Medina's Muslims and the Quraysh tribe of Mecca in which he refused to initiate violence. Instead he prayed and looked for a sign from God, and his men did not attack until they themselves were attacked. The Prophet Muhammad's seven rules for just war, then, appropriately begin with not attacking others first.

1. **Do not initiate war.** War must be a last resort, once all peaceful alternatives are exhausted. Even then, Muslims should refrain from aggression if the opponent also refrains.

2. **Fight only men on a battlefield.** Women, children, and the elderly are to be excluded and should not be pursued. The conflict should not extend to villages and sanctuaries.

3. **Respect the wounded.** Injured combatants no longer able to fight should not be pursued or killed.

4. **Refrain from environmental warfare.** The Prophet Muhammad forbade the cutting of trees and the spreading

of poison in the land of the enemy—the poisoning or filling of wells, for example. In modern times the proscription would apply to chemical, biological, and nuclear weapons.

5. **Treat combatants and captives humanely.** Their basic needs should be met, and they should remain free of torture or physical coercion.

6. **Respect houses of worship.** Conflict should not extend to mosques, churches, or synagogues, or to priests, monks, or other clergy.

7. **Avoid using deception to overcome the enemy.** Trickery, such as attacking at night when others are sleeping, is immoral.

Under these rules, it's easy to see that few wars fought then or now could qualify as just. In Islam, just wars are decreed to be such by the highest Muslim religious authority (presently Ayatollah Sistani for Shia; for Sunnis, a senior religious authority such as the Grand Sheikh of Al-Azhar in Cairo).

Whether a war is just also depends on the Prophet Muhammad's command to consider injustice or oppression on the part of the enemy. If the enemy will not rectify an injustice it commits, one has a duty to fight to correct that. The Bosnia war is one modern example. One hundred thousand people died in Bosnia and Kosovo as a result of war and ethnic and religious cleansing, so although the United Nations and United States were not attacked, they were right to send troops to prevent more mass deaths.

5. WHY DO MUSLIMS NOT CONDEMN ACTS OF TERRORISM?

Muslims in fact frequently and strenuously condemn terrorist acts all over the world, though those condemnations are not always reported. The acts themselves and the extremists who applaud them seem to gain all the attention of American media, while the moderate, prudent voice of the scholar falls on deaf ears. After the 9/11 attacks, Muslims in greater Detroit, my home, gathered for numerous candlelight vigils, and they have gathered to denounce terrorist tactics several times since. First-generation Muslim Americans often have immigrated here to escape just that sort of barbarism and hatred, and they appreciate the peaceable and orderly nature of life in the United States.

6. WHAT IS ISLAM'S VIEW OF CHRISTIANS AND JEWS?

Many I speak to are surprised to learn of the respect Islam has for Christians and Jews. In the Qur'an they are called the People of the Book, meaning that they subscribe to the core ideas and traditions espoused in the Torah and the Bible, which Islam is based on. Like Judaism and Christianity, Islam is an Abrahamic faith. The last of the three divinely revealed, monotheistic religions, Islam reveres Adam, Noah, Abraham, Moses, Jesus, and many other prophets. The Prophet Muhammad himself was a descendant of Abraham through his first son, Ishmael. "And dispute ye not with the People of the Book," the Qur'an says in chapter 29, verse 46, "except with means better [than mere disputation], unless it be with those of them who inflict wrong [and injury]; but say, 'We believe in the revelation which has come down to us and in that which came down to you; Our God and your God is One; and it is to Him we bow [in submission].' "

All of the prophets mentioned above are named in the Qur'an. It devotes an entire chapter to Mary (chapter 19), in which God chronicles Jesus' virgin birth and the reaction from Mary's contemporaries, and He speaks of Jesus 124 times, while the Prophet Muhammad is mentioned by name only four times. Non-Muslims in the West, however, hear talk of "infidels" and "disbelievers." The Qur'an also speaks of infidels, but in very specific terms. "Infidel" does not refer to just any Christian or Jew but to someone who aims to harm or kill Muslims for practicing their faith. The Prophet Muhammad lived in an adversarial world where some coexisted peacefully and others, including some Jews and smaller numbers of Christians, were combative. He accommodated the People of the Book where possible and allowed them to live as protected peoples (*dhimmi*) in Muslim communities and worship privately in their own fashion. In exchange, they paid a nominal protective tax but were not expected to defend the community in battle, no doubt a fair tradeoff.

Another passage from the Qur'an (3:113–15) shows the Prophet Muhammad's nuanced, open-minded outlook on Christians and Jews: "Of the People of the Book are a portion that stand [for the right]; they rehearse the Signs of God all night long, and they prostrate themselves in adoration. They believe in God and the Last Day; they enjoin what is right, and forbid what is wrong; and they hasten [in emulation] in [all] good works: They are in the ranks of the righteous. Of the good that they do, nothing will be rejected of them; for God knoweth well those that do right."

7. DON'T TODAY'S MUSLIMS HATE JEWS?

As explained in Question 6, Jews have always enjoyed an excellent status in Muslim countries, as People of the Book, and Muslims are therefore called upon to demonstrate respect and tolerance for both the people and their faith. Chapter 7, verse 159 of the Qur'an says, "Of the people of Moses [that is, the Jews] there is a section who guide and do justice in the light of truth." Muslim states have never experienced what we know as anti-Semitism. That was a product of Christian Europe, a religiously motivated bias that many scholars believe led directly to the Holocaust.

Arab history is rich in Jewish poets, physicians, and politicians—being both Arab and Jewish is not a contradiction—and prominent Jewish communities exist in many Muslim countries, including Iraq, Iran, Syria, Yemen, and many others. They have the same rights as any other citizen and attend synagogues and, if they wish, private schools. In Iraq, the minister of finance was traditionally Jewish, at least until 1948 and the establishment of Israel.

The animosity between certain Jews and Arabs—not Muslims only—exists because of real estate, not religion. Palestinians whose ancestors had lived on their lands for centuries have been the subjects of systematic crackdowns by the Israeli government since that country's founding. Over the years, hundreds of thousands of Palestinians, especially Christians, have fled. The tragic irony of the Holocaust is that a genocide against Jews gave way to terrible crimes against Palestinians: militias threatened and murdered people. Farms were destroyed. Terrorist groups set off bombs in crowded marketplaces and worked to assassinate opposition leaders. More than a hundred Palestinians died in 1948 at the massacre of Deir Yassin, a village outside Jerusalem taken over by Zionist forces. In 1982, during the Lebanese civil war, Israeli troops helped facilitate the massacre of thousands at Sabra and Shatila, two refugee camps on the southwest side of Beirut.

Over seven decades, the attacks and reprisals carried out against the respective opponents have many backstories, complexities, and shades of gray. No one is without fault. But, likewise, no one can credibly deny that before all the wanton bloodshed, a diverse population of Palestinians had been living together peacefully in their homeland for centuries. In the relative blink of an eye, they saw entire towns leveled, their livelihoods eliminated, and fences constructed to keep them at bay. Perhaps 750,000 were forced out of Palestine. Today, 3 million Palestinians live as refugees, many of them in miserable conditions.

Meanwhile, Israel opens its doors to Jews from around the world to live on and profit from the lands usurped from its prior inhabitants. At least 2 million Palestinians are living in the diaspora while Israel still occupies territories in the West Bank (Palestinian), Golan Heights (Syrian), and Shebaa Farms (Lebanese).

Peace between Arabs and Jews will be possible and lasting only if it is combined with justice. The entire world needs to appraise the events taking place there with fresh eyes and work to correct the policies behind them. I pray that one day peace and justice will return to this part of the Middle East.

8. IS IT TRUE THAT THE PROPHET MUHAMMAD KILLED SEVEN HUNDRED JEWS?

The story of the Banu Qurayza (a tribe of Arabian Jews contemporary with the Prophet Muhammad, and different from the Banu Quraysh of Mecca) is much cited among those who wish to believe that he had a vendetta against the Jews. As the Prophet Muhammad's power in Medina grew, various tribes and factions in the city and surrounding areas had to choose sides: with the Muslims of Medina or with the wealthy Quraysh, the traders of Mecca. Some of the Jewish clans of Medina were also traders and were reluctant to jeopardize their trade relations with the Quraysh. They continued to do business with them and, more alarmingly for Muslims, relayed military intelligence to them.

The Prophet Muhammad, aware of the duplicity going on around him, developed a document called the Constitution of Medina whose signers pledged their mutual loyalty and, at minimum, financial aid to the people of Medina in the event of outside attack. The Prophet Muhammad wanted assurance that his neighbors would not betray him in the ongoing battles with Mecca. Twice Jewish tribes violated the constitution, once attempting to assassinate the Prophet, and yet he allowed them to leave Medina with most of their property despite the Arab custom of killing the offending men and enslaving women and children for committing such treason. Prior to a landmark engagement with the Quraysh called the Battle of the Trench, the Muslims had been defeated badly, and one of the most prominent Jewish tribes of Medina, the Banu Qurayza, anticipated the Muslims' imminent demise. During the Battle of the Trench, so called because of the strategic defensive trench the Prophet Muhammad ordered dug around the perimeter of Medina, the Banu Qurayza overtly sided with the Quraysh and even resupplied them, an important advantage since the battle lasted for a month.

The Quraysh did not win as expected, however. They were routed and the remaining soldiers forced to retreat to Mecca. The Prophet Muhammad knew he would have to confront those who had violated the Constitution of Medina and had banked on the Muslims' annihilation, but because he had a clear interest in the dispute, he allowed the Banu Qurayza an arbiter to determine their fate. Both sides agreed to honor the decision of a man named Sa'd ibn Mu'adh, a Muslim native of Medina whom the Banu Qurayza considered a friend. Sa'd was not as forgiving as the Prophet Muhammad had been toward the previous conspirators, and he decreed that the men be executed and the women and children be made captives. The highest historical estimates place the number of Banu Qurayza killed at 700, but more authoritative sources say 350 were killed. It is important to note that they were executed for treason, not for being Jews. The Constitution of Medina did not forbid its Jewish signers from practicing their religion, and some non-Jewish allies of the Banu Qurayza who also violated the treaty were executed as well.

9. IS HEAVEN ONLY FOR MUSLIMS?

None of us can say for sure who will and won't be in heaven until the day of God's Judgment, but Islam's close ties to Judaism and Christianity signal a heaven that is open to the People of the Book (see Question 6). In chapter 2, verse 62 of the Qur'an, God says, "Those who believe [in the Qur'an], and those who follow the Jewish [scriptures], and the Christians and the Sabians—and who believe in God and the Last Day, and work righteousness, shall have their reward with their Lord; on them shall be no fear, nor shall they grieve."

10. WHAT IS THE DIFFERENCE BETWEEN SHIA AND SUNNIS?

Shia and Sunnis are not as different as some people believe. Westerners sometimes compare the two groups to Catholics and Protestants, but our differences do not reach even that level and are more historical than theological. The split between Shia and Sunnis dates to the end of the Prophet Muhammad's life. Shia believe that Imam Ali, who was the Prophet's cousin and son-in-law, as well as the first man to convert to Islam, was his designated successor. Numerous traditions attest to this, but perhaps the most famous and persuasive is the story of Ghadir Khum, a stream where the Prophet Muhammad gave a sermon after his last pilgrimage to Mecca. Tens of thousands of Muslims heard him name Imam Ali as the next leader of all Muslims. Two months later, the Prophet Muhammad died.

Sunnis assert that this and other traditions have been misinterpreted and that the Prophet wanted his companions to decide for themselves who ought to lead them. Shortly after the Prophet's death, a few of his most prominent companions held a small, secret council and made a pact to name Abu Bakr as caliph, the Prophet Muhammad's successor. Under the caliphate no Muslim had a divine right to rule, but there also was no established provision for how the leader ought to be selected. Various disputes arose as the balance of power swung to this or that tribe, and as the Muslim community grew, the most ambitious and calculating leaders began dominating the caliphate and ruling Muslims more as emperors than as benevolent religious figures.

In the Shia school of thought, a divine spark passed from the Prophet Muhammad to Imam Ali, his closest male heir, and down to generation after generation of this line of the Prophet's descendants, known as the twelve Shia Imams. Imam Ali was the first Imam and, with his wife Fatima (who was the Prophet Muhammad's daughter), begat this line of Shia leaders. They were not messengers of God as was the Prophet, but their leadership was divinely inspired and infallible, and they flawlessly transmitted his teachings to subsequent generations of Muslims with the same wisdom and piety. Many Muslims, though not most, saw them as the true and rightful leaders of Muslims. As one might imagine, the later emperor-caliphs viewed the Shia Imams as dangerous rebels and continually suspected them of plotting to overthrow the caliphate. Many of the Imams were imprisoned, poisoned, or both.

The political differences between Shia and Sunnis engendered some differences in custom, as both branches have their own collections of texts and traditions they recognize as valid. Sunni legal rulings rely heavily on the work of four esteemed eighth- and ninth-century scholars, while in Shi'ism the highest scholars have more flexibility to interpret existing law. Today Sunnis generally recognize Al-Azhar University in Cairo as the highest seat of Sunni scholarship while Shia authority has resided in various cities and with various scholars over time but at present rests with Ayatollah Sistani in Najaf, Iraq.

Shia and Sunnis agree on 90 percent of Islamic practices. Both Shia and Sunnis pray five times a day, for example, but Shia pray on three occasions, combining the noon and afternoon prayers and the dusk and night prayers. Shia and Sunnis frequently worship at each others' mosques, a practice one would rarely see among Catholics and Protestants. Intermarriage is common between Shia and Sunnis, and many are reluctant to distinguish themselves as one or the other. Rather, they prefer, as I do, simply to be called Muslim.

11. IS GOD MALE OR FEMALE?

As an intangible, omnipotent supreme force, God is neither male nor female. Arabic, like English, has separate pronouns for masculine and feminine, and the Qur'an refers to God using masculine pronouns, as most holy books do. Arabic also distinguishes between the one almighty God (*Allah*) and generic references to any god, whether male (*elah*) or female (*aleha*). The use of masculine pronouns reflects the limitations of language to describe God and also the early influence of men in discussions of God. Historically, people have ascribed feminine qualities, somewhat arbitrarily, to countries, ships, and the moon, associations that still crop up in English today. All manner of inanimate objects take masculine or feminine pronouns that differ from language to language and seem to bear no correlation to their actual traits. Who can say why?

The Qur'an also frequently uses the plural pronouns "We," "Us," and "Our" in place of "He," "Him," or "His." This is not meant to be taken literally as an indication of multiple gods. Kings of old used the same "royal we," which I think of as "we the magnificent." Like the male singular pronouns used, these pronouns do not reflect the actual nature of God.

12. HOW DOES ISLAM VIEW WOMEN?

Islam has a long history of promoting women's rights. Like many societies of fourteen hundred years ago, pre-Islamic Arabia displayed an appalling attitude toward women. They were regarded as property with no legal standing, and fathers were therefore reluctant to accept the burden of raising daughters when they could have sons. Female infanticide was common and accepted. The Prophet Muhammad's teachings about the place of women in society, like those on the poor and enslaved, were nothing short of revolutionary. He himself had four daughters; both of his sons died in infancy. "He who is given three daughters, he feeds them, he takes care of them, and he accords benevolent treatment toward them, they will be protection against Hell-Fire," he said. A man asked him, "What about two?" The Prophet Muhammad said, "Two as well" (from Musnad Ahmad, hadith no. 22881).

The Prophet Muhammad granted Muslim women the right to marry and divorce as they wished, to inherit money and property, and to participate as citizens in the community. He accorded them a position of honor and respect within the family that they still hold today. I counsel many people and bring young men and women together in marriage, but it is my wife who holds our family together and instills the highest ideals in our children. The history of Islam is filled with the contributions of great women. The Prophet Muhammad's first wife, Khadijah, was a wealthy merchant in Mecca who had hired him as an employee. She spent untold amounts of her wealth in spreading Islam and sustaining its supporters. Fatima, the daughter of the Prophet Muhammad, is exalted for challenging the political establishment after her father's passing and as the revered wife of Imam Ali and the mother of Imam Hasan and Imam Husayn.

There can be no doubt that Islam's perspective on women differs from that of contemporary Christians and secular westerners. The Islamic position is admittedly more traditional. A quick comparison between Islamic and western Christian cultures shows that the latter have changed much more rapidly in the past hundred years than has the former, but historically the Islamic view of women has not been dramatically different from that of other religions. While American women gained the right to vote in 1920, women in Islam have had full rights, including the right of political participation, since the faith's early days. We have yet to see a female president in the United States, but numerous women have assumed top leadership roles in several Muslim countries: Prime Minister Khaleda Zia in Bangladesh; Prime Minister Benazir Bhutto in Pakistan; President Megawati Sukarnoputri in Indonesia; and Prime Minister Tansu Çiller in Turkey. Today women make up 25 percent of Iraq's parliament. Shirin Ebadi, a Muslim Iranian attorney, won the Nobel Peace Prize in 2003 for her humanitarian work on behalf of women.

As with other political and social issues, a certain contingent of Muslims has always interpreted the Qur'an and sayings of the Prophet Muhammad in the most misogynistic manner possible to suit their own agendas, but Islam's fundamental commitment to improving women's lives still holds. While morality and tradition will remain an important part of Muslim teachings and culture, I expect that women in the Muslim world will continue to gain more access to political, social, and philanthropic life.

13. WHY DO MANY MUSLIM WOMEN WEAR HEAD SCARVES?

Modesty is incumbent upon both Muslim men and women, and head scarves are a traditional component of conservative public dress for women, which is known as hijab. The Arabic word *hijab* may be translated as "covering" or "concealing." Hijab covers the entire body save for the hands, face, and sometimes feet. Muslim women don their hijab only in public or before men outside their family. They need not wear it in the company of women, their husbands, or their relatives, such as their children, fathers, fathers-in-law, or sons-in-law.

Women living in the time of the Prophet Muhammad wore hijab to adhere to the Qur'anic verses and sayings of the Prophet Muhammad promoting modesty and chastity. Several verses in the Qur'an speak to modest covering for women, such as chapter 24, verse 31: "And say to the believing women that they cast down their looks and guard their private parts and do not display their ornaments except what appears thereof, and let them wear their head-coverings over their bosoms . . ."

Chapter 33, verses 32 and 33 of the Qur'an says, "O wives of the Prophet! you are not like any other of the women: If you will be on your guard, then be not soft in [your] speech, lest he in whose heart is a disease yearn; and speak a good word. And stay in your houses and do not display your finery like the displaying of the ignorance of yore." The Prophet Muhammad's wives and daughters were seen as the best examples for women of the period, so other women readily adopted their habits and styles.

The passages are not unlike those given at points in the Bible, which expresses many of the same views on morality as the Qur'an. First Corinthians, chapter 11, verses 4–6 reads: "Every man praying or prophesying, having *his* head covered, dishonoureth his head. But every woman that prayeth or prophesieth with *her* head uncovered dishonoureth her head: for that is even all one as if she were shaven."

Muslims and non-Muslims alike recognize that women are symbols of attraction and temptation in society. Whether in liberal societies or conservative ones, women are viewed differently from men. Even in the United States, women are not permitted to go topless as a man might because to do so is considered distracting and immodest. No one says this infringes upon women's rights. Muslims also believe in increased modesty for women, with the difference being that they expand the area necessary for coverage to emphasize inner beauty over superficial beauty.

I would think this appreciation for a woman's intrinsic worth is an attitude feminists would support, but in the United States many seem to equate wearing revealing attire with liberation and a head covering with oppression. Women's groups in the West have spoken out loudly and clearly about violations of women's rights in Iran, Afghanistan, and Saudi Arabia, but they fell silent when France forced hundreds of thousands of Muslim girls and women to remove hijab in public schools. In addition to infringing on freedom of worship, the policy forced females to choose between their religion and their education. German legislators and courts have wrestled with similar legislation for public school teachers. I confess bewilderment as to why women's groups eagerly defend Muslim women's rights in Tehran, Kabul, and Riyadh, but not in Paris and Berlin.

Islamic scholars disagree somewhat about the specific requirements of hijab. Muslim women wear many varieties of modest clothing, and there is a range in the amount of coverage these clothes provide. In certain very conservative areas, women will wear a hijab that covers the entire body, including the face, but even conservative Saudi Arabia does not require the face veil, and in the majority of the Muslim world, it's safe to say that women wear their hijab voluntarily and proudly, declaring not their subjugation to men but their submission to God.

14. WHY CAN'T MUSLIM WOMEN LEAD THE CONGREGATIONAL PRAYER, AND WHY DO WOMEN HAVE TO PRAY IN THE BACK OF THE MOSQUE?

Actually, women can lead the congregational prayer, provided that they are leading a group made up only of women. The reason for barring them under other circumstances is not prejudice but modesty. Prayer involves bowing and prostrating, and asking women to position themselves in front of men in this situation would not only be demeaning to the women but could also present a distraction for the men. The distinction comes naturally to both genders: notice that the man who drops his car keys on the ground thinks nothing of bending at the waist to retrieve them, whereas a woman will discreetly bend at the knees.

For the same reason, men pray in front of women when both genders are present at a mosque. Newscasters reported during the 2000 election campaign that the vice presidential nominee, Senator Joe Lieberman, attends a Modern Orthodox synagogue in Stamford, Connecticut, Agudath Sholom, that divides men and women for prayer, and I saw no eyebrows raised as a result of the report. Where Muslims are concerned, on the other hand, the protocol somehow feels more threatening. I should point out that Muslim men and women are *separated,* not necessarily *segregated,* though some mosques do use partitions between the genders during prayer. If the partition runs down the middle, placing men and women on opposite sides, there is no reason for women to pray in the back. Few mosques in Michigan that I know of use partitions, however; the Islamic Center of America does not. This also was the case in the Prophet Muhammad's mosque, and is what I would like to see in all mosques: Muslims praying together in the same room, without segregation, and with women positioned behind men to preserve the modesty and dignity of all.

15. WHY ARE WOMEN FORBIDDEN FROM ENTERING SOME MOSQUES?

Islam itself does not prevent women from entering mosques. As I mentioned in answer to the previous question, women prayed together with men in the Prophet Muhammad's mosque, and he welcomed and encouraged the practice. Refusing women entrance to mosques is a case of culture overshadowing religion. I have not encountered any mosques in the United States that do not permit women to pray there, and those abroad that do not allow women are in a distinct minority. The only reason I can think of for this, other than excessive conservatism, is that mosques in many countries are neighborhood entities. They serve a highly local population that strives to attend a mosque for as many of the five daily prayers as possible. Mosques located in industrial areas made up overwhelmingly of laboring men could create an unsafe or inhospitable environment for women to attend, and so those mosques might head off any potential problems by disallowing women.

16. DID THE PROPHET MUHAMMAD HAVE MULTIPLE WIVES?

Custom in seventh-century Arabia permitted a man to marry as many women as he was able to care for, and although the Prophet Muhammad did not forbid polygamy, he did limit it and regulate it in the Muslim community. In chapter 4, verse 3 of the Qur'an, God says, "If you fear that you cannot act equitably towards orphans, then marry such women as seem good to you, two and three and four; but if you fear that you will not do justice [between them], then [marry] only one or what your right hands possess; this is more proper, that you may not deviate from the right course." Another verse, 129 in chapter 4, discourages polygamy more directly: "You have it not in your power to do justice between wives, even though you may wish [it]."

The Prophet Muhammad was monogamously married to his first wife, Khadijah, for about twenty-five years. After she died, he did take other wives simultaneously, up to eight, but for altruistic reasons. Frequent warfare and strife in Arabia at the time left many women as widows without the means to support themselves and otherwise unmarriageable. Through marriage, the Prophet Muhammad ensured that they and their children would be taken care of. He also married the daughters of neighboring tribal leaders so as to secure peace with those tribes and to strengthen relations with them. His marriages to Safiyah bint Hoyay bin Akhtab, who was Jewish, and Mary the Copt, who was a Christian from Egypt, demonstrated for Muslims that they should not be hostile to Jews and Christians. Both women converted to Islam after marrying the Prophet Muhammad.

Because of the risk in war to men and the vulnerability of women at that time, society looked upon polygamy differently, as it did in the Christian and Jewish traditions. Abraham, for example, had two wives at the same time. Yet polygamy is very rare among Muslims today. Only a tiny percentage of Muslims practice it, while the vast majority recognize that monogamous marriages are the soundest and most rewarding.

17. DID THE PROPHET MUHAMMAD MARRY A NINE-YEAR-OLD GIRL?

Arab custom did not permit that a girl be married before she reached puberty. These stories concern Aisha, the Prophet Muhammad's third wife and the daughter of Abu Bakr, a longstanding companion of the Prophet. High status was accorded women who married younger—they tended to be the most attractive and received marriage proposals from many men—so the assertion that Aisha was married at age nine is a way of expressing her beauty and desirability in the community. Many scholars believe there were political reasons for the marriage, a way for the Prophet Muhammad to strengthen his relationship with the Adeey, a strong subtribe of the Quraysh that Abu Bakr belonged to. Regardless, there is no compelling evidence that the Prophet Muhammad consummated his marriage to Aisha while she was underage.

18. DO MUSLIMS BELIEVE THAT THEY WILL BE REWARDED WITH SEVENTY-TWO VIRGINS IN HEAVEN?

The idea of seventy-two virgins in a Muslim paradise has captured the public's imagination and might be one of the first concepts that come to mind when an American thinks about Islam. It is also a fabrication. The myth originated with a few passages from the Qur'an, which devotes several chapters to the afterlife. In chapter 56, verses 17–24, the Qur'an describes what awaits those who make it to heaven: "Round about them shall go youths never altering in age, with goblets and ewers and a cup of pure drink; they shall not be affected with headache thereby, nor shall they get exhausted, and fruits such as they choose, and the flesh of fowl such as they desire. And *pure, beautiful ones,* the like of the hidden pearls: A reward for what they used to do" [emphasis added].

Chapter 3, verse 15 says, "For the righteous are Gardens in nearness to their Lord . . . with Companions pure [and holy] and the good pleasure of God."

The standard interpretation of such verses is that good female believers will reach a perfected "virgin-beautiful" state in heaven, and good Muslim men will dwell there with their perfected spouses. Any speculation about the number of partners is completely arbitrary. Yet the Qur'an itself emphasizes the fantastic nature of heaven's contents, that people cannot imagine the spiritual and earthly riches that it holds but that they will be incredible and blissful in whatever capacity.

19. DOES ISLAM ACCEPT DEMOCRACY?

Some people, including some hard-line Muslims, argue that democracy is contrary to Islamic principles. I disagree. Islam did not take shape in a democratic environment—neither did many other religions—but there is nothing in Islam that precludes Muslims from embracing democratic governments. Predominately Muslim countries such as Bangladesh and Indonesia have elected governments, and millions of Muslims in other democratic countries eagerly participate in their countries' elections. In Iraq's December 2005 parliamentary elections, despite threats of violence and calls for a boycott, turnout was about 70 percent—roughly 25 percent higher than is seen in a U.S. presidential election.

The pessimism about Islamic democracy comes from Arab history. It is true that Arab countries historically have been plagued by corrupt, absolutist governments, which can be attributed to a variety of complicated factors: the Arab cultural tradition of deferring to respected, senior leaders rather than holding popular elections; wariness of colonial rule; the false belief of some Muslims that they must accept unjust rulers or be considered disloyal; and politically expedient U.S. support of tyrannical Middle East regimes. Unfortunately, the United States promotes democracy in Latin America, eastern Europe, and elsewhere, but it prefers to deal with dictators in Muslim countries when those leaders acquiesce to U.S. interests, regardless of the consequences for the dictators' subjects. Not surprisingly, then, many Arabs see in U.S. attempts to facilitate Middle East democracy the pulling of more strings, not sincere concern for the welfare of the people.

Regardless of these discouraging factors, Arabs are eager for democracy. As the vast, diverse international community of Muslims continues to debate the politics of religion from all sides, more and more Muslims, especially in the Middle East, will see that they do not have to sacrifice their religious and cultural values in order to institute free, responsive, democratically elected governments.

20. HOW DOES ISLAM VIEW HOMOSEXUALITY?

Islam's position on homosexuality is essentially the same as that of Judaism and Christianity. All three Abrahamic faiths disapprove of homosexuality, but many Protestants and Jews have adopted a modern reinterpretation of homosexuality as an equal, alternative form of love and sexual expression. At an annual interfaith forum I attended in 2004, a twelve-member panel debated issuing a statement against same-sex marriage. Hawaii and Nevada were considering allowing it at the time. One rabbi unequivocally opposed making the statement and called the Torah a historic book, not a divine book, arguing that its proscription against homosexuality was outdated. Like all Muslims, I believe that the words of the Qur'an come directly from God, and therefore I cannot share the same sentiment.

The Islamic belief is that homosexuals who act on their urges suffer from an improper upbringing or lack of balance. In Middle Eastern culture, there is strong disapproval of homosexuality. The inclination itself is not a sin, but I advise those who are unable to resist it to seek spiritual counseling.

Glossary

Abaya: A long, formal woman's robe worn in public in Arab countries. Often black, the abaya is one form of hijab.

Abbasid dynasty: Succession of Baghdad-based rulers (A.D. 750–1268) who laid claim to the caliphate through descent from the Prophet Muhammad's uncle Abbas. The Abbasids succeeded the Umayyads (see *Umayyad dynasty*) and ushered in a golden age of science, mathematics, and philosophy that transmitted much ancient Greek and Hindu learning, as well as new Persian and Arab knowledge, to Europe in later years.

Ahlul-bayt: Literally, "People of the House." Refers to the Prophet Muhammad's family.

Allahu akbar: "God is greatest" or "God is great." Used in the call to prayer and also by Muslims before they begin any of the daily prayers.

Ashura: The holiday marking Imam Husayn's martyrdom at Karbala in A.D. 680 on the tenth of Muharram, the first month of the year. *Ashura* means "tenth" in Arabic.

As-salaamu alaikum: The traditional, formal Arabic greeting meaning "Peace be with you."

Ayatollah: An esteemed title granted by popular consensus to the most learned Muslim clerics. "Sign of God" in Arabic. The highest of these leaders, known as grand ayatollahs, number only a few dozen worldwide.

Banu Hashim: The Prophet Muhammad's clan, a small but prestigious group and part of the larger Quraysh tribe of Mecca. Hashim, the founder of the tribe, was a great-grandfather of the Prophet Muhammad.

Caliph: Successor to the Prophet Muhammad and head of the caliphate, the historical government of the Islamic world.

Dhimmi: Historically, Jews and Christians living in predominately Muslim societies who paid a nominal tax to live as protected people.

Eid al-Adha: The Feast of Sacrifice, which begins during the pilgrimage to Mecca, on the tenth day of Thul al-Hijja, the last Islamic month. The three-day holiday commemorates Abraham's readiness to sacrifice his son Ishmael (not Isaac, as in Jewish and Christian tradition) for God, and millions of Muslims worldwide sacrifice a sheep in honor of Abraham's obedience.

Eid al-Fitr: The holiday feast that breaks the fast at the end of Ramadan, a joyous occasion marked by prayer, reflection, celebration, and visiting of family.

Enshallah: "God willing."

Fattoush: Lebanese salad made of seasonal vegetables, such as cucumbers and tomatoes, tossed with pita bread, spices, and lemon juice.

Fatwa: A legal ruling on Islamic law issued by a master of jurisprudence, a mujtahid.

Hadith: A narration of Islamic tradition distinct from the Qur'an. In Sunni Islam, a hadith can come only from the Prophet Muhammad. In Shia Islam, the sayings of the Twelve Revered Imams, which are based on the Prophet Muhammad's teachings, also qualify.

Hajj: The pilgrimage to Mecca, made in the last month of the Islamic calendar year, Thul al-Hijja. One of the Five Pillars of Islam.

Hajj/hajji: Male/female courtesy titles for Muslims who are preparing for or making the hajj, or who have completed it.

Halal: In conformance with Islamic law; often applied to Islamically permissible foods.

Haram: Forbidden by Islamic law.

Hejaz: The western region of today's Saudi Arabia, including Mecca and Medina, and the primary regional identifier in the Prophet Muhammad's time. In the 1920s, the Saudi ruling family changed the name of the Hejaz; it is now called the Western Province.

Hijab: Proper, modest dress for women. The word often refers specifically to a head covering.

Hummus: A traditional Middle Eastern food made of puréed chickpeas, sesame seed paste, olive oil, garlic, and other seasonings.

Iftar: Any dinner eaten during the holy month of Ramadan to break the ritual daytime fast.

Ihram: The simple white wardrobe worn by male pilgrims on the hajj to Mecca.

Ijtihad: The interpretation of Islamic law conducted by a mujtahid. Ijtihad has ceased among Sunnis, who rely on four primary schools of thought (Hanafi, Hanbali, Maliki, and Shafei) from the eighth and ninth centuries A.D., but ijtihad is still open in the Shia tradition.

Imam: (1) In Shia Islam, the honorary title for any of the twelve divinely inspired descendants of the Prophet Muhammad, starting with Imam Ali ibn Abi Talib and ending with Imam Muhammad Al-Mahdi. In this usage, the word is capitalized. (2) A title for the leader of a congregational prayer in progress. (3) An honorary title for founders of Sunni schools of thought and for certain scholars of hadith. (4) Any Muslim religious leader, particularly in the West.

Istikhara: A random consultation of the Holy Qur'an seeking guidance.

Jihad: Struggle or striving. Non-Muslims commonly know of what the Prophet Muhammad termed the lesser jihad, the armed defense of Islam against outside threats. More important for Muslims is the greater jihad, the personal reckoning necessary to behave morally and improve oneself. Only a mujtahid can declare a lesser jihad.

Kaaba: The cube-shaped holy house at the center of the Grand Mosque in Mecca. Built by Adam and rebuilt by Abraham, it lies at the center of Islamic history and is the structure toward which Muslims around the world pray. It also holds the Black Stone, which the Archangel Gabriel gave to Abraham. In pre-Islamic times, the Kaaba housed various idols for the tribes of the Hejaz.

Muethin or muezzin: One who calls Muslims to the five daily prayers (*salat*). Many now use a public address system, while in the West, certain mosques use the call only inside, since Muslims are unlikely to hear it from their homes anyway. Professional muethins are selected for their beautiful voices and are held in high esteem.

Mujtahid: A master of Islamic jurisprudence. Only a mujtahid can issue a fatwa or declare a jihad.

Mukhabarat: Secret police; in this book, the term refers to the agents of Saddam's Baathist regime.

Mushrik: Those who commit *shirk,* defined as the holding of illegitimate beliefs about God, which could include polytheism, paganism, atheism, and anthropomorphism (the humanization of God).

Mutawa: The religious police of the Saudi government; they enforce Wahhabi standards.

Quraysh: The wealthy tribe of the Prophet Muhammad, which controlled trade in Mecca and also maintained the Kaaba and hosted the annual pilgrimage, even in pre-Islamic times. His clan, the Hashim, were members of the Quraysh tribe. The Prophet's denunciation of the Quraysh's pagan rites and of their disregard for Mecca's poor upset the status quo and led to his exile to Medina.

Ramadan: The holy month, the ninth of the Islamic calendar, in which the Holy Qur'an was first revealed to the Prophet Muhammad. Observant Muslims focus their thoughts on others' suffering and fast during the days of Ramadan.

Saei: During the pilgrimage to Mecca, the ritual reenactment of Hagar's search for water in the desert by walking between two hills, Safa and Marwa.

Sayed: A male descendant of the Prophet Muhammad. Female descendants are sayyidas. Often used alone as a title to address a person with respect.

Seera: The biography of the Prophet Muhammad and stories of his life.

Sharia: Islamic law governing both religious obligations and the rules of society, derived from the Qur'an, the sayings of the Prophet (and, according to the Shia, the sayings of the Twelve Imams), scholarly consensus, and intellect. Muslim scholars and schools of thought differ on the validity of certain sources for determining sharia and might consult others.

Sharif: The governor of Mecca, who used to be a descendant of the Prophet Muhammad. Sunnis use "sharif" as an honorific title for descendants of Imam Hassan and Imam Husayn.

Sheikh: Literally translated as "old man," this versatile term can refer to a Muslim clerical leader, tribal leader, tribal elder, or other respected elder, whether Muslim or Christian.

Shia: The sect of Islam asserting the right of succession for the Prophet Muhammad's family and comprising about 15 percent of Muslims. Derived from "Shi'atu Ali" in Arabic: "the party of Ali."

Shura: In ancient Arab culture, community consultation in decision making and selection of tribal leaders, a concept that points to Islam's compatibility with western-style democracy.

Sufism: A small, diverse branch of mystical Islam that views Islam as a means to becoming one with God.

Sunna: The traditions of the Prophet Muhammad and, in Shia Islam, the Twelve Revered Imams as revealed through the hadith.

Sunni: Followers of the Islamic establishment that succeeded the Prophet Muhammad and was ruled by the Four Rightly Guided Caliphs: Abu Bakr, Umar, Uthman, and Imam Ali. They comprise about 85 percent of Muslims.

Tabbouleh: A Lebanese salad made with cracked bulgur wheat, mint, tomatoes, onions, parsley, seasonings, and olive oil.

Tabligh: Missionary work within the Muslim community.

Tawaf: Repeated circumambulations of the Kaaba; called "Turning" in English. Often performed with thousands of people, *tawaf* is the first rite of the hajj.

Umayyad dynasty: The Damascus-based caliphate that ruled Muslims from A.D. 661 to 750; under the Umayyad caliphs, Muslim lands expanded greatly, but Shia suffered considerably.

Umrah: The lesser pilgrimage to Mecca (the hajj being the greater pilgrimage), which lasts not more than a few hours and can be performed at any time of year.

Wahhabism: An extreme interpretation of Islam based on the teachings of the fourteenth-century scholar Ibn Taymiyya and the eighteenth-century preacher Muhammad ibn Abd al-Wahhab. Wahhabis preach return to a nonexistent "pure" Islam and view non-Wahhabi Muslims as deviants. Wahhabis self-identify as Salafis.

Principles of Islam

THE FIVE PILLARS OF ISLAM

In the century after the Prophet Muhammad's death, Muslim religious scholars (*ulama*) organized the essence of Islam into five components, called the Five Pillars of Islam. These were judged to best encapsulate the core beliefs and actions that define Muslims. The Five Pillars are mandatory and are vital to Islam, but they are not the only obligations. Muslims do not gamble or consume alcohol or pork, for example; they embrace fellow Muslims as brothers or sisters regardless of race or status; and they are expected to be humble and honest in all their dealings, among many other principles.

The first pillar, *shahadah,* is the most important in that it defines Muslim belief: God is one, has created all before us, and has no likeness, partners, or human qualities. The other four pillars are demonstrative outgrowths of that faith, the actions that profession of faith requires. The importance of community is evident in every pillar, even in the seemingly personal act of prayer.

1. **Shahadah** (*testimony*): The profession of faith recited daily in Muslim prayers and also by new converts before witnesses: "I bear witness that there is no god but God and that Muhammad is the Messenger of God."

2. **Salat** (*prayer*): Compulsory prayer, usually the five daily prayers, which are recited from memory in Arabic.

3. **Sawm** (*fast*): The requisite daytime fast during the holy month of Ramadan. This is a complete fast; Muslims must refrain from all drinks as well as food and from sexual intercourse as part of the daytime fast. Shia wait fifteen minutes after sunset to break the fast, while Sunnis break it immediately.

4. **Zakat** (*poor rate*): Annual charitable tithing amounting to 2.5 percent of net worth.

5. **Hajj** (*pilgrimage*): The two-week pilgrimage to Mecca, made in the last month of the Islamic calendar year, Thul al-Hijja. Physically and financially capable Muslims must perform the hajj once in their lifetime.

SHIA THEOLOGY

The Five Pillars of Islam are just one way of describing Muslims' beliefs and practices. Shia Muslims also adhere to two other sets of principles, which either restate or complement the Five Pillars of Islam. The first set, the Five Roots of Religion, addresses beliefs; the second, the Ten Branches of Religion, deals with practices, four of which are also pillars of Islam.

The Five Roots of Religion

1. **Tawhid** (*oneness*): Tawhid is the core belief acknowledged in the *shahadah* by saying, "There is no god but God." God has prophets and messengers, but no equal.

2. **Adalah** (*justice*): Although Muslims should work for justice, they also know that God is just and merciful and that He has designed a world in which justice will prevail.

3. Nubuwwah (*prophethood*): God has sent prophets to humanity to carry his message. The Qur'an names twenty-five but makes clear there are others. Adam was the first, and Muhammad was the last, the "Seal of the Prophets."

4. Imamah (*leadership*): "The Imams [successors] after me are twelve," the Prophet Muhammad said. "The first of them is Ali son of Abu Talib and the last of them is the Qaem [Al-Mahdi]. They are my successors, trustees, guardians, and the proofs of God on my nation after me."

5. Qiyamah (*Judgment Day*): All people will be called to answer for their lives on this earth when this world ends and the last Imam, Al-Mahdi, returns with Jesus to restore justice and favor.

The Ten Branches of Religion

1. Salat (*prayer*): Compulsory prayer, usually the five daily prayers.

2. Sawm (*fast*): The requisite daytime fast during the holy month of Ramadan.

3. Hajj (*pilgrimage*): The two-week pilgrimage to Mecca, performed at least once in a Muslim's lifetime.

4. Zakat (*poor rate*): Annual charitable tithing whose form depends on the school of thought: Sunnis pay 2.5 percent of gross annual income; Shia may pay 2.5 percent of the total worth of a designated good, commonly cattle. If paid in cash, Shia combine *zakat* with *khums* (see number 5) and pay 20 percent of surplus annual income.

5. Khums (*one-fifth*): Tithing of 20 percent of surplus annual income, paid in addition to *zakat* by Shia.

6. Jihad (*struggle*): The ongoing perfection of oneself and pursuit of a just world.

7. Amr-bil-ma'ruf (*enjoining what is good*): Chapter 3, verse 104 of the Qur'an says, "Let there arise out of you a band of people inviting to all that is good, enjoining what

is right, and forbidding what is wrong: They are the ones to attain felicity."

8. Nahi-anil-munkar (*forbidding what is evil*): In addition to the above verse, the Qur'an says, in chapter 9, verse 71, "The Believers, men and women, are protectors one of another: they enjoin what is just, and forbid what is evil."

9. Tawalla (*love of God's patrons, mainly the Prophet Muhammad's family*): Chapter 42, verse 23 of the Qur'an mandates love of the Prophet's family in return for his delivering God's word: "No reward do I ask of you for this except the love of those near of kin."

10. Tabarra (*disassociation from opponents of God, and from the Prophet Muhammad and his family*): This logically corresponds to *tawalla,* above; though it does not entail hatred, it does mean active disassociation from both people and actions contrary to the Prophet Muhammad and his family.

The Twelve Revered
Shia Imams

1. Ali ibn Abi Talib (A.D. *600–661*)*

Imam Ali's father, Abu Talib, also raised the Prophet Muhammad, who served as a father figure while Imam Ali, his cousin, was growing up. Imam Ali was the first male convert to Islam and went on to marry the Prophet Muhammad's daughter Fatima. Imam Ali was the father of Shia Islam and the rightful successor to the Prophet, who was his only earthly superior in the annals of Islamic spirituality and philosophy. Imam Ali is buried in Najaf, Iraq.

2. Hasan ibn Ali (A.D. *625–669*)

Imam Ali's eldest son by Fatima, Imam Hasan is known for his battles with Mu'awiyah, a companion of the Prophet Muhammad from the Umayyad clan who claimed the caliphate for himself from Damascus. Imam Hasan reached a peace agreement with him in 668 that ceded the caliphate to Mu'awiyah but re-

*Because of historical uncertainties and the differences between the solar and lunar calendars, birth and death years for the Imams are inexact.

260 The Twelve Revered Shia Imams

quired that a council of Muslim delegates select the next caliph. Shia believe that Mu'awiyah poisoned Imam Hasan soon after. Imam Hasan is buried in Medina, Saudi Arabia.

3. Husayn ibn Ali (A.D. 626–680)

The charismatic Imam Husayn, brother of Imam Hasan, formalized a Shia identity of justice through sacrifice at the Battle of Karbala. Greatly outnumbered by armies from the illegitimate empire that demanded his allegiance, Imam Husayn accepted their vengeance upon him, and we commemorate his martyrdom annually during the holiday Ashura, mindful that the evil carried out against him still exists. Imam Husayn is buried in Karbala, Iraq.

4. Ali Zain al-Abedeen (A.D. 658–713)

Imam Ali Zain al-Abedeen escaped death at Karbala because he was ill during the battle. He became known as an esteemed scholar and he mourned the slaughter of his family for a lifetime. The son of Imam Husayn and the daughter of the last Sassanid (Persian) emperor, he published a collection of supplications called *Psalms of Islam,* regarded among Shia as the third most sacred Islamic text, after the Qur'an and Imam Ali's *Peak of Eloquence.* Imam Ali Zain is buried in Medina.

5. Mohammad al-Baqir (A.D. 676–732)

Imam Mohammad al-Baqir was the first Imam to descend from the Prophet Muhammad through both his maternal and paternal lines. Many gravitated to him for his high scholarship and caring demeanor. After the tragedy at Karbala he shed new light on the persecution and deeply held beliefs of the Shia. He is buried in Medina.

6. Jafar al-Sadiq (A.D. 702–765)

Imam Jafar al-Sadiq is famous as the founder of the Jafari school of thought, the primary Shia interpretation of Islamic law. The four major Sunni schools are Hanbali, Hanafi, Maliki, and Shafei, all named after their respective founders. Imam Jafar al-Sadiq, in fact, taught two of them, his contemporaries Abu Hanifah and Malik ibn Anas. Sunnis and Shia alike recognize his legal brilliance. Imam Jafar al-Sadiq is buried in Medina.

7. Musa al-Kadhim (A.D. 745–799)

Imam Musa spent thirty-five years as the head of the Imamate, more than any of the other first eleven Imams. One Shia sect believes that Imam Musa's older brother Ismail was the rightful Imam; they are known as the Ismailis, or Seveners. Ismail died young during his father's imamate. Imam Musa lived in a time of great conflict and suspicion about the Imams. The Abbasid ruler Harun al-Rashid imprisoned him in Baghdad multiple times, and finally he died in prison. He is buried in Baghdad with the ninth Imam, Imam Muhammad al-Jawad.

8. Ali ar-Rida (A.D. 765–818)

Like so many Muslim rulers before him, the Abbasid caliph Ma'mun, son of Harun al-Rashid, feared a revolt of the people under the Imams. To prevent such a fate, Ma'mun forced Imam Rida to leave his home in Medina and live under the caliphate in Khorasan, a far eastern Persian province. Ma'mun hoped to gain favor with Shia by naming Imam Rida as his successor, but the Imam did not outlive Ma'mun. He died after being poisoned by Ma'mun while traveling with him near Tus, in Iran. Imam Rida is buried in Mashad, Iran.

9. Muhammad al-Jawad (A.D. 810–835)

Imam al-Jawad assumed the mantle of the Imamate at age nine and, despite his youth, developed a reputation as a formidable public debater, besting the most respected scholars of his day. He married the daughter of the Abbasid caliph Ma'mun, who was overjoyed to have his lineage merged with the family of the Prophet Muhammad. Imam al-Jawad spent his final years in Baghdad under Ma'mun's successor before passing, apparently of poisoning (as with many of the Imams), at age twenty-five. He is buried in Baghdad, near his grandfather Imam Musa.

10. Ali al-Hadi (A.D. 828–868)

Imam al-Hadi is known as a great teacher and source of spiritual wisdom, yet he spent the last half of his life either imprisoned or under house arrest in Samarra, Iraq, then the seat of the caliphate. He is buried in Samarra at Al-Askari, the Golden Mosque, near his son, Imam Hasan al-Askari. Their shrine was bombed by foreign insurgents in February 2006, which set off waves of sectarian violence throughout Iraq. In June 2007, insurgents destroyed the two minarets, which survived the 2006 attack.

11. Hasan al-Askari (A.D. 846–874)

Imam al-Askari spent his entire life either under house arrest or in prison, under the close watch of a succession of Abbasid caliphs in Samarra and Baghdad. Though his contact with almost all Shia was limited, he was able to transmit his knowledge discreetly to the Shia elite and in turn to a growing Shia population. Imam al-Askari died young and is buried alongside his father in Samarra.

12. Muhammad ibn Hasan (Al-Mahdi) (A.D. 868–)

Caliphs of the time knew that the twelfth Imam would be the savior and took elaborate precautions to prevent Imam al-Askari from having a successor. Nevertheless, Imam al-Mahdi was born, undetected by those in power, and he went into occultation at the age of six, upon the death of his father. In exceptional circumstances he maintained contact with the Shia community through his deputies. He is still among us but remains hidden until God chooses for him to return at the end of days together with Jesus to launch a campaign of justice and reform.

Select Time Line of Islamic and Middle East History

A.D. 570   The Prophet Muhammad is born into the Hashim clan of the Quraysh tribe, the dominant religious, social, and political force in Mecca.

610   The Prophet Muhammad receives his first revelation from God.

619   Abu Talib, the Prophet Muhammad's uncle and the leader of the Hashim clan, dies, leaving the Prophet vulnerable to attacks from Meccans opposed to Islam. The Prophet's wife, Khadijah, also dies around the same time.

622   Under threat of assassination, the Prophet Muhammad flees to Yathrib, which he renames Medina, to lead an independent Muslim community. Year 0 of the Islamic calendar.

628   The Prophet Muhammad, refused entry to Mecca to perform the annual pilgrimage, signs the Treaty of Hudaybiyyah with Meccans. The treaty postpones his pilgrimage until the following year and requires an end to all hostili-

	ties between Meccans and Medinans and their respective allies.
630	After a Meccan violation of the Treaty of Hudaybiyyah, the Prophet Muhammad conquers Mecca peacefully, grants its inhabitants amnesty, and returns to Medina.
632	The Prophet Muhammad makes his Farewell Pilgrimage to Mecca and proclaims Imam Ali ibn Abi Talib his successor. Two months later, the Prophet passes away.
632–634	Abu Bakr, a prominent companion of the Prophet Muhammad, assumes leadership of the Muslim community as the first caliph. The Muslims who would become known as Shia dispute his ascension, believing Imam Ali to be the rightful caliph.
634–644	Umar ibn al-Khattab rules as the second caliph.
ca. 636–640	Arab Muslims defeat the Persian Sassanian empire at the Battle of Qadisiyyah, in southern Iraq, marking the beginning of Persia's Islamization. Saddam Hussein would compare his war with Iran in the 1980s to Qadisiyyah.
644–656	Uthman ibn Affan, an aged merchant from the Umayya clan, serves as the third caliph.
656–661	Imam Ali, the first Shia Imam, becomes the last of what Sunnis call "The Four Rightly Guided Caliphs" (Abu Bakr, Umar, and Uthman being the first three). By the end of Imam Ali's rule, Islam reaches from Tripoli, in present-day Libya, to Central Asia.
661	Imam Ali is killed by a hard-line former supporter for failing to adequately punish the Umayyad adversary Mu'awiyah. Mu'awiyah claims the caliphate from Damascus.
661–750	Rule of the Umayyad dynasty. The Umayyads compete with the Prophet Muhammad's clan, the Hashim. Under the Umayyads, the new Islamic empire expands to include Spain, all of North Africa, and most of Central Asia.
668	Imam Hasan, Imam Ali's eldest son, negotiates a treaty with Mu'awiyah under which the next caliph will be chosen by a council of Muslim delegates.

669	Imam Hasan dies of poisoning in a plot by Mu'awiyah.
680	Mu'awiyah declares his son Yazid to be his successor, thus abrogating his earlier agreement with Imam Hasan. After refusing to pledge allegiance to Yazid, Imam Husayn (Imam Hasan's brother) is slain at Karbala by Umayyad armies.
691	Muslims complete the Dome of the Rock mosque in Jerusalem, the third holiest city in Islam. The mosque marks the spot where the Prophet Muhammad ascended to heaven and returned to earth with knowledge of the required five daily prayers.
750–1258	Rule of the Abbasid dynasty. The Abbasids move the caliphate from Damascus to Baghdad. Much of their influence wanes within a century after they take power, with continual fragmentation of an expansive empire.
756	Abd al-Rahman, of the Umayyad ruling family, claims a separate caliphate from Córdoba, Spain.
874	The twelfth and last Imam, Imam Al-Mahdi, goes into occultation (see "The Twelve Revered Shia Imams," p. 259).
971	The Fatimid dynasty of Egypt completes the Al-Azhar Mosque in Cairo. Once Shia, Al-Azhar is now the center of the world's most prestigious Sunni university.
977	The Imam Ali Holy Shrine is built over Imam Ali's tomb in Najaf, Iraq.
1005	Al-Sheikh al-Tusi founds the Shia seminary, the Hawza, at Najaf.
1037	The great Muslim physician, poet, and philosopher Ibn Sina (Avicenna) dies in Hamedan, Persia.
1095–1272	Crusades in the Holy Land.
1099	European crusaders conquer Jerusalem.
1245	Muslims retake Jerusalem.
1254–1517	Rule of the Mamluk dynasty over Egypt and Syria.
1258	Mongols put an end to the waning Abbasid empire by sacking Baghdad.

1263–1328	The lifetime of the anti-Shia scholar Ibn Taymiyya, whose texts Wahhabis still use in classrooms today.
1286–1922	Foundation and end of the Ottoman empire.
1492	The fall of Granada ends Muslims' ruling presence in Spain. Ferdinand and Isabella expel Spanish Jews who refuse to convert to Christianity.
1654	The Taj Mahal is completed in Agra, India.
1683	Central and eastern European forces unite to defeat the Ottomans at the Battle of Vienna.
1703	Muhammad ibn Abd al-Wahhab, the founder of Wahhabism, is born in the Najd region of central Arabia. He would partner with Muhammad ibn Saud, a tribal sheikh, to control Najd's political and religious life.
1801–1804	Wahhabis take over Mecca and raid Najaf and Karbala, Iraq.
1917	The Balfour Declaration articulates Britain's support for a permanent Jewish homeland in Palestine.
1920	Iraqis revolt against British occupation.
1921	King Faisal I becomes king of Iraq under British authority.
1922–1946	French Mandate Period: the San Remo agreement gives France control of Syria in 1920; months later, France establishes Lebanon as a separate country.
1922–1948	British Mandate Period: Great Britain controls Jordan, Palestine, and, at various times, Iraq.
1923	The Shia seminary at Qum is founded.
1932	King Abdul Aziz ibn Saud consolidates the kingdoms of Najd and Hejaz to form the Kingdom of Saudi Arabia. Iraq achieves independence from Britain under King Faisal, a Hashemite whose father was Grand Sharif of Mecca.
1938	Oil is first discovered in Saudi Arabia.
1941	Britain invades Iraq and remains until 1947.
1948	Israel is established as an independent state.

1958	Abdul Karim Qasim overthrows Iraq's Hashemite monarchy and draws power from the Iraqi Communist party in attempting to form a populist regime. Nearly all of the royal family is assassinated.
1959	Saddam Hussein takes part in a Baathist plot to assassinate Prime Minister Qasim and is shot in the leg. He flees to Egypt and is supported by U.S. intelligence.
1963	With help from the CIA, the Baathists and Abdul Salam Arif overthrow Prime Minister Qasim. Arif soon purges Baath party members from the government.
1966	Abdul Salam Arif dies in a helicopter crash. His brother, Abdul Rahman Arif, succeeds him.
1967	Skirmishes and simmering tensions between Israel and Arab states (Egypt, Syria, and Jordan) erupt into the Six-Day War, from which Israel emerges with a decisive victory and occupies territory in the West Bank, Jerusalem, Gaza, and the Golan Heights that becomes a subsequent source of conflict with Palestinians.
1968	The Baathists in Iraq regain power in a bloodless coup. Ahmed Hassan al-Bakr is named president. Saddam Hussein heads the new regime's security forces.

Notes

Chapter 1: Husayn vs. Hussein

1. Muhammad Ali, *A Manual of Hadith,* p. 332. Drawn from Tirmidhi and Mishkat hadith.

2. A Shi'ite Encyclopedia, chapter 3, "Ghadir Khum," Part I (al-islam .org/encyclopedia/). (Brackets in the sourced quotation.)

3. Ibid.

4. Shakir, *The Qur'an Translation,* 5:3.

5. A Shi'ite Encyclopedia, chapter 3, "Ghadar Khum," Part I (al-islam.org/encyclopedia/). (Brackets added.)

6. Ibid., chapter 5, "Tragedy of Karbala as Reported by the Sunnis," Part VI (al-islam.org/encyclopedia/). (Brackets in the sourced quotation.)

7. Al-Jibouri, *Kerbala and Beyond,* p. 59.

8. Mackey, *The Reckoning,* p. 70.

9. Farouk-Sluglett and Sluglett, *Iraq Since 1958,* pp. 115–16; Sada, *Saddam's Secrets,* pp. 69–70.

10. Farouk-Sluglett and Sluglett, *Iraq Since 1958,* pp. 116, 135.

11. Ibid., pp. 198–99; Tripp, *A History of Iraq,* p. 216.

12. Farouk-Sluglett and Sluglett, *Iraq Since 1958,* p. 199.

13. Tripp, *A History of Iraq,* p. 217.

Chapter 2: Struggle in Iran

1. Shakir, *The Qur'an Translation,* 84:6.

2. Percentage for 1975. United Nations Population Division, 1994.

3. Hunter, *Islam, Europe's Second Religion,* p. xiii.

4. Ibn Asaker, *Tareekh Madeenat Dimishq* [History of the City of Damascus], vol. 42 (Beirut, Lebanon: Dar Al-Fikr, 1994), p. 61.

5. Al-Sadouq, *Man La Yahtharahol Faqeeh,* 2nd ed. (Qum, Iran: Al-Nashr Al-Islami Institute, 1984), vol. 4, p. 180.

6. Aslan, *No God but God,* p. 67.

7. Ibid., p. 163.

8. Al-Jibouri, *Kerbala and Beyond,* p. 30.

9. Al-Sadouq, *Man La Yahtharahol Faqeeh,* vol. 1, pp. 240–41.

10. Kinzer, *All the Shah's Men,* p. 4.

11. Baqer Moin, *Khomeini: Life of the Ayatollah* (New York: Thomas Dunne Books, 2000), p. 104. (Bracketed material added.)

12. These figures are unofficial estimates based on conversations with staff at the respective seminaries.

13. Farouk-Sluglett and Sluglett, *Iraq Since 1958,* p. 258.

14. Hiro, *The Longest War,* p. 250.

15. Campbell, *Desert War,* p. 2. Campbell estimates 500,000 injured and 250,000 dead for Iran and 150,000 injured and 100,000 dead for Iraq.

16. "Whatever Happened to the Iraqi Kurds?" Human Rights Watch Report, March 11, 1991 (www.hrw.org/reports/1991/IRAQ913.htm #_ftn11).

Chapter 3: Sacred Journey

1. Yusuf Ali, *An English Interpretation of the Holy Qur'an,* 22:27.

2. Al-Kulayni, *Al-Kafi,* 3rd ed. (Tehran, Iran: Dar Al-Kotob Al-Islamiyya, 1987), vol. 5, p. 329.

3. Yusuf Ali, *An English Interpretation of the Holy Qur'an,* 22:78.

4. Ibid., 37:105.

5. Al-Nouri, *Mustadrak Al-Wasa'el,* 2nd ed. (Beirut, Lebanon: Alul Bayt Institute, 1988), vol. 12, p. 409.

6. Michael Wolfe, ed., *One Thousand Roads to Mecca: Ten Centuries of Travelers Writing About the Muslim Pilgrimage* (New York: Grove Press, 1997), pp. 226–27.

7. Shakir, *The Qur'an Translation,* 28:85.

8. Ibn Hisham, *Assiyrarah al-Nabawya* (Beirut: Dar Elia Al-Turath Al-Arabi, 1995), vol. 2, p. 125.

9. A Shi'ite Encyclopedia, chapter 3, "Ghadir Khum," Part I (al-islam.org/encyclopedia/).

10. Michael Z. Wise, "Mecca's Makeover," *Travel+Leisure,* February 2004, p. 106 (www.travelandleisure.com/articles/meccas-makeover/).

11. Muhammad Howydi, *Al-Tafseer al-Moeen* (Qum, Iran: Dar Al-Fiqh, 2003), p. 236.

Chapter 4: The Idea of America

1. Martin Luther King, Jr., *Where Do We Go from Here: Chaos or Community?* (New York: Beacon Press, 1968), p. 167.

2. Sylviane A. Diouf, *Servants of God: African Muslims Enslaved in the Americas* (New York: New York University Press, 1998), p. 48. Figures are estimates based in part on research by Philip Curtin and Stanley Engerman.

3. Robert Lipsyte, "Clay Discusses His Future, Liston and Black Muslims," *The New York Times,* February 27, 1964.

4. Ali ibn Abi Talib, *Nahjul Balagha,* vol. 4, p. 103, short saying no. 442. Passage translated by Imam Qazwini.

5. Tom Kenworthy, "Bush Daughters Cited in Texas," *USA Today,* May 31, 2001 (www.usatoday.com/news/washington/2001-05-31-bushdaughters.htm); "Jeb Bush's Daughter Charged with Prescription Fraud," CNN.com, January 29, 2002 (archives.cnn.com/2002/US/01/29/jeb.bush.daughter.drugs/).

6. Hunter, *Islam, Europe's Second Religion,* p. xiii. BBC News, "Muslims in Europe."

7. Council on American-Islamic Relations, "American Muslims."

8. Shakir, *The Qur'an Translation,* 24:31.

9. **$3 billion:** Dan Ackman, "How Big Is Porn?" *Forbes,* May 25, 2001 (www.forbes.com/2001/05/25/0524porn.html). **$10 billion:** Steve Kroft, "Porn in the U.S.A.," *60 Minutes,* September 5, 2004 (www.cbsnews .com/stories/2003/11/21/60minutes/main585049.shtml). **$12 billion:** Jane Lampman, "Churches Confront an 'Elephant in the Pews,' " *Christian Science Monitor,* August 25, 2005 (www.csmonitor.com/2005/0825/ p14s01-lire.html?s=widep).

10. Ali ibn Abi Talib, *Nahjul Balagha,* vol. 3, letter 31, p. 56. Passage translated by Imam Qazwini.

11. David Masci and Gregory A. Smith, "God Is Alive and Well in America," Pew Research Center, April 4, 2006 (pewresearch.org/pubs/15/ god-is-alive-and-well-in-america); Jeffrey L. Sheler, "Faith in America," *U.S. News & World Report,* May 6, 2002, pp. 40–49.

12. Yusuf Ali, *An English Interpretation of the Holy Qur'an,* 19:16–25, 27–34.

13. Ibid., 3:64.

Chapter 5: Bridge Building

1. H.A.R. Gibb, *Whither Islam? A Survey of Modern Movements in the Muslim World* (New York: Routledge, 2002 [originally published 1932]).

2. Yusuf Ali, *An English Interpretation of the Holy Qur'an,* 2:278.

3. Mark 2:15–17.

4. Henry David Thoreau, *Walden and Other Writings.* Brooks Atkinson, ed. (New York: Modern Library, 2000), p. 77.

5. Lynette Clemetson, "U.S. Muslims Confront Taboo on Nursing Homes," *The New York Times,* June 13, 2006.

6. Ibid.

7. Yusuf Ali, *An English Interpretation of the Holy Qur'an,* 17:23.

8. "A Killer More Deadly Than AIDS, Cancer, Etc.—Combined," *Chicago Defender,* January 7, 2002.

9. Helena Oliviero, "South Leads Trend of Motherhood Without Marriage," *Atlanta Journal-Constitution,* October 13, 2005; Ashley Estes, "Births to Unwed Mothers Rise in Utah," *Salt Lake Tribune,* April 15, 2001.

10. Bagby, Perl, and Froehle, "The Mosque in America."

11. For the quotation from the Prophet ("The seeking of knowledge . . ."), see Muhammad Ali, *A Manual of Hadith,* p. 33. Drawn from Bhq. and Mishkat hadith. The verse from the Qur'an ("Whoever is given knowledge . . .") is from Shakir, *The Qur'an Translation,* 2:269.

Chapter 6: The Muslim Capital of the West

1. Pope John Paul II, homily delivered at Oriole Park at Camden Yards, Baltimore, October 8, 1995. Reprinted in the *New York Times* as "Words of Faith and Freedom: The Text of the Homily Delivered in Baltimore," October 9, 1995.

2. Al-Kulayni, *Al-Kafi,* vol. 2, 3rd ed. (Tehran: Dar Al-Kotob Al-Islamiyya, 1987), p. 77.

3. Associated Press, "A Daughter, 4 Men Arrested in Circumcision of 10-Year-Old Girl," *The Washington Post,* September 13, 1994.

4. UNICEF Iraq Child and Maternal Mortality Surveys, 1999, www .unicef.org/newsline/99pr29.htm. The surveys estimated that post–Gulf War sanctions had reversed the downward trend of infant and child mortality in the 1980s and that, absent UN sanctions, 500,000 fewer children in Iraq would have died. Because the estimates applied only to 1991–1998, it's likely that another 200,000 to 300,000 children died as a result of sanctions between 1999 and 2003.

5. "American Muslim PAC Endorses George W. Bush for President," *American Muslim Perspective,* October 23, 2000 (ampolitics.ghazali.net/html/ampcc_endorses.html).

Chapter 7: Paranoid America and "Islamofascists"

1. Benjamin Franklin, *Historical Review of Pennsylvania,* 1759. Quoted in John Bartlett, *Familiar Quotations,* edited by Emily Morison Beck (Boston: Little, Brown, 1980), p. 348.

2. Unger, *House of Bush, House of Saud,* p. 86. Unger is citing *The Rise, Corruption, and Coming Fall of the House of Saud,* by Said Aburish (New York: St. Martin's Press, 1995), pp. 24, 27.

3. Mona Eltahawy, "They Died for Lack of a Head Scarf," *The Washington Post,* March 19, 2002.

4. Shakir, *The Qur'an Translation,* 5:32.

5. Ali ibn Abi Talib, *Nahjul Balagha,* vol. 2, speech no. 224, p. 218. Passage translated by Imam Qazwini.

6. "Forensic Identification of 9/11 Victims Ends," ABC News, February 23, 2005, placed the number of World Trade Center deaths at 2,749 (abcnews.go.com/WNT/story?id=525937&page=1); a CNN.com special, *War Against Terror,* cited 125 Pentagon deaths on the ground and 64 from American Airlines Flight 77 (www.cnn.com/SPECIALS/2001/trade.center/victims/main.html). For the number of Muslim victims, see "After 9/11 Muslims Have a Vital Mission to Reach Out," *Washington Report on Middle East Affairs,* vol. 22, no. 3, April 2003, p. 82.

7. See Bush's "Address to a Joint Session of Congress and the American People," September 20, 2001 (www.whitehouse.gov/news/releases/2001/09/20010920-8.html).

8. CBS News, "Poll: Sinking Perceptions of Islam."

9. National Geographic–Roper Public Affairs 2006 Geographic Literacy Study. "Study: Geography Greek to Young Americans," CNN.com, May 4, 2006 (www.cnn.com/2006/EDUCATION/05/02/geog.test/).

10. Al-Kulayni, *Al-Kafi,* vol. 2, 3rd ed. (Tehran: Dar Al-Kotob Al-Islamiyya, 1987), hadith of Imam Mohammad al-Baqir, p. 426.

11. Wilgoren, "Islam Attracts Converts."

12. Ibid.

13. Yusuf Ali, *An English Interpretation of the Holy Qur'an,* 13:7.

14. Erik Lord, "Maida Visits Mosque in Show of Solidarity," *Detroit Free Press,* December 15, 2001.

15. Unger, *House of Bush, House of Saud,* pp. 2, 7–9.

16. Ackerman, "Arrested for Driving While Muslim."

Chapter 8: Carrying the Mission to the Halls of Power

1. Letter to William Roscoe, Dec. 27, 1820, in Albert Ellery Bergh, ed., *The Writings of Thomas Jefferson* (Washington, D.C.: issued under the auspices of the Thomas Jefferson Memorial Association of the United States, 1907), vol. 15, p. 303 (www.monticello.org/reports/quotes/uva.html).

2. Mahajan, "We Think the Price Is Worth It."

3. Sayed Hassan al-Qazwini, "Opening Dialogue with Our Enemies Is

Often Our Only Option," *Arab American News,* May 27, 2006 (www
.arabamericannews.com/newsarticle.php?articleid=5383).

4. Friedman, "If It's a Muslim Problem."

5. "The CIA's Intervention in Afghanistan: Interview with Zbigniew
Brzezinski, President Jimmy Carter's National Security Adviser," Center
for Research on Globalisation. *Le Nouvel Observateur* (Paris), January
15–21, 1998, Bill Blum, trans. (www.globalresearch.ca/articles/BRZ110A
.html).

Chapter 9: Our American bin Ladens

1. Aron Kahn, "Ellison Breaks Ground as Muslim, Black," *St. Paul Pioneer
Press,* November 8, 2006.

2. Ann Coulter, "This Is War," *National Review,* September 13, 2001
(www.nationalreview.com/coulter/coulter.shtml).

3. Jonah Goldberg, "L'Affaire Coulter," *National Review,* October 3, 2001
(www.nationalreview.com/nr_comment/nr_comment100301.shtml).

4. NBC Nightly News, interview with Franklin Graham, November 16,
2001.

5. *700 Club,* February 22, 2002.

6. Ibid., March 13, 2006.

7. *Nightline,* ABC News, March 15, 2006.

8. Graham, "My View of Islam."

9. Matthew 5:44.

10. Kevin Phillips, *American Dynasty: Aristocracy, Fortune, and the Politics of
Deceit in the House of Bush* (New York: Viking, 2004), p. 222.

11. *700 Club,* November 11, 2002.

12. "President Bush, Secretary Annan Discuss Iraq," transcript, November 13, 2002 (www.whitehouse.gov/news/releases/2002/11/20021113
-10.html).

13. Cal Thomas, "Men of Faith in Washington, D.C., Need Our Prayers,"
Crosswalk.com, November 9, 2001 (www.crosswalk.com/1108858/).

14. Guy Taylor, "Boykin Sparks Status Debate," *Washington Times,* October 27, 2003.

15. Hersh, "The Gray Zone."

16. Deborah Caldwell, " 'Poised and Ready,' " Beliefnet (www.beliefnet .com/story/123/story_12365_1.html).

17. Steven Waldman, "Why Is Bush Afraid of Franklin Graham?" Beliefnet (www.beliefnet.com/story/124/story_12422_1.html).

Chapter 10: Lines in the Sand

1. John Milton, *Samson Agonistes,* 1771. Quoted in *The International Thesaurus of Quotations,* compiled by Eugene Ehrlich and Marshall De Bruhl (New York: HarperCollins, 1996), p. 659.

2. Dobbins, "Nation Building."

3. Bor, "654,000 Deaths Tied to Iraq War."

4. "Wolfowitz Defiant After Hotel Rocket Strike," CNN.com, October 26, 2003 (www.cnn.com/2003/WORLD/meast/10/26/sprj.irq.hotel/index.html).

5. James Gerstenzang, "At a Michigan Grill, an Arab-American Voice Quizzes Cheney," *Los Angeles Times,* September 22, 2004.

Chapter 11: Return to the Cradle

1. Quoted in the *Encyclopedia of Religious Quotations,* edited by Frank S. Mead (Westwood, N.J.: Fleming H. Revell Co., 1965), p. 230.

2. Friedman, "A Nobel for Sistani."

3. Stephanie Strom, "What Is Charity?" *The New York Times,* November 14, 2005.

4. Sunan Abu Dawood, *Kitab Al-Adab* (Beirut, Lebanon: Dar Al-Fikr, 1990), vol. 2, p. 464, hadith no. 4941.

Chapter 12: The Islamic Frontier

1. Reza, *Peak of Eloquence,* p. 595.

2. CBS News, "Poll: Sinking Perceptions of Islam."

3. Ibid.

4. Elias, "USA's Muslims under a Cloud."

5. 2006 CAIR Civil Rights Report (www.cair.com/cair2006report/).

6. Ibid.

7. Yusuf Ali, *An English Interpretation of the Holy Qur'an,* 42:36, 42:38.

8. Ibn Abi Al-Hadeed, *Sharh Nahjul Balagha,* 2nd ed. (Qum, Iran: Dar Ihya' Al-Kotob Al-Arabiyya, 1927), vol. 20, p. 267.

Epilogue

1. Shakir, *The Qur'an Translation,* 10:90–92.
2. Jodi Wilgoren, "On Campus and on Knees, Facing Mecca," *The New York Times,* February 13, 2001.
3. Wilgoren, "Islam Attracts Converts."

Selected Bibliography

Books

Abdullah, Thabit A. J. *A Short History of Iraq: From 636 to the Present.* Essex, England: Pearson Education, 2003.

Ali ibn Abi Talib, Imam. *Nahjul Balagha* [Peak of Eloquence]. Qum, Iran: Dar Al-Thakha'ir, 1991.

Aslan, Reza. *No God but God: The Origins, Evolution, and Future of Islam.* New York: Random House, 2005.

Campbell, John T. *Desert War: The New Conflict Between the U.S. and Iraq.* New York: New American Library, 2003.

Chirri, Mohamad Jawad. *Inquiries About Islam.* 5th ed. Updated by Adnan Chirri and Kassem Allie. Self-published, 2005.

Esposito, John L. *Islam: The Straight Path.* 3rd ed. New York: Oxford University Press, 1998.

————. *What Everyone Needs to Know About Islam: Answers to Frequently Asked Questions from One of America's Leading Experts.* New York: Oxford University Press, 2002.

Farouk-Sluglett, Marion, and Peter Sluglett. *Iraq Since 1958: From Revolution to Dictatorship.* London: I. B. Tauris, 1990.

Feldman, Noah. *What We Owe Iraq: War and the Ethics of Nation Building.* Princeton, N.J.: Princeton University Press, 2004.

Hiro, Dilip. *The Longest War: The Iran-Iraq Military Conflict.* London: Routledge, 1991.

Holy Bible, King James Version. Uhrichsville, Ohio: Barbour Publishing, 2002.

Hunter, Shireen T. *Islam, Europe's Second Religion: The New Social, Cultural, and Political Landscape.* Westport, Conn.: Praeger Publishers, 2002.

Jibouri, Yasin T. al- *Kerbala and Beyond.* Qum, Iran: Ansariyan Publications, 1999.

Kinzer, Stephen. *All the Shah's Men: An American Coup and the Roots of Middle East Terror.* Hoboken, N.J.: John Wiley & Sons, 2003.

Mackey, Sandra. *The Reckoning: Iraq and the Legacy of Saddam Hussein.* New York: Norton, 2002.

Mamdani, Mahmood. *Good Muslim, Bad Muslim: America, the Cold War, and the Roots of Terror.* New York: Pantheon, 2004.

Muhammad Ali, Maulana, ed. *A Manual of Hadith.* Dublin, Oh.: Ahmadiyya Anjuman Ishaat Islam Lahore USA, 2001.

Nakash, Yitzak. *The Shi'is of Iraq.* Princeton, N.J.: Princeton University Press, 1994.

Reza, Sayed Ali, trans. *Peak of Eloquence: Sermons, Letters and Sayings of Imam Ali ibn Abi Talib [Nahjul Balagha].* Elmhurst, N.Y.: Tahrike Tarsile Qur'an, 2002.

Sada, Georges, with Jim Nelson Black. *Saddam's Secrets: How an Iraqi General Defied and Survived Saddam Hussein.* Brentwood, Tenn.: Integrity Publishers, 2006.

Shakir, M. H., trans. *The Qur'an Translation,* 10th ed. Elmhurst, N.Y.: Tahrike Tarsile Qur'an, 1999.

Tripp, Charles. *A History of Iraq.* Cambridge, England: Cambridge University Press, 2000.

Unger, Craig. *House of Bush, House of Saud: The Secret Relationship Between the World's Two Most Powerful Dynasties.* New York: Scribner, 2004.

Yusuf Ali, Abdullah, trans. *An English Interpretation of the Holy Qur'an.* 3rd ed. Lahore, Pakistan: Shaikh Muhammad Ashraf, 1995.

Periodicals

Ackerman, Spencer. "Arrested for Driving While Muslim." AlterNet/*The Nation,* September 28, 2006 (www.alternet.org/story/42235/).

Bor, Jonathan. "654,000 Deaths Tied to Iraq War." *Baltimore Sun,* October 13, 2006.

Dobbins, James. "Nation Building: The Inescapable Responsibility of the World's Only Superpower." *RAND Review,* Summer 2003 (www.rand .org/publications/randreview/issues/summer2003/nation5.html).

Elias, Marilyn. "USA's Muslims under a Cloud." *USA Today,* August 10, 2006 (www.usatoday.com/news/nation/2006-08-09-muslim-american -cover_x.htm).

Friedman, Thomas. "If It's a Muslim Problem, It Needs a Muslim Solution." *The New York Times,* July 8, 2005.

———. "A Nobel for Sistani." *The New York Times,* March 20, 2005.

Graham, Franklin. "My View of Islam." *The Wall Street Journal,* December 9, 2001.

Hersh, Seymour M. "The Gray Zone." *The New Yorker,* May 24, 2004.

Lord, Erik. "Maida Visits Mosque in Show of Solidarity." *Detroit Free Press,* December 15, 2001.

Mahajan, Rahul. "We Think the Price Is Worth It: Media Uncurious About Iraq Policy's Effects—There or Here." *Extra!* (Fairness & Accuracy in Reporting), November/December 2001 (www.fair.org/ index.php?page=1084).

Wilgoren, Jodi. "Islam Attracts Converts by the Thousands, Drawn Before and After Attacks." *The New York Times,* October 22, 2001.

Online Sources

Bagby, Ihsan, Paul M. Perl, and Bryan T. Froehle. "The Mosque in America: A National Portrait." Council on American-Islamic Relations, 2001 (www.cair-net.org/mosquereport/Masjid_Study_Project_2000_ Report.pdf).

BBC News. "Muslims in Europe: Country Guide." December 23, 2005 (news.bbc.co.uk/2/hi/europe/4385768.stm).

CBS News. "Poll: Sinking Perceptions of Islam." April 12, 2006 (www.cbsnews.com/stories/2006/04/12/national/main1494697.shtml).

Council on American-Islamic Relations. "American Muslims: Population Statistics" (www.cair-net.org/asp/populationstats.asp).

———. Civil Rights Report, 2006 (www.cair.com/cair2006report/).

A Shi'ite Encyclopedia. Chapter 3, "The Major Difference Between the Shia and the Sunni" (al-islam.org/encyclopedia/).

UNICEF. "Child and Maternal Mortality Survey 1999," Iraq (www.childinfo.org/iraq.htm).

About the Authors

IMAM HASSAN QAZWINI is descended from seven generations of prestigious Islamic scholars. He was born in Karbala, Iraq, in 1964 and moved to the United States in 1992. He serves as the spiritual leader of the Islamic Center of America in Dearborn, Michigan, regularly meets with presidents and other politicians, and has appeared on CNN, NPR, and the BBC and in *The New York Times, The Wall Street Journal, The Washington Post, The Christian Science Monitor,* the *Detroit Free Press, The Detroit News,* and a wide range of other media outlets.

BRAD CRAWFORD, the co-author of *American Crescent,* is the author of *Compass American Guides: Ohio* and the co-author of *My Sister Is Missing: Bringing a Killer to Justice.* A graduate of the University of Missouri's School of Journalism, Crawford freelances full-time from Cincinnati, Ohio. His website is www.bradcrawford.net.

About the Type

This book was set in Schneidler, a typeface originally designed in 1936 by F. H. Ernst Schneidler for the Bauer Typefoundry. The typeface is based on the fonts of Venetian printers from the Renaissance period, and possesses those earlier fonts' grace beauty, and classical proportions. Schneidler was initially released only as a roman design, and its current italic companion, sometimes called Amalthea, was not issued until 1956, a year after Ernst Schneidler's death.